An Garda Síochána and the Scott Medal

An Garda Síochána
and the Scott Medal

GERARD O'BRIEN

FOUR COURTS PRESS

Set in 11 on 13.5 point Ehrhardt for
FOUR COURTS PRESS LTD
7 Malpas Street, Dublin 8, Ireland
e-mail: info@fourcourtspress.ie
and in North America for
FOUR COURTS PRESS
c/o ISBS, 920 NE 58th Avenue, Suite 300, Portland, OR 97213

A catalogue record for this title
is available from the British Library

ISBN 978-1-84682-124-0

Printed in Great Britain
by Athenaeum Press, Gateshead, Tyne & Wear.

CONTENTS

ILLUSTRATIONS

occur between pages 96 and 97.

ABBREVIATIONS

D/J	Department of Justice
DMD	Dublin Metropolitan Division
ER	East Riding
GA	Garda Archives
IRA	Irish Republican Army
NAI	National Archives of Ireland
RIC	Royal Irish Constabulary

In loving memory
of Doris Brooks
(1938–2008)

ACKNOWLEDGMENTS

Commissioner Noel Conroy, now retired, graciously gave his permission for this project to be undertaken, and Commissioner Fachtna Murphy gave it his blessing at its conclusion. To both men the author extends his sincere gratitude and appreciation. The project itself would have foundered at several stages but for the guidance and assistance of Inspector Pat McGee of the Garda Museum, whose unflagging enthusiasm and perseverance were exceeded only by his courtesy and readiness to help wherever and whenever. The biographical details which turned this book from a dry account of events and medals into a story about real people and their bravery were supplied at the cost of considerable labour by Donal Kivlehan, also of the Garda Museum. Donal also searched garda records for the author at a time when they were still in the process of being organized, and slaved long over the photocopier in the service of this project. Encouragement was provided and inquiries undertaken at the crucial early stage of the work by Inspector Della Murray (formerly of Human Resources Management, Garda Headquarters). Important details regarding the procedures connected with the Scott Medal were furnished by Assistant Commissioner Catherine Clancy. The passing of material to and from the Garda Museum was facilitated, always cheerfully, by Sergeant Niall Cody of Burnfoot Garda Station, County Donegal. Gerry J. Shannon of the Department of Justice, at a time when he was particularly busy, advised the author on the quantity, nature and likely content of various files which had been deposited in the National Archives of Ireland. Jenny Moran of the National Archives provided me with photocopies of many of those files with commendable speed, efficiency and courtesy. Two men who contributed greatly to this book never knew of either its inception or completion: the late Gregory Allen left behind not only the finest history of the Garda Síochána ever written, but also a small but invaluable file of papers relating to the Scott Medal. The late Paddy Hanley, son of a Garda, published during 1959–60 in the periodical *Iris an Gharda* an extremely useful and interesting series of articles and lists regarding Scott Medal recipients and their deeds. I am grateful to his sisters, Ms Ann McKeigue and Ms Gertie Hanly, both of Tullamore, for sharing their memories of him with me. Closer to home, Frank and Marie D'Arcy, Dennis Orsi, and James Loughlin have at different times listened patiently to the verbal outpourings of the author on the subject of Scott Medals. My children, Aoibhinn and Aodhan, have endured many a hurried microwave dinner while their father typed and shuffled papers. As ever, Michael Adams, Martin Healy and Martin Fanning of Four Courts Press have demonstrated extraordinary stoicism in the face of the author's inability to interpret style sheets, read proofs or keep his pages in the correct order. Finally, though not least, sincere appreciation is extended to the very many recipients of Scott Medals who responded (either directly or via Pat McGee) to the author's requests for details of life-threatening experiences which, in some instances, they would perhaps rather have forgotten.

INTRODUCTION

The Irish of the revolutionary and post-revolutionary periods were slow to award themselves medals. The trinklets and watchchain fobs which were presented as momentoes to the members of the first and second Dála were not followed by campaign medals for combatants until almost a generation had passed.[1] When these finally emerged during the 1940s they were poorly designed and produced in the cheapest of metals. The first gallantry medals, issued exclusively for the Irish army in 1944, were issued so sparingly that little is known of them.[2] Despite the significant role played by the state's new police force, An Garda Síochána, in winning the peace after 1922, no Irish government ever seriously considered celebrating its courage and steadfastness with a medal as in other countries.

But the long years of conflict, and the civil war in particular, had brought the new Irish Free State perilously close to insolvency. It was an Ireland in which everyone seemed to be casting about in increasing desperation for either a pension or a job.[3] In such an atmosphere medals were not going to be any minister's priority. The IRA had won the War of Independence and the National Army had won the civil war. These conflicts were now in the past, and the morale of either veterans or serving soldiers was no longer, it seemed, a matter of importance to the overworked government. For the unarmed Gardaí, however, (and for the Dublin Metropolitan Police in its last years) the 'war' went on in the forms of continuing social unrest and violent criminal and subversive activity. The failure to manage effectively the awkward transition from the Royal Irish Constabulary to the new Garda Síochána was demonstrated tellingly by the 'Kildare Mutiny' and the consequent resignation of the force's first commissioner, Michael J. Staines, in 1922. The new force had been in existence only a short time when its members began to be murdered.[4] In the circumstances the maintenance of the force's morale must

1 During 2006 and 2007 a few small silver 'watchchain-fob' medals, unnamed but inscribed in Irish with the title and year of the first or second Dáil appeared in local and internet auctions. For details of the four small gold medals issued by Michael Collins to 'four members of his munitions team who were responsible for the design, manufacture and issue of explosives during the War of Independence', see James J. Hogan, *Badges: Medals: Insignia, Oglaigh na hEireann (Irish Defence Forces)*, (Dublin, 1987), 77. 2 Medals for those who took part in the 1916 Rising, and for veterans of the War of Independence, were finally issued in 1941–2. The Military Medal for Gallantry was produced in 1944. See Hogan, *Badges*, 71–2. 3 The matter of Volunteer pensions was high on the agenda and began to feature in legislation as early as 1924. 4 Gregory Allen, *The Garda Síochána:*

have been a matter of some concern to the government and, in particular, to its new commissioner (from September 1922) Eoin O'Duffy.

Colonel Walter Scott was another man who certainly understood the importance of maintaining morale. Born in Canada of Scottish parents in 1861, Scott rose from modest beginnings to a position of considerable wealth and influence in the hard-nosed business world of nineteenth-century America; it was a time and a place in which the preservation of a positive attitude was very often an essential pre-requisite for survival. Nobody knows precisely why Scott became fascinated by police and firemen, but it may have dated from his time as honorary police commissioner of New York City. He originated the award of Scott Medals in various police departments, New York, Boston, Worcester, Holyoke, Detroit and Buenos Aires. His view of the importance of such awards was summed up by him as he donated medals in Boston in 1922:

> while I feel that it is not necessary that medals be offered as an incentive to the performance of one's duty, yet it has always been a practice of mine to present flowers during one's lifetime, while one can inhale their fragrance and enjoy their beauty. Hence the gift of the medals.[5]

In the early years of the twentieth century, Irish immigrants or their sons made up a significant proportion of both the police and fire services of New York.

In May 1923 O'Duffy, during his attendance at the third international police conference in New York, addressed the assembled delegates. Afterwards he was approached by Scott who expressed a keen interest in the manner in which the new Irish force had been organized and trained and displayed a keen awareness of the political background to its establishment. He was, he said, an 'ardent admirer' of the late Michael Collins, and was anxious to help the fledgling force in some 'enduring' way. By O'Duffy's account it was Scott who suggested the endowment in perpetuity of a gold medal for bravery 'to be presented annually to the member of the Garda who in my opinion most deserved the distinction'.[6] Once back in Dublin O'Duffy lost no time in engaging the services of John Francis (Sean) Maxwell

---

policing independent Ireland, 1922–82 (Dublin, 1999), 31–48 for the 'Kildare Mutiny', and 231–3 for the Roll of Honour. Garda Henry Phelan was the first member of the force murdered, on 28 October 1922. **5** Garda Archives (hereinafter GA), small file of material on the Scott Medal collected by the late Gregory Allen, including an unpublished typescript by Charles P. McDowell, 'Walter Scott and the Scott Medal for Valour' [c.1977]. **6** *Garda Review*, January 1932, 133–7.

(1880–1948), a local art teacher who had designed the Garda badge.[7] As soon as the proposed design was ready it was dispatched to Scott for approval. Scott responded early in January 1924 not only with the dies for the medal and the first gold medal to be struck from them, but also with the financial underpinning for the award, 'a $1,000 six per cent gold bond of the Detroit Edison Company, Detroit, Michigan, (B12096), maturing in 1940, this bond to be held by your Department or City Treasurer, the interest therefrom to pay for the gold medal annually'.[8] The medal was struck in 18 caret solid gold, and Scott concluded his letter with his Boston comments of 1922 regarding medals and flowers.

Scott himself in the same letter made it clear that the medal was to be awarded by the commissioner 'or your Department' to a Garda 'who in your judgment, or that of your cabinet [sic.], has … especially distinguished himself for valour in the performance of duty'. If in any particular year or years no Garda was believed to have so distinguished himself, then Scott was happy for 'the unused interest' to 'become part of the principal'. The passing of a mere eight months between the arrival of Scott's letter, the dies and the first medal, and the presentation ceremony in August 1924, suggests that little time was lost in selecting potential candidates for the award. The details of the process by which Garda James Mulroy emerged as the first recipient of the Walter Scott Medal are few but intriguing. Soon after receiving the dies and medal O'Duffy issued a circular to superintendents and chief superintendents emphasizing that the medal was only for those who had demonstrated 'exceptional proof of bravery and heroism, and have shown outstanding and exceptional courage involving the risk of life in the interests of the public'. Each chief and other superintendent was to give 'this highly important matter his close personal attention'; he was to 'carefully weigh and consider the merits of each case and submit the whole circumstances … for the information of the Commissioner'. According to an article published in one of the first garda periodicals, *Guth an Gharda*, in August 1924, some 100 files had to be examined before a shortlist of 19 gardaí could be compiled. Among those passed over in a further pruning were four guards who had been killed during the previous two years. Mulroy's name eventually emerged from a final list of four.

A Reward Fund and a set of regulations by which it could be administered had to wait upon the passing of the Garda Síochána Act of 1924, when such machinery was set up under Section 18 of that Act. This provided for the

7 Allen, *Garda Síochána*, 21.   8 *Garda Review*, January 1932, 133, Scott's letter to O'Duffy of 8 January 1924 (mis-typed '1922'). The dies for the medal were made by Dieges and Clust of New York City.

establishment of a Reward Board consisting of at least two officers of not lower than assistant commissioner rank who were to be nominated by the commissioner. These two officers would consider cases referred to them and recommend to the commissioner that rewards be issued by him to any member of the force up to (and including) the rank of chief superintendent. Germane to the award of the first Scott Medal, however, was the inclusion of the provision that, 'the Commissioner shall have power, subject to the approval of the Minister for Justice, to grant individual rewards in exceptional cases without previous reference to the Reward Board'.[9] Other than O' Duffy's circular and the *Guth an Gharda* article there remains today of that initial reward process only the short note from Eoin O'Duffy to Mulroy's chief superintendent at Ennis: this asked that Mulroy and Garda John Donlon (who was with Mulroy during the incident) be told of 'my appreciation of their coolness and bravery ... in defending themselves against armed robbers one of whom was disarmed by Garda Mulroy after a shot had passed through his frock'.[10]

At a well-attended and well-publicized ceremony on 18 August 1924 Garda Mulroy was presented with his medal by Walter Scott himself in the presence of the President, W.T. Cosgrave, and the Ministers for Justice and Finance, Kevin O'Higgins and Ernest Blythe, along with Commissioner O'Duffy. The following year Garda John Rooney was awarded the medal, followed by Sergeant Peter O'Reilly a year later. The presentation ceremony at Garda Headquarters in Dublin's Phoenix Park became an annual moment of celebration and the pinning-on of the medal by the minister for justice (Scott did not attend after the first year) a veritable tradition. But in 1925 a further refinement was introduced. Again, beyond O'Duffy's personal account, little trace remains of the stages by which the Scott Silver and Scott Bronze Medals came into being. O'Duffy met Walter Scott again at the 1925 international police conference. So impressed was he by the commissioner's account of 'how much the prize was coveted' that Scott apparently 'handed me a 500 dollar bond to endow in perpetuity a silver and bronze medal' for those 'who came second and third respectively in the Scott Medal list'; or, if the gold medal wasn't awarded, to those who came first and second. A letter written by O'Duffy as he was handing over the reins as commissioner to his successor in 1933 makes it unambiguously clear that he had asked Scott to finance the silver and bronze

---

9 The circular by O'Duffy is quoted in *Iris an Gharda*, January 1959, 155. See GA, Gregory Allen file, for a copy of the 'Garda Síochána Reward Fund (administration) Regulations, 1925', signed by Kevin O'Higgins, Minister for Justice, 10 February 1925.   10 National Archives of Ireland (hereinafter NAI), D/J[ustice] 2005/147/160, Eoin O'Duffy, commissioner, to chief superintendent, Ennis, 13 November 1923.

medals.[11] In the absence of any other evidence the reviewers of the procedures during the 1950s concluded that their predecessors of the 1920s had not regarded Scott's original stipulation that the awardee must have 'especially distinguished himself' as an 'absolute' interpretation, 'but meaning any member who had distinguished himself according to a standard in an especial manner. The subsequent provision for silver and bronze medals clearly indicates this'.[12] The first Scott Silver Medal went to Garda John Whelan and the first Bronze to Detective Garda James Hanafin. A year later, in 1927, O'Duffy found himself unable to 'differentiate in merit' between the second and third candidates and so 'I had the Scott funds supplemented [he did not say how] and a second silver medal cast instead of a bronze one'. A precedent thus having been set, it was possible to have two gold medals cast for presentation in 1932 when two gardaí, Charles Connell and Michael Hayden, involved in the same incident, tied for first place.[13]

In 1933 Eoin O'Duffy surrendered the commissionership of the Garda Síochána to Eamonn Broy.[14] A year before O'Duffy left office the practice of rewarding Scott Medal winners with money in addition to their medals was introduced. A gold medallist could expect to receive £30, a silver medallist £20, and a bronze winner £15.[15] The various procedures associated with the award of the medal were now well in place and little change took place during the sometimes-turbulent 1930s. In 1937, for the first time, no deed of valour was performed which met the Reward Board's standards for the award of any Scott Medal. In 1938, also for the first time, no gold medal was awarded though there were two silver and two bronze awards. In 1939 there were no Scott Medals awarded. A resurgence in subversive activity in 1940 saw the award of five gold medals, an unprecedented number for any one year. A year later one of the gold medallists of 1940, Detective Sergeant John Collins, received a Scott Bronze Medal, and became the first garda ever to receive a second such award. But 1942 came and went with no award, as did the years 1944, 1945 and 1946. Two medals, both gold, were awarded in 1947 and thereafter no further Scott Medal awards were made until 1958.

Despite the short-lived IRA campaign of the early war years it seems generally true that in comparison with earlier and later periods, the country

11 *Garda Review*, January 1932, 137. GA, Gregory Allen file, Eoin O'Duffy, commissioner, to P[atrick] Walsh, assistant commissioner, 31 May 1933. 12 GA, Gregory Allen file, [unsigned], assistant commissioner, to commissioner [Daniel Costigan], 26 November 1956. 13 *Garda Review*, June 1933, 773. 14 For a recent and authoritative view of O'Duffy's career, see Fearghal McGarry, *Eoin O'Duffy: a self-made hero* (Oxford, 2006). 15 Paddy Hanley, 'The bravest of the brave', in *Iris an Gharda*, February 1959, 241.

saw less criminal activity and less social unrest during the 1940s and 1950s. But this in itself would not explain the sudden falling-off in Scott Medal awards. Throughout its history the medal has been awarded very frequently in connection with rescues from drowning and house fires – which are perennial occurrences. It is tempting for the historian to seek to locate some speculative explanation in the straitened economic circumstances of the time. Colonel Scott had died in 1935 and his original bond had matured in 1940. It was inevitable that the financial underpinnings of the medal would grow weaker with the passing of the years. But then, there was always the Reward Fund, replenished, according to section 18 of the Garda Síochána Act, 1924, with 'all fines, penalties ... damages awarded ... or otherwise payable to any member of the Garda Síochána on any summary conviction'. As we have seen, the award of the Scott Medal was administered through the Reward Fund; as long as sufficient money existed therein it was surely but a short step to financing the award through the Fund also, as Scott's bond became progressively exhausted. The medals, it was true, were not cheap in any sense, but there were only a few in each year and none at all in those years when the Reward Board decided that the conditions for an award had not been met.

A few weeks after the war in Europe ended the Irish government decided to introduce a scheme to recognize and reward with medals and certificates 'all efforts to save human life which involve serious personal risk'. Civilians performing such deeds within the state, and even crews of Irish ships or anybody rendering assistance to them, were eligible for the awards. Only members of the defence forces who were 'on active service' were excluded. The Deeds of Bravery Act, 1947, as the eventual legislation was entitled, did not exclude members of the Garda Síochána. The new award machinery was to be administered by a council (Comhairle na Mire Gaile) consisting of the ceann comhairle of the Dáil, the cathaoirleach of the Seanad, the chairmen of the Red Cross and General Council of Galway Councils, the lord mayors of Cork and Dublin, and the commissioner of the Garda Síochána.[16] The bill had been introduced by the Minister for Justice, Gerald Boland, one of whose annual functions was to present Scott Medals to deserving gardaí. During the early Dáil discussions on the measure he remarked that

in the case of persons who risked their lives my own personal idea would be to provide one medal – a good one. I felt the same about the Gardaí.

16 *Dáil Debates* (hereinafter *DD*), vol 97, 27 June 1945, cols 1716–28; vol 104, 20 March 1947, cols 2520–6. *Seanad Debates*, vol 33, 25 March 1947, cols 1402–10; 16 April 1947, cols 1494–7.

When handing out a bronze medal, I certainly did not like it. There is no doubt about it, there were some outstanding deeds of gallantry, and others may not have been quite the same, but I always thought it was hard luck on the man who got the bronze medal. That was my personal view.[17]

Of course the decisions regarding the award of Scott Medals rested not with the Minister for Justice but with the Garda Reward Board. But 1947, the year which saw the introduction of a new bravery award system which included the Garda Síochána, not only as potential awardees but also, through the commissioner, as a voice on the Comhairle na Mire Gaile, was also the last time for many years that the Scott Medal was awarded.

Besides the Scott Medal itself, gardaí were eligible for and had received down the years many awards from bodies such as the Royal Humane Society, as well as monetary awards from the Garda Reward Fund itself. Members of the force were amongst the earliest recipients of Comhairle certificates and thereafter scarcely a year went by that did not see a garda listed, and his heroism described, in the Comhairle's published annual report. The Comhairle's *Thirteenth Annual Report*, for 1959, included an account of how Detective Sergeant James Mulroy of Ennis had on 28 April that year rescued from drowning a young woman who was attempting to commit suicide; he was awarded a certificate. But the Guards were not involved with the Comhairle merely in the guise of heroes: The bringing of deserving cases to the Comhairle's attention and the verification of the circumstances of those cases became an additional part of a garda's duty. At the beginning of the Comhairle's existence the garda commissioner, Michael J. Kinnane, had argued in vain for the appointment of a civilian inspector.[18]

The continuing 'failure' to award Scott Medals was by the mid-1950s becoming a source of concern, however, and in 1956 pressure (almost certainly from within the force) led to a review of the system. Replying to a query from the Minister for Justice who had asked why no awards had been made for nine years, the commissioner, Daniel Costigan, pointed out that he had received no recommendations for the years 1952, 1953 or 1955. Two recommendations had reached him in respect of 1954 but he 'did not consider that the cases came up to the standard which had been set in the past'. One of these cases, he added, had been considered also (before it was submitted to the Reward Board) by the Comhairle na Mire Gaile and was not thought worthy

---

17 *DD*, vol 97, 27 June 1945, col 1726.   18 NAI, D/J 90/116/13, minutes of third meeting of Comhairle na Mire Gaile, 1 October 1947, item 10.

of an award. It was, however, his intention, Costigan assured the minister, 'to review the present arrangements for the award of the Scott Medal'.[19]

Within six weeks Deputy Commissioner Garret Brennan had been asked to ascertain if, and how, practices surrounding the award of Scott Medals had changed or evolved over time.[20] In late November Costigan was informed that no substantive change had taken place in the interpretation of Scott's original letter of 1924 to Eoin O'Duffy. Colonel Scott's wishes were still being complied with, including his stipulation that no medal need be granted if 'in the opinion of those awarding the medal no one is entitled to it'. The intentions of Colonel Scott, as well as the essence of O'Duffy's first circular on the matter in 1924, were properly represented in the latest relevant circular, Routine Order 50/1942, paragraphs 7(b) and 8(p). The Reward Board, having considered the matter, saw no reason why the same arrangements should not be followed in the future.[21] Costigan accepted the Board's view that no medal should be awarded unless a certain standard had been reached, but with reluctance – 'I have serious doubts as to whether it was the original intention of Colonel Scott'.[22]

The year following the review went by also with no award, but in the autumn of 1959 Commissioner Costigan was able to inform the Department of Justice that Scott Bronze Medals were to be awarded to to four gardaí in respect of courageous actions during 1958. Gardaí John Moynihan, Thomas Slattery and Vincent Nolan had been concerned in the rescue of women and children from a burning building. Garda Patrick Ryan had rescued a man from drowning. All four had received certificates from Comhairle na Mire Gaile in respect of their deeds. A sour note was struck (though temporarily) when the Minister for Justice, Oscar Traynor, initially expressed the view that the presentation of mere bronze medals was a function more suited to the commissioner but that he would be quite happy to officiate if there were gold or silver medals involved. Traynor agreed to attend once it had been explained to him by Costigan that (amongst other things) 'the Force might misinterpret the Minister's reasons, if he did not make the presentations', and that the event would attract considerable press attention.[23] The presentation – 'one of

19 NAI, D/J 4/438, part 1, D. Costigan, commissioner, to Thomas J. Coyne, Department of Justice, 30 June 1956. 20 GA, Gregory Allen file, D. C[ostigan], commissioner, to [Garret] Brennan, deputy commissioner, 15 August 1956. 21 GA, Gregory Allen file, [unsigned] assistant commissioner, to commissioner [Daniel Costigan], 26 November 1956. 22 GA, Gregory Allen file, D. C[ostigan], commissioner, to [Garret] Brennan, deputy commissioner, 11 December 1956, and Brennan's temporising reply of 21 December 1956 on behalf of the Reward Board. 23 See the award recommendations and related correspondence in NAI, D/J 4/438, part 2.

the most impressive ceremonies ever held at the Depot' – was held on 8 April 1960: The Scott Medal was back.[24]

And it has never gone away. Since 1960 more than 300 Scott Medals have been awarded. For the most part the pattern laid down in the early period of the award whereby only a few are issued each year has been adhered to. The upsurge of terrorist activity at the start of the 1970s was reflected in a few minor adjustments which had to be made to the award process. Because Colonel Scott's original approval of the medal design had arrived in January 1924 the selection process for the first recipient had focussed on courageous acts performed during the previous year. This pattern of awarding medals not for the current year but in respect of the year preceding the presentation was closely followed thereafter. This not only allowed time for the selection process itself but for the preparation of the presentation ceremony (which took place at the Training College at Templemore from the mid-1960s). A potential legal complication, of which the Reward Board had always been aware, began to affect the citations (usually published in the Garda periodical and often in the newspapers) which accompanied the award. These gave a detailed account of the incident in which the recipient had been involved.[25] In certain circumstances the publication of such information before or during the trial of any persons charged with offences in connection with the incident could conceivably have compromised the case against them. In earlier years there was less sensitivity on this matter (Mulroy's assailants were not brought to trial until 1926, three years after their attack on him), but in the more tense social and political atmosphere of the 1970s the issue had to be addressed more carefully. On a few occasions (as in 1975 for instance) the presentation of a number of medals was delayed by legal problems surrounding the prosecution of accused persons. When clearance was finally received for the release of the awards a back-log of some twenty medals had built up (nine of them gold) which had to be presented, and paid for, in one year.[26] Citations recording full details of the relevant incidents were issued where possible, but with increasing frequency, 'short' citations, which acknowledged the guards' bravery but withheld all other details, began to be produced to coincide with the presentation of the medals.

As crime rates rose during the 1970s alongside the concurrent terrorist outrages more and more gardaí became involved in incidents which ended up

---

24 *Garda Review*, May 1960, 449–53. 25 See GA, Gregory Allen file, [unsigned] assistant commissioner, to [Daniel Costigan], commissioner, 21 December 1956. 26 NAI, D/J 2005/147/159, G. Kenny [Department of Justice] to Secretary, Department of Finance, 11 August 1975.

in front of the Reward Board in the form of recommendations for Scott Medals. While there is no evidence that the standards in place since the foundation of the award were in any sense diluted (not even death on duty entitles a guard to the *automatic* award of a Scott Medal) the circumstances of that troubled period made almost inevitable the award of a greater number of medals in some years than had ever before been seen. The Conroy Commission which in 1970 had reported on pay and conditions in the force had recommended a large increase in the monetary rewards payable to Scott Medal recipients; these had not been raised for some time.[27] From 1972 onwards recipients of gold medals received £300, silver medallists £200 and bronze medallists £100. (The amounts were increased again in 2004 to €1,500, €11,000, and €750 respectively.) The steadfastness of the Reward Board in awarding increased numbers of medals and higher monetary grants where clearly they were well deserved was admirable, but the economy was depressed and prices for precious metals as well as production costs had risen alarmingly since the early days of the award. By the mid-1970s the Scott Medal was enmeshed in a brief but alarming financial crisis.

As stated earlier, the basic financial underpinning for the award was the interest from Colonel Scott's bond. By the 1970s the bond had been invested in the National Loan and was accruing interest on deposit under the quaint title of the Scott Medal Post Office Savings Account. But, half a century after Colonel Scott's largesse the account hovered at around £300, and the senior officers responsible for arranging payment for the preparation of the medals were reluctant to 'denude' the account 'which is of historic significance to the Garda Síochána'.[28] In 1927–8 the Oireachtas made a modest contribution of £415 to the Reward Fund as part of the Garda Vote. This was included automatically in the Vote each year thereafter, but the sum was not increased; in 1975 it was still £415.

Additional support for the medal awards had long been provided also by the various fines, penalties and damages awarded on foot of summary convictions. But the main source of revenue for the Garda Síochána Reward Fund

---

27 NAI, D/J 2005/147/158, notes 'For Minister's Information' in connection with a parliamentary question by Hugh Byrne TD, 22 June 1972, stating that until the 1972 increase, Scott Medal monetary awards were £100 (gold), £60 (silver), and £40 (bronze). The award of a Scott Medal did not *automatically* bring promotion in its wake. It was noted (in 1972) that only a handful of guards – 1 in 1935, 2 in 1940, 2 in 1948 and 1 in 1967 – had been thus 'specially promoted'. The commissioner in 1972 (Michael J. Wymes) was 'not in favour of … automatic promotion' for Scott Medal recipients. 28 NAI, D/J 2005/147/160, John Fenning, assistant commissioner, to Secretary, Department of Justice, 2 December 1977.

Deposit Account is derived from the expected surplus credit balance in the Weight[s] and Measures Fees Suspense Account and the monies in the Reward Fund Deposit Account are subsequently used to defray the cost of Scott Medals and to provide the accompanying monetary rewards. This arrangement dated back to the days of the Royal Irish Constabulary and the relevant legislation, the Weights and Measures Act, 1889, was condensed appropriately in section 80 of the Garda Síochána Code which in turn was based on the RIC Finance Code. For the Reward Board the crisis began in July 1974 when the Department of Industry and Commerce, home of weights and measures inspection, decided to deduct the *actual* costs connected with the inspection duties performed by its ex-officio staff, who were members of the Garda Síochána. (The subsistence allowances and fees payable to these staff-members had not been raised since 1945 and potential difficulties with the National Prices Commission discouraged any application for a revision.) The knock-on effect was to severely reduce the amount of revenue filtering into the Garda Reward Fund.[29]

With the presentation of an unprecedented number of medals looming on 10 October 1975 and a severely overdrawn Reward Fund Deposit Account (by £3,400), a tense struggle got under way to persuade the Department of Finance to sanction the additional funds needed (some £5,500) to pay for the Scott Medals and related monetary rewards. The manner in which Industry and Commerce had passed its problem to the Department of Justice also involved the Garda Reward Fund in a shortfall of £9,000 which was due to those gardaí who served as weights and measures inspectors – sanction for this amount was requested also from Finance. Some 53 garda sergeants were involved in inspection work and the rewards (a maximum of £190 in 1975) were 'considered an essential part of the job … [v]ery few of the inspectors are able to earn overtime and they do not qualify for any of the weekend allowances'.[30] The fact that the silversmiths needed ten weeks to prepare the medals made it imperative that the problem be resolved quickly. Worse still, the tendency of the price of metals, particularly gold, to fluctuate, raised the possibility that a sudden market shift would in the event of any delay render inadequate the sum approved by Finance. Eventually, following a protracted correspondence between the Minister for Justice, Patrick Cooney, and the

29 NAI, D/J 2005/147/159, memo by 'JB', accountant [Department of Justice], 26 July 1974; Sean O Muiri, Department of Industry and Commerce, to Secretary, Department of Justice, 6 February 1975; T.F. Brady, Department of Justice, to Secretary, Department of Finance [?] July 1975.
30 NAI, D/J 2005/147/159, internal memo, T.F. Brady, Department of Justice, to Miss Griffin, 14 July 1975.

Taoiseach, Liam Cosgrave (who was standing in temporarily at Finance for the Minister, Richie Ryan), the Department of Finance agreed to sanction the payment of £1,300 for medals and £4,200 for monetary rewards. The question of the £9,000 for the overworked sergeant-inspectors, however, was deliberately left unresolved.[31]

As Eoin O'Duffy remarked to Colonel Scott in 1925, the Scott Medal was a most coveted award; and so indeed it remains. The task of the Reward Board is an unenviable one in that it is partly a process of elimination: In most years there may be several or many recommendations, but only a few Scott Medallists. In the wake of the Conroy recommendations of the early 1970s the type of monetary award which had been associated with excellent or exceptional police work in Ireland, even as far back as the RIC days, came to an end and was replaced by a system of commendations. From 1972 onwards only the award of the Scott Medal has been accompanied by a monetary reward. Such is the value placed on the award and such is the esteem accruing to its recipient that the decisions of the Reward Board have not invariably met with the agreement of those not privy to its deliberations. Manifestations of dissatisfaction or private protests inside the force have been very uncommon but far from non-existent. Those which have occurred tend to reflect the genuine incomprehension of members who were involved in the same incident but only one, or some, of whose number was adjudged worthy of a Scott Medal.

At the time of the incident in 1923 in respect of which he received his medal, Garda Mulroy was in the company of Garda John Donlon who, at a certain point, left Mulroy to seek help. It was rumoured that, during the presentation ceremony the following year, Commissioner O'Duffy had uttered some remarks which reflected unfavourably on Donlon's conduct during the incident. Whether or not there was any truth in these stories the suspicion that he had cravenly left Mulroy to his fate dogged Donlon for decades. Finally in 1954 he appealed to his superiors for vindication, specifically in the form of a Scott Medal which, he felt, would prove to all detractors that his part in that long-ago incident had been no less meritorious than Mulroy's. He referred to the short note of 13 November 1923 which had been placed in his file (quoted above, 14), in which O'Duffy had congratulated not just Mulroy but Donlon as well on their 'coolness and bravery'. Donlon's appeal was taken very seriously and his case reviewed by the Reward Board who reported on it

31 NAI, D/J 2005/147/159, Patrick Cooney, Minister for Justice, to Richie Ryan, Minister for Finance, 13[14] August 1975; Liam Cosgrave, Department of Finance, to Patrick Cooney, 1 September & 10 September 1975.

to the commissioner. It was a difficult matter, not least because the Board 'was unable to locate the original report from [the] Chief Superintendent, Ennis, on which the award of [the] Scott Medal to Garda Mulroy was based'. All other available documents, however, including press reports and crime branch files on the incident, had been examined. Donlon was advised that it was simply not possible for the matter to be re-examined after a lapse of thirty years.[32] In the spring of 1978 former Sergeant James Mulroy agreed to give his Scott Medal as a permanent exhibit to the embryo Garda Museum. The commissioner, Patrick McLaughlin, when requesting the minister's attendance and conveying the details of the intended occasion to the officials at Justice, carefully drew attention to the 'delicate issues' raised by Donlon's appeal and copied to them the papers on the 1954 appeal. John Donlon, who had 'retired with an exemplary record of service', had in fact died on 16 March 1978.[33]

Other such appeals surfaced occasionally over the years, usually in the form of representations from members of the Dáil, from the garda representative bodies, and even from concerned members of the public. They date for the most part from the post-1970 period since which awards to groups of gardaí involved in the same incident have become increasingly common.[34]

The pages that follow constitute as complete a record as the sources allow of the incidents which resulted in the award of Scott Medals to members of the Garda Síochána. These represent solid gold, silver and bronze benchmarks in the force's continuing struggle against crime and high watermarks of its enduring commitment to the safety and well-being of the state and its citizens. They represent also the reality that courage is not confined to any particular generation or gender or age or rank but is a permanent and integral feature of the Garda Síochána and of all who have the honour to wear its uniform. Now let their stories speak for themselves.

---

32 NAI, D/J 2005/147/160, Garda J[ohn] Donlon to superintendent, Tramore, 8 September 1954; [signature illegible] assistant commissioner, to commissioner [Daniel Costigan], 13 December 1954.
33 NAI, D/J 2005/147/160, James Mulroy to Sergeant Gregory Allen, Garda Headquarters, 2 June 1978; P[atrick] McLaughlin, commissioner, to A. Ward, Department of Justice, 7 June 1978.
34 These may found scattered through NAI, D/J files 2005/147/158 to 160. See also *Garda News*, November 1991, 5, 7.

THE SCOTT MEDAL RECIPIENTS

James Mulroy, Garda 1264

Garda Mulroy was the first recipient of the Scott Medal. Born at Coolkevane, Straide, County Mayo on 17 August 1899, he had been a labourer before he joined the Guards on 19 May 1922.

He was on his first posting at Broadford Garda Station, County Clare on 26 May 1923 when the incident occurred for which he was awarded his medal. Together with a colleague he was on his way back to the station at Broadford when, in a lonely spot some four miles from home they were waylaid by two armed assailants. Both attackers were armed, one brandishing a revolver and the other a shotgun. The object appeared to have been simple robbery as both Guards were ordered to surrender all possessions even including their uniforms. It is unclear whether Mulroy's colleague complied, but Mulroy himself refused to be intimidated and his attackers then forced him at gunpoint further along the road in the direction of Broadford. The two robbers then tried to force Mulroy up an even more-deserted laneway, but Mulroy, realizing that they were seeking a quiet spot to murder him, again refused, challenging them to kill him where he stood. The revolver was then placed against his chest and the robbers gave him five minutes in which to comply, reinforcing their clear threat to kill him by counting off the minutes and seconds. In the course of this their attention strayed and Mulroy sprang at the man holding the revolver, pinning him down on the road. The other assailant then fired at Mulroy, causing a flesh wound to his shoulder. The shotgun was single-barrelled and so, unable to fire again, the man then began to beat Mulroy over the head with the weapon until the stock broke away. Maintaining his hold on the man he had pinned to the ground, Mulroy with his other hand gripped the shotgun barrel. The shotgun-bearer then took to his heels, leaving his colleague in Mulroy's grip. Mulroy was then able to disarm the assailant beneath him. At this point Mulroy momentarily lost consciousness. When he recovered he was still clutching the shotgun barrel and the revolver, but his captive had taken the opportunity to flee. Mulroy made his way back to Broadford Station arriving at 5a.m. As soon as his wounds had been attended to by a local doctor he went immediately with another Guard and managed to arrest one of the two assailants.

Garda Mulroy received his Scott Gold Medal from Colonel Scott himself at a presentation ceremony at the Depot in Dublin's Phoenix Park on 18 August 1924 in the presence of a distinguished company. Mulroy continued his career later in the Special Branch at Limerick, retiring on 16 August 1962 after 40 years and 9 months service. His achievement as the first Guard to receive the Scott Medal was remembered in 1978 when he was feted at a special dinner during which he presented the medal to the Garda Museum. James Mulroy died on 7 August 1986 ten days short of his 87th birthday.[1]

John Rooney, Garda 3378

John Rooney had been born in Glasgow on 4 October 1902 but had family links with Derry. He was an engineer's apprentice at the time he joined the Guards on 10 February 1923.

Rooney was on duty as Barrack Orderly at Tirconnaill, Castlefin, County Donegal, when a man reported that his car had just been stolen by an armed man. Leaving the station in the hands of his complainant, Rooney immediately set out in pursuit of the thief. When sighted by Rooney the thief (one Maguire, well-known to the Gardaí) was still in the village, again in the act of robbing passers-by at gunpoint and clearly intending to use the stolen car as a getaway vehicle. Rooney crept up behind the man, pausing only to allow Maguire's latest victims to get clear. The thief, however, spotted him at the last moment. Ignoring the gun, now being pointed directly at him, Rooney seized hold of Maguire, struggling with him for possession of the revolver which he eventually succeeded in wresting from the man's grasp. The Guard then marched the whining, threatening and cajoling thief to the station and secured him.

Garda Rooney received his Scott Gold Medal from the Minister for Justice, Kevin O'Higgins, on 9 December 1925, at what was now to become an annual presentation ceremony. Rooney went on to serve at Kanturk, County Cork, but resigned on 23 September 1927. He had served for 4 years and 7 months. Nothing is known of his life thereafter.[2]

Peter O'Reilly, Sgt. 1873

Peter O'Reilly, born on 17 April 1891 at Leitrim, Upper Mullagh, Kells, County Meath, left his occupation as a farmer to join the Guards on 6 October 1922.

He was sergeant on duty at Raheny Station (then part of the Dublin/ Wicklow Division) on the night of 10 October 1925 when he received a report that a masked man brandishing a revolver had held up the staff at the Howth Railway Station's parcels office. The thief had been unable to breach the office safe, however, and had made off instead with items of clothing. O'Reilly, who had already spotted a man cycling at speed through the village without lights, took off immediately after the robber, although knowing him to be armed. Overtaken by O'Reilly a mile outside Raheny, the thief, one Christopher Farnan, was seized by the Guard and a vicious struggle took place lasting some thirty minutes in which O'Reilly frustrated the man's efforts to draw his gun. O'Reilly sustained facial injuries as Farnan (a member of a Dublin boxing club) grabbed at his lip and attempted to gouge out one of his eyes. At length O'Reilly got possession of the gun and marched Farnon back to Raheny Station.

O'Reilly received his Scott Gold Medal from the President of the Irish Free State, William T. Cosgrave, at a presentation ceremony in August 1926. He continued at Raheny until his retirement on 16 April 1948, having served 25 years and 193 days. He died on 9 February 1976.[3]

John Whelan, Garda 11825 (106A Dublin Metropolitan Police)

Born at Clonegal, Carlow, on 21 June 1901, John Whelan forsook farming for a career in the police on 20 March 1923.

He had been on patrol in Inchicore on the night of 14 April 1925 when a resident on the licensed premises of Mr Patrick Guinan, Tyrconnell House, called to him from a window that two armed men had broken in. Whelan immediately entered the building by forcing the front door and was confronted by an armed assailant who fired at him but missed. The Guard then seized and overpowered the man but was beaten almost unconscious by the man's accomplice who struck him repeatedly with the butt of a revolver. Whelan, despite his injuries, attempted to pursue the robbers and reached Kilmainham Station where he was able to give an accurate description of them. That same night both assailants, Patrick King and Sean Costello, were arrested by a team of Gardaí which included Whelan. When Whelan was finally taken to hospital the wounds to his head required six stitches.

Garda Whelan received his Scott Silver Medal from the President of the Irish Free State, William T. Cosgrave, at a presentation ceremony in August 1926. Thereafter he continued in the Dublin Metropolitan Division until he retired on 28 December 1944, having served 21 years and 9 months. (The date of his death does not appear in the records).[4]

James Hanafin, Garda, 4797

James Hanafin was born at Tubber, Lispole, County Kerry, on 8 March 1904. He left farming to become a Guard on 23 June 1923.

He was on duty at his first posting in Belderrig, County Mayo, on the morning of 30 March 1925 when he heard revolver shots. The culprit, he quickly ascertained, was one Martin Hegarty, who had discharged the revolver outside the home of a Mr Caulfield of Belderrig. Though unarmed, Hanafin pursued and caught up with Hegarty a short distance away. Ignoring the levelled revolver and an explicit threat to shoot him, Hanafin seized both the assailant and the loaded firearm. An accomplice of O'Hegarty's attempted to rescue him but, with the help of Garda Kelly 4181, who arrived fortuitously on the scene, Hanafin managed to arrest both men.

Garda Hanafin received his Scott Bronze Medal from the President of the Irish Free State, William T. Cosgrave, at a presentation ceremony in August 1926. By the time he received the award Hanafin had become a Detective Officer attached to the Special Branch at Cork. Here he was to remain until he retired on 23 June 1954, having served 31 years and 1 day. He died on 2 June 1958.[5]

John J. Ward, Garda 12491 (Dublin Metropolitan Police)
John Ward, born in Derry's Waterside district on 14 January 1897, joined the police on 15 July 1924.

He was off duty and had just looked in at Terenure Station on the early evening of 23 March 1926 when he heard of an attempted robbery at Kimmage Post Office. Two men had presented revolvers at the counter assistant and demanded cash, but fled when the lady screamed loudly for help. Once the postmistress had telephoned the details to Terenure Station an immediate search was put in hand, in which Ward, though in plain clothes and unarmed, willingly joined. As he cycled along the Canal between Harold's Cross Bridge and Parnell Bridge he spotted two men approaching who matched the description of the would-be robbers. Both had their right hands in their pockets and Ward formed the opinion that they were armed. Having cycled past them he dismounted and called on them to halt. Both men instantly fired on him from a distance of about eight yards, but missed. Ward began to weave to avoid presenting a standing target. The men began to move apart and one of them demanded that Ward put his hands up, cocking and pointing the gun as he did so. When Ward ignored the threat and advanced on the men one of them again fired, the bullet passing between Ward's legs and through his overcoat. The two assailants then fled past Harold's Cross Bridge and along Harold's Cross Road and into a lane off the Canal, turning to fire yet again at the pursuing Ward. Catching sight of Garda Michael North, 11550, of Rathmines Station, in the near-distance Ward drew his attention to the two men and quickly appraised him of the situation. Although likewise off duty, unarmed and in plain clothes, North joined Ward in the pursuit. As they followed the assailants into the lane the Guards saw one of them fling his overcoat over a wall as he ran. North stopped to pick up the coat but Ward continued and apprehended the man who had abandoned it. The man's revolver was discovered later near the discarded coat, but Ward had continued and seized the man in the belief that he was still armed. The captured robber was then handed by Ward and North to a group of detectives who had joined them at the scene. The second man's escape was but temporary; he was arrested a few days later.

Garda Ward received his Scott Gold Medal from the Minister for Justice, Kevin O'Higgins, at a presentation ceremony on 22 June 1927. Later, Ward left 'E' District for Kevin Street and remained there until he retired on 27 March 1958, having served a total of 33 years and 256 days. He died on 9 June 1969.[6]

Francis O'Donoghue, Garda 2943

Garda O'Donoghue was born in Virginia, County Cavan, on 30 April 1902, and had been a student before joining the Guards on 20 December 1922.

He was on duty in the dayroom of Midleton Station, County Cork, on the evening of 10 November 1926 when a telephone message was received from Carrigtwohill Station alerting him that a party of IRA men had driven through the town at high speed apparently heading towards Midleton. Detective (or 'S' Branch) Units at Cobh and Midleton had already been instructed to intercept these evidently-frequent forays across the county by the IRA, and the uniformed Gardaí (of which O'Donoghue was one) had orders to co-operate with the detectives and keep them informed of such movements. On the night in question, however, no detective was available to accompany O'Donoghue who, being unarmed, would not normally have been expected to halt the IRA men's car in the absence of an armed detective. Undaunted, however, by the dangers of which he was well aware (having previously taken part in such stop-and-search operations), O'Donoghue, accompanied only by Garda Michael Mason, 5687, immediately proceeded to take up a position on the bridge at Midleton. Within minutes the car came speeding towards them. The motorists evaded O'Donoghue's signal to halt and his attempt to block their passage. Instead they drove into an adjacent road only to be impeded by a set of railway crossing gates. The two Guards, aware that a train was due and that the gates would be shut across the road, hotly pursued the car, coming level with it as it's driver attempted to turn it around. Garda O'Donoghue, his renewed call to the driver to stop again having been ignored, leaped onto the running board and seized the steering wheel. The front-seat passenger grabbed him by the throat and tried to push him off the car, but O'Donoghue persisted and wrenched the wheel of the vehicle (then moving at some 20 miles per hour) in an attempt to run it into a wall. The passengers at this point lost their collective nerve and pleaded with the Guard not to 'kill' them. O'Donoghue then managed to grab and apply the hand-brake, bringing the car to a halt despite some residual resistance from its occupants. At this stage O'Donoghue, who had now placed the car's occupants under arrest, was assisted by Detective Officer Lynch, who had arrived on the same Cork train which had initially prevented the IRA men's escape and whose attention had been attracted by the commotion. Beneath the car's front seat a fully-loaded Webley revolver was discovered together with nine rounds of ammunition and a number of seditious documents. The occupants of the (unlicensed) car were discovered to be four members of what was then known as the Irregular Battalion Staff, all from Cobh, and on their way to a Battalion Council meeting. The meeting, it subsequently emerged, had been called to plan the series of raids on Garda Stations which took place a few days later, during which two Gardaí, Sergeant Fitzsimons and Garda Ward, were murdered.

Garda O'Donoghue received his Scott Silver Medal from the Minister for Justice, Kevin O'Higgins, at a presentation ceremony on 22 June 1927. He later moved to the Special Branch in Dublin, and had served 41 years and 6 days when he retired on 29 April 1965. Garda O'Donoghue died on 21 September 1983.[7]

Charles Scully, Garda 12428 (Dublin Metropolitan Police)
Charles Scully was born at Foynes, County Limerick on 2 March 1904, and left his labouring job to join the police on 12 June 1924.

He was on duty in the vicinity of North Clarence Street, Dublin on the evening of 26 June 1926, when he was alerted by a shopkeeper and a group of by-standers to an attempt which had just been made to rob a nearby shop. The robber was armed and a shot had already been fired. Garda Scully joined the by-standers in pursuit of the robber, one William Cooney, but was virtually alone when, after a chase of 440 yards, he cornered Cooney in a cul-de-sac off Railway Street. Ignoring the revolver pointed at him from a distance of five yards, Scully grappled with the robber who then fired the gun missing the Guard by inches, and disarmed him. With the assistance of one of the original by-standers who had arrived on the scene (but who took no part in the actual struggle) Scully conveyed his prisoner to the Station.

He received his Scott Silver Medal from the Minister for Justice, Kevin O'Higgins, at a presentation ceremony on 22 June 1927. Garda Scully later moved to Fitzgibbon Street Station, but his remaining career was all too short. Sadly, he died of tuberculosis on 10 July 1936 having served 11 years and 66 days. He was 32 years old.[8]

John Kelly, Sgt. 3656
M.J. Ellis, Garda 6848

John Kelly, born at Ballymurray, County Roscommon, on 10 May 1900, exchanged the life of a student for that of a Guard on 8 March 1923.

M.J. Ellis, born at Clonmellon, Drumlish, County Longford, on 21 May 1905, left farming to become a Guard on 23 July 1925.

Sergeant Kelly and Garda Ellis were prominent among a group of volunteers (including an ex-RIC man) who rescued the crew of a stricken vessel at Killala Bay on the night of 6 November 1927. The ship, a Danish schooner named the *Sine* had left Poltenhugh, Sweden, early in October with a cargo of 450 tons of timber bound for Ballina. She had laid at anchor for over a fortnight in Killala Bay waiting for a tide high enough to allow her to proceed up the river Moy to Ballina. But, under gale-force conditions on the afternoon of 6 November, the ship's two anchors gave way and she was swept outward until she lay off Barrtra Island 1.5 miles from Killala Pier. When rockets and distress signals were spotted and it became clear that the crew were in great danger Sergeant Kelly took the initiative and organised a rescue party comprising Garda Ellis and eight civilians. The volunteers took possession of the only craft available – two leaky fourteen-foot rowing boats. Soon after setting out the boat carrying the two Guards was discovered to be taking in water so fast that a sod of turf had to be used to plug the leak. In darkness, high wind and seas, and in constant danger of capsizing, the rescuers reached the small island after two gruelling hours rowing, only to face a mile walk across sandbanks in order to get near as possible to the ship. Kelly was almost immediately caught up in a lengthy but successful struggle to get possession of a life buoy which had been thrown from the ship into the wild sea. After wading in almost five feet of water for half an hour Sergeant Kelly secured the buoy which had a vital durable lifeline attached. This enabled the exhausted ship's crew to clamber to safety along the hundred-foot rope which the rescue team weighed down with their bodies. Another gruelling hike across the sandbanks followed, this time dragging with them the shattered crew-members, and a return sea-journey no less arduous than the first. Rescuers and crew reached the safety of Killala at 11p.m.

The heroic rescue was the subject of much attention locally as well as at Garda Headquarters. At a presentation ceremony at Killala Schoolhouse on 5 April 1928 both Guards and ex-RIC Sergeant James Pryal were each given inscribed binoculars and the three were also included in the award of certificates made to all the volunteers by the Lifeboat Institution. During a garden party at the Depot on 4 July 1928 Sergeant Kelly's initiative and leadership on the fateful night were rewarded further with the presentation of a Scott Gold Medal. Garda Ellis, who supported his sergeant so magnificently, was awarded a Scott Silver Medal. Both medals were presented by the Minister for Justice, James Fitzgerald-Kenney. John Kelly rose to the rank of Inspector in April 1943 and to that of Superintendent in July 1957. He spent the latter part of his service in Wexford and retired on 9 May 1963, having spent 40 years and 63 days in the force. He died on 10 June 1978. M.J. Ellis continued in the west of Ireland, serving in the May and Galway Districts until his retirement on 28 August 1955. He had served a total of 30 years and 17 days. Garda Ellis died on 9 June 1989.[9]

John O'Brien, Garda 5846

Born at Rathmore, County Kerry, on 6 March 1905, John O'Brien had been a labourer before joining the Guards on 10 July 1924.

He was returning from a long swim at Courtown Harbour, County Wexford, on 13 July 1927 when his attention was attracted by a man still in the water and about 25 yards from land who appeared to be in difficulties. The man, Nicholas Scallon of Gorey, had remained too long in the water in an area plagued by a strong undercurrent and had no strength left to reach the shore. Garda O'Brien hurriedly undressed again and went to his aid. Mr Scallon was near the end of his endurance when Garda O'Brien reached him and his panic-stricken struggles made it difficult for the Guard to effect the rescue. By the time he was brought to shore the man had lost consciousness and Garda O'Brien had to resort to artificial respiration to revive him. At length Mr Scallon recovered sufficiently to make his way home.

Just over a month later, on 18 August 1927, when Garda O'Brien was swimming at the same spot, this time in the company of the Revd Mr McNabney, Methodist minister of Gorey, the minister, notwithstanding the Guard's warning to him to stay near the shore as the sea was very rough that day, accidentally strayed too far out. Finding himself some 70 yards from the shore and growing exhausted, McNabney called for help and Garda O'Brien yet again swam to the rescue. Again there was the desperate struggle to effect the rescue against the frenzied clutching of a drowning man and a rough sea, and again the successful delivery of a man from certain death. In the aftermath of the McNabney rescue Gorey's Methodist community presented Garda O'Brien with a gold watch.

In recognition of both acts of gallantry John O'Brien received the Scott Silver Medal from the Minister for Justice, James Fitzgerald-Kenny, during a garden party at the Depot on 4 July 1928. Garda O'Brien continued his career in the Wexford Division, becoming Sergeant in August 1959 and retiring on 24 March 1967, having served 42 years and 258 days. He died on 19 April 1978.[10]

David Hannon, Garda 12253 (Dublin Metropolitan Police)

David Hannon was born in Bray, County Wicklow, on 15 June 1903, and had followed the occupations of labourer and butcher before joining the police on 11 April 1924.

He was on duty at Dun Laoghaire Station on 7 August 1927 when he noticed a young girl fling her hat and handbag on the ground on a green plot near to the Royal Yacht Club and run towards the edge of the embankment with the obvious intention of throwing herself into the water. The tide was high at the time and the water at least 14 feet deep. Garda Hannon was separated from the girl by some 300 yards and was unable to reach her before she entered the water. Once he had reached the spot, however, and despite being in full uniform, he immediately jumped in to save her. That the girl intended to drown herself was apparent from the desperate struggle she put up against the Guard's efforts, endangering both their lives. Hannon persisted and got her back to the shore with the greatest difficulty. It later emerged that the girl was mentally ill. Garda Hannon would later receive a Certificate from the Royal Humane Society, presented to him by the Senior District Justice, Mr Cussen.

During a garden party at the Depot on 4 July 1928 he received the Scott Silver Medal from the Minister for Justice, James Fitzgerald-Kenny. Garda Hannon later transferred to Lad Lane in the Dublin Metropolitan Division. He retired on 4 August 1955, having served 31 years and 116 days, and died on 24 February 1984.[11]

Victor S.C. Lockhart, Garda 12221 (Dublin Metropolitan Police)

Born at Langton, Howth Road, Dublin, on 4 October 1897, Victor Lockhart left a position as clerk to enter the police on 27 March 1924.

Garda Lockhart was just coming on duty on 18 October 1928 when his Station at Clontarf was alerted by telephone of a raid on James Corbett's Public House in Howth Road by three armed men. Lockhart, though unarmed and alone, immediately went to the scene and, having obtained such few details as were known, set off on his bike to a prominent spot in the Clontarf Golf Links from which he was able to see three men moving at speed across the fields towards Artane. Returning to the road he cycled to a point in Killester Lane where he believed he would intercept them. Soon the three robbers approached, and as they came abreast of him Lockhart emerged from the hedge where he had lain hidden and demanded that they surrender. All three responded by drawing their revolvers, and as Lockhart rushed forward to seize the nearest assailant two shots rang out. Undaunted the Guard proceeded to disarm and subdue not only the man in his grasp but the second of the robbers also. The third robber, stunned by what had occurred, surrendered his gun without further resistance. Lockhart then marched the three at gunpoint back to the scene of the robbery where, before his amazed colleagues who were still making inquiries, the robbers were divested of the cheques and £50 in money which they had taken from the safe and cash register no more than half an hour previously. One of the raiders was found to be still in possession of a fourth revolver and some forty rounds of ammunition.

Garda Lockhart received his Scott Gold Medal from the President of the Irish Free State, William T. Cosgrave, during a garden party at the Depot on 13 August 1929. He later transferred to the College area of the Dublin Metropolitan Division but retired early on 6 March 1941, having served 16 years and 340 days. Nothing is known of his life thereafter.[12]

Thomas P. Scully, Garda 4708

Thomas Scully was born on 19 February 1904 at Cragganock, Cree, County Clare, and had worked on the railway before entering the Guards on 15 June 1923.

He was stationed at Ferrybank in Waterford and was at the Tramore Races on 15 August 1928 when an incident occurred which, but for his personal intervention, would have ended in tragedy. A lady spectator attempted to cross the track just before the start of a steeplechase. Suddenly realizing that the race was about to begin and that horses were almost upon her she collapsed in a faint behind a jump and out of view of the jockeys. Garda Scully ran forward as the horses approached and pulled the unconscious lady close into the jump where they both lay until the horses had passed over them. Had she been allowed to remain where she had fallen she would certainly have been trampled.

Garda Scully was presented with his Scott Silver Medal by the President of the Irish Free State, William T. Cosgrave, during a garden party at the Depot on 13 August 1929. He was later moved to Blarney, County Cork, where he was still stationed when he retired on 18 February 1967, having served 43 years and 249 days. Garda Scully died on 12 July 1982.[13]

Charles Manning, Garda 11771 (Dublin Metropolitan Police)
Born on 19 February 1898 at 25 South William Street, Dublin, Charles Manning left labouring for a career in the Dublin Metropolitan Police on 2 September 1921. In the early hours of 24 February 1928 he was on duty near Burgh Quay when he saw a woman throw herself into the River Liffey. Garda Manning immediately plunged in and managed to effect a rescue with the greatest difficulty as the woman fought strenuously against his efforts to keep her head above water. It emerged subsequently that the woman was mentally ill.

Garda Manning received his Scott Bronze Medal from the President of the Irish Free State, William T. Cosgrave, during a garden party at the Depot on 13 August 1929. He was still stationed at Store Street when he retired early on 28 September 1934, having served 13 years and 26 days. Nothing is known of his life thereafter.[14]

Thomas Mahon, Garda 3981
Hugh Semple, Garda 343
Garda Mahon and Garda Semple both came from County Offaly, Mahon having been born at Newtown, Rahan, on 10 March 1897, and Semple at Moneygall on 11 July 1895. Semple had been an early recruit, joining the force on 18 March 1922, and Mahon a year later on 6 April 1923. Before joining up both men had been labourers.

They were stationed at Kilmanagh, County Kilkenny, on the afternoon of Sunday 10 March 1929 when a series of disturbing incidents which had occurred that morning were brought to their attention. A man who the previous year had been under treatment in a mental hospital entered Ballycallion Church during Mass armed with a shotgun which, at one point, he appeared to brandish. After the service he discharged the gun over the heads of a curious crowd which had gathered outside the church. He later withdrew to a location named known as Ballyfunk and walked endlessly back and forth to the Ballycallion Church. Gardaí Mahon and Semple located the man who had by then taken refuge inside a house at Ballycudihy. Alarmed local people warned the two Gardaí that he was threatening to shoot anyone in uniform who approached him. Refusing several offers of firearms and the advice that they should shoot him through a window, the Gardaí calmly assessed the situation. The man, though still armed and apparently waiting for some assault from without, had not menaced the householder (an 85-year-old woman) or attempted to repulse neighbours or other usual callers at the house. Mahon and Semple, therefore, having persuaded a neighbour to open the door, rushed into the house behind him and, with the neighbour's help, managed to overpower the man whose gun was found to be fully loaded and cocked. The two Gardaí's difficulties were not at an end, however. As they set off on the five-mile journey to Kilmanagh Station they were obliged to draw their batons to keep at bay an incensed crowd of locals intent on attacking the handcuffed man in their custody. On his appearance before the District Court the man was committed to Kilkenny Mental Hospital.

For the first time since the introduction of the Scott Medal neither Mahon nor Semple nor any of the several Gardaí who that year had saved lives and disarmed mentally disturbed persons armed with knives were considered suitable for the award of a gold medal. The incident at Ballycudihy, however, had involved firearms. Mahon and Semple, therefore, received their Scott Silver Medals from the Minister for Justice, James Fitzgerald-Kenney, during a garden party at the Depot on 24 June 1930. Thomas Mahon resigned voluntarily from the force some two months later, on 26 September 1930, having served 7 years and 5 months; nothing is known of his life thereafter. Hugh Semple, one of the force's earliest recruits, stayed on, serving later in Galway, until his retirement on 7 October 1954 after a service of 32 years and 204 days. He died on 29 June 1958.[15]

Michael Mullane, Sergeant 1905
Brian Connaughton, Garda 4447

Sergeant Mullane was born in Burnfoot, Mallow, County Cork, on 8 October 1899, and entered the force on 12 October 1922, having previously been a labourer. Garda Connaughton, from Ballinglas, Mountbellew, County Galway, was born on 15 March 1902, and left his occupation as a farmer to join the Gardaí on 18 May 1923.

Both men were serving at Drumshambo, County Leitrim, in 1930, when, with great perseverance, they tracked down two armed men, members of an illegal organization, in the townland of Dromod. Three rifles were seized and the men arrested and returned to Drumshambo Station.

Mullane and Connaughton respectively received their gold and silver Scott Medals from the Justice Minister, James Fitzgerald-Kenney, at a Depot garden party on 28 July 1931. Both men continued to serve in the Sligo/Leitrim Division. Mullane, sadly, died in harness on 1 October 1957, after serving 34 years and 355 days. Garda Connaughton, who was promoted to Sergeant in the summer of 1951, retired on 14 March 1965, having served 41 years and 301 days. He died on 26 March 1983.[16]

James Scott, Garda 4173

James Scott, born on 24 May 1899, at Accony, Louisburg, County Mayo, left farming for the Gardaí on 25 April 1923.

While stationed at Cobh, County Cork, on 21 December 1930, he displayed exceptional courage in rescuing a German sailor from drowning.

He received his Scott Silver Medal from the Justice Minister, James Fitzgerald-Kenney, at a Depot garden party on 28 July 1931. Later he was awarded the Medal of the German Red Cross, together with a diploma and a personal letter of appreciation from the German Minister in Dublin. Garda Scott continued to serve in Cork until his retirement on 23 May 1962, having served 39 years and 29 days. He died on 10 May 1966.[17]

Arthur Cullen, Garda Sergeant 1938
James Leddy, Garda 1894
Joseph Kelly, Detective Garda 4317

Born on 1 April 1898 at Kiltimagh, County Mayo, Arthur Cullen was a grocer's assistant until he joined the force on 14 October 1922. Garda Leddy had been born at Gowna, County Cavan on 3 May 1902 and had been a barman before joining on 11 October 1922. Detective Garda Kelly, born on 31 October 1903 at Eyeries, Castletown, County Cork, had worked in farming before becoming a Guard on 5 May 1923.

Sergeant Cullen received his Scott Silver Medal from the Justice Minister, James Fitzgerald-Kenney, at a Depot garden party on 28 July 1931, for his courage and skill in rescuing a young man and woman from two armed kidnappers at Cappawhite, County Tipperary, in 1930. Scott Bronze Medals were awarded on the same occasion to Garda Leddy and Detective Garda Kelly for their assistance to Garda Cullen during the incident. A young pregnant domestic servant was rejected by the father of her unborn child. The girl's relatives, several of them members of the IRA, kidnapped the man in question and attempted to force the pair to marry literally at gunpoint. Acting on a tip-off the three Guards intercepted the armed wedding party as it approached the Church in Cappawhite. When challenged, the relatives surrendered their weapons and were taken into custody. Of the three officers only Detective Garda Kelly was armed. Sergeant Cullen later served in the Louth Division until his retirement on 19 June 1953, after serving 30 years and 74 days. He died on 19 April 1971. Garda Leddy went on to serve in the Limerick District and retired on 2 May 1965, having served 42 years and 204 days. He died on 19 November 1976. Detective Garda Kelly served in Tipperary and Bray, County Wicklow, and retired on 30 October 1966 after a service of 43 years and 179 days. He died on 21 May 1982.[18]

Charles Connell, Garda 2980
Michael Hayden, Garda 726

Garda Connell was born at Williamstown, Moate, County Westmeath, on 15 September 1899, and had been a farmer before joining the force on 3 January 1923. Michael Hayden, born on 6 June 1892 at Kilcool, Greystones, County Wicklow, left labouring for the Gardaí on 6 April 1922.

Both men were stationed in the Cavan–Monaghan Division on the night of 6–7 November 1930 when a Mrs Margaret McCabe of Castleblaney informed them that her husband had become insane and was threatening her, her 4-year-old son and their servant boy, with a loaded shotgun. They escaped, managing to lock him inside the house, but his elderly mother was trapped within. Realizing that the situation, however dangerous, would brook no delay, Connell and Hayden decided not to wait on the arrival of other Gardaí to assist. Having learned from Mrs McCabe the general lay-out of the house they effected an entry and overpowered the disturbed man, seizing his gun and cartridges. It was, sadly, too late to save the man's 75-year-old mother; he had battered her to death.

In the first ceremony in which two Scott Gold Medals were awarded for the same incident, Connell and Hayden received their medals from the Minister for Justice, Patrick J. Ruttledge, on his first official visit to the Depot in June 1933 (the presentation ceremony of 1932 had been postponed). Both men continued to serve in Cavan–Monaghan. Garda Connell retired after 39 years and 255 days on 14 September 1962, and Garda Hayden after 32 years and 61 days on 5 June 1954. Connell died on 24 April 1984, predeceased by his colleague Michael Hayden who had died on 17 July 1968.[19]

Martin Langton, Garda 3617

Born at Gowran, County Kilkenny, on 2 March 1902, Martin Langton worked in farming before joining the force on 6 March 1923.

He was on duty at Howth, County Dublin, on 7 November 1931 when he heard screams of distress from the East Pier. Two girls were in difficulties at a distance from the pier. Garda Langton threw them a mooring rope, but the girls could not reach it. Langton was a very poor swimmer but, seeing one of the little girls sink, he left his tunic and greatcoat on the pier and dived in and brought her to the surface. He then seized hold of the other struggling child and kept all three of them afloat while he waited for help. A local man, seeing the incident, made his way to them in a punt. Despite his exhaustion Garda Langton gave artificial respiration to one of the girls who had lost consciousness, enabling her to recover.

He received his Scott Silver Medal from Justice Minister Patrick J. Ruttledge at the Depot in June 1933. Garda Langton continued to serve in the Dublin/Wicklow Division until he retired on 30 May 1952 after a career lasting 29 years and 86 days. He died on 30 October 1991.[20]

Patrick Sweeney, Garda 1277

Garda Sweeney was born at Glenapadden, Annacarty, County Tipperary, on 20 April 1901, and was a labourer before joining the Gardaí on 22 May 1922.

He was stationed at Dungarvan, County Waterford, and was playing handball when a passer-by alerted him to the fact that a man (later discovered to be suicidal) had just thrown himself from the quayside into the outgoing tide and was being swept away. Sweeney immediately dived in and made his way to the man, reaching him at a dangerous point near the opening of the bay. Turning the drowning man (who weighed 14 stone) onto his back and gripping him securely with one hand, the Guard fought his way back to safety using one hand against the current. On reaching dry land Garda Sweeney then revived the man through artificial respiration.

The Minister for Justice, Patrick J. Ruttledge, presented Sweeney with his Scott Bronze Medal at the Depot in June 1933. Patrick Sweeney continued his career in later years at Kilkenny Station, from where he retired on 1 November 1963, having served 41 years and 164 days. He died on 10 September 1973.[21]

Laurence Fennelly, Sergeant 114

Sergeant Fennelly, born at Esker, Timahoe, Leix, on 22 November 1901, had been a carpenter before entering the force on 2 March 1922.

He and Sergeant M. Dolan were on duty in Clonmel soon after 10pm on the night of 17 January 1932 when they were informed of a fire at a house in Ann Street. The two sergeants entered the house and noted that the upper floors were ablaze and that the stairwell was filling with thick smoke. From onlookers they learned that children were trapped upstairs. Both men immediately made their way to the landing of the first floor and discovered that the source of the fire was in a room on the next floor above them. Fennelly made a bold attempt to reach the room but was driven back by the heat and smoke which momentarily made his senses swim. On recovering he attempted the ascent again only to meet Sergeant Dolan coming down the stairs with a child in his arms. On reaching safety Dolan also needed time to recover. Meanwhile his colleague after four attempts managed to get past the blazing room on the second floor and reached the third floor where he could hear a child crying.

Pinned to the stairhead by the thick smoke he tried to persuade the child to come to him. When this failed Fennelly plunged towards the sound of the crying, located the child and carried her back downstairs past the second-floor inferno to safety. It was then that the two policemen learned from a maid that another child, a baby six months old, was still trapped on the top floor. The maid, who had left the children alone in the house, was too distraught to give a clear description of the lay-out of the top floor. With some difficulty a wet cloth was procured, and Fennelly again mounted the stairs and reached the top floor through the ever-thickening smoke. It was now necessary for Sergeant Dolan to remain some distance below him on the stairs, calling repeatedly so that Fennelly would be guided back to the stairhead. Reacting to a noise on his right Fennelly felt his way along a corridor and into a room where he stumbled over the baby's cot. Guided by Dolan's voice from below Fennelly again reached the staircase and eventual safety past the veritable inferno on the second floor landing. All three children, particularly the baby, were suffering severely from smoke inhalation, but all made a full recovery.

Sergeant Fennelly received his Scott Gold Medal from the Minister for Justice, Patrick J. Ruttledge, at the Depot on 20 August 1933 during the Aeridheacht of the Aonach an Gharda. Both Fennelly and Dolan were also enrolled in the Carnegie Hero Trust from which, in addition, they received silver watches. Sergeant Dolan also received a monetary grant from the Garda Reward Fund for his part in the rescue. Sergeant Fennelly continued to serve in Clonmel, rising to Inspector (1942) and later to Superintendent (1952). He retired on 21 November 1964 having served 42 years and 265 days, and died on 29 August 1975.[22]

Henry L. Smith, Garda 1969

Born at Salthill, County Galway, on 24 January 1898, Henry Smith had worked in farming before joining the force on 18 October 1922.

He was stationed at Killaloe, County Clare, on 13 August 1932, when the area suffered a cloud burst of unusual severity. A message was received to the effect that a Mrs Woodroofe was trapped by rising flood waters at her home about a mile from the Garda Station. Together with his colleagues Sergeant Staunton and Garda Connolly, Garda Smith persuaded a reluctant lorry driver to take them to the scene. Mrs Woodroofe's house was set in a hollow which, under the impact of torrential rain, was fast becoming a lake. When the three Gardaí arrived they found her clinging to the upper edge of her front door in an effort to avoid being swept away, while on-lookers stood by in apparent helplessness. Within the house lay her bedridden husband and their baby. Realizing that not a moment was to be lost, Garda Smith plunged through the torrent, risking the treacherous pot-holes which surrounded the building, seized Mrs Woodroofe and passed her to his colleagues who had followed him. Smith then returned again to the house through the still-rising water. This time he managed to secure Mrs Woodroofe's baby; tragically the child had drowned. For the third time, accompanied on this occasion by Garda Connolly, Smith re-entered the house and found Mr Woodroofe in a room off the kitchen. Despite their imminent danger of being cut off by the water (which had now risen to a height of more than five feet), both men got Mr Woodruffe onto a mattress which they then used as a raft to float him through the front door and to safety.

Along with a testimonial from the Royal Humane Society – one was received also by Garda Connolly – Garda Smith was awarded the Scott Silver Medal. He received his medal at the Depot from Justice Minister Patrick J. Ruttledge on 20 August 1933. Garda Smith spent much of his later career in the Tipperary Division, from which he retired on 9 January 1954 having served 31 years and 61 days. The date of his death is not known.[23]

Michael J. Brady, Garda 7505

Michael Brady was born in Monaghan's High Street on 29 October 1903, and had been a labourer before joining the Gardaí on 27 January 1927.

He was Barrack Orderly and on his own at Edgeworthstown Station, County Longford, on 17 November 1932, when he was informed by the porter of the National Bank that an armed robbery was in progress. He sent the porter to fetch two off-duty Gardaí who were at home, left the Station in the hands of the Sergeant's wife, and made his way, alone and unarmed, to the bank. Meeting on route one of the off-duty Guards, Garda McLoughlin, who then accompanied him, Garda Brady arrived at the bank to find the manager and an assistant being held up by one man. The robber made up for his lack of support, however, by brandishing both a knife and a gun. Pointing both weapons at the two Guards, the robber got through the door of the bank and tried to escape on a bicycle. Garda Brady thrust his foot through one of the wheels causing the robber to fall to the ground. The man then recovered himself sufficiently, however, to attempt to stab Garda Brady who had (almost unavoidably) got his foot caught in the spokes of the damaged wheel. Garda McLaughlin then closed with the robber causing him to drop the knife. Freeing himself after a fierce scuffle the man then fled across an adjacent field only to run into the arms of Garda Breen, the other off-duty Garda alerted by the bank porter. All the money taken from the National Bank was safely recovered.

Garda McLoughlin later received a monetary grant from the Reward Fund. Garda Brady was awarded the Scott Bronze Medal, which he received from Patrick J. Ruttledge, Minister for Justice, at the Depot, on 20 August 1933. Michael Brady continued to serve in the Longford/ Westmeath Division until his premature death from heart failure on 3 November 1941. He had served 14 years and 278 days.[24]

Thomas J. O'Rourke, Garda 6453

Garda O'Rourke, born on 6 November 1905 at Courtmacsherry, County Cork, had been a motor driver before joining the force on 15 January 1925.

He was on duty in the Cork ER Division on the night of 16 November 1932 when he and two colleagues were summoned to a house-fire at Blackrock Road. When they arrived they were loudly called upon by a gathered crowd to save the life of a man believed trapped upstairs by the flames. The three Gardaí forced open the front door and Garda O'Rourke immediately made his way to the kitchen, where he soaked his handkerchief prior to making his way upstairs. After a search fraught with danger (nobody was actually in the house after all) Garda O'Rourke was overcome by smoke and heat and barely made his way back to the front door before he collapsed. Thereafter he spent over three weeks in hospital and it was a further month before he was fit to return to duty.

Garda O'Rourke's selfless bravery and promptitude were recognized by the Carnegie Hero Trust whose directors included him on the Trust's Roll of Honour and presented him with a silver watch. On 20 August 1933 he received the Scott Bronze Medal at the Depot from Justice Minister Patrick J. Ruttledge. Garda O'Rourke went on to enjoy a distinguished career, becoming Sergeant in 1942, Inspector in 1961, and Superintendent in 1964. He retired after 42 years and 298 days on 5 November 1968, and died on 1 March 1992.[25]

John Wynne, Sergeant 289

Born at Cloonloo, Gurteen, County Sligo, on 1 April 1900, John Wynne was no stranger to police work when he transferred from the Royal Irish Constabulary to the new force on 16 March 1922.

Normally stationed in the Carlow/Kildare Division, Sergeant Wynne was on temporary duty at Templemore, County Tipperary, on 14 August 1933 when he received word that a man, Thomas Ryan, engaged in sinking a pump on farmland, had become trapped. An escape of foul gases had rendered him unconscious and all attempts by his workmates to rescue him had failed. Sergeant Wynne, pausing only to equip himself with a set of metal butcher's hooks and a length of rope, sped to the scene. Ryan was deeply unconscious and the surrounding air foul and suffocating as the Sergeant had himself lowered into the shaft. An attempt to raise Ryan by putting him into a tub had to be abandoned due to the unfortunate man's excessive weight, the narrowness of the shaft and the foulness of the air. Wynne's effort to have the man raised to the surface by tying him to the tub was no more successful, as Ryan's weight caused the tub to overbalance. This led to both men becoming trapped temporarily in the shaft. Wynne directed that the tub be lowered to the bottom again. Once this had been done he was able to re-adjust Ryan's position. Finally the tub, with Ryan and the Sergeant on board, was drawn to the surface. Along with the effects of suffocation Wynne had been severely cut and bruised during the rescue, not least through his efforts to protect Ryan's head during the ascent from various stones which projected from the sides of the hole. Sadly, Ryan died shortly after being hauled to the surface.

Sergeant Wynne received the Scott Gold Medal from the Minister for Justice, Patrick J. Ruttledge, at the Depot on 8 July 1934. In addition he later received a silver watch from the Carnegie Hero Trust. Wynne was later stationed at the Depot in Dublin. He was still serving at the time of his death on New Year's Day 1962, a career that had lasted 39 years and 213 days.[26]

Henry Gillespie, Garda 7659

Garda Gillespie was born at 6 Academy Terrace, Derry, on 24 April 1906, and had been a teacher before joining the force on 27 October 1927.

Whilst stationed in the Mayo Division he was participating in a diving competition on 17 August 1933, a particularly stormy day, in Enniscrone, County Sligo. The weather had caused the abandonment of most of the planned events when Gillespie became aware that a man was drowning in the comparatively sheltered area of the pier. Responding to the officials' calls through the megaphone for volunteers to assist the hapless man, the Garda dived in and made his way through enormous waves towards the man who now appeared to be unconscious. Because of the strong current between him and the shortest journey back to the pier, Gillespie with his senseless charge was forced to undertake a 250-yard swim to reach safety. The effort proved too severe, and, unable to reach the shore after several attempts, the Garda seized a rope the end of which had been thrown to him and tied the unconscious man's hands with it. This enabled those on the pier to pull the man to safety and allowed Gillespie to save himself.

Garda Gillespie, the only person amongst the fifty onlookers who was prepared to risk his life in the waves, was presented with his Scott Silver

Medal at the Depot on 8 July 1934 by the Minister for Justice, Patrick J. Ruttledge. Gillespie went on to serve in later years at Letterkenny Station, County Donegal. He retired on 8 April 1950 having served 22 years and 6 months. The date of his death is unknown.[27]

Andrew Quinn, Garda 4846

Andrew Quinn was born at 6 Albert Street, Belfast, on 4 September 1897, and worked as an engineer before joining the Guards on 4 July 1923.

He was on traffic duty near Portobello House, Dublin, early on the evening of 15 November 1933 when he went to the aid of the fire brigade as they attempted to rescue bedridden patients from a fire at the nearby nursing home. Assisted by the firemen Garda Quinn succeeded in rescuing some twelve patients, most of them from the upper floor of the blazing building. In addition to the hazards of heat and smoke there was a gas escape inside the premises, the electricity fused and the water-pipes burst. When, at the conclusion of the main rescue effort, it was suggested that one woman patient was still unaccounted for, Garda Quinn immediately re-entered the building and searched every room until he was satisfied that there was nobody left within. As he retreated down the stairs part of the roof collapsed on top of him, breaking his leg and forcing him to drag himself the rest of the way to the first-floor landing from which firemen carried him to safety. He spent five weeks in hospital recovering not only from his damaged leg but from the many scorch-marks on his face and hands.

Garda Quinn received his Scott Silver Medal from Justice Minister Patrick J. Ruttledge at the Depot on 8 July 1934. After his heroic endeavour Andrew Quinn continued his career as a detective in Dublin Castle, retiring on 7 December 1954 having served 31 years and 1 day. He died on 30 May 1979.[28]

Timothy Mahony, Garda 2376
Laurence Neill, Garda 5357
Patrick Quinn, Garda 1700

Garda Mahony was born on 8 February 1900 at Rylane, Coachford, County Cork and had been a farmer before joining the force on 15 November 1922. Garda Neill, born on 28 September 1902 at 32 McDermott Street, Waterford, had worked as a moulder before joining up on 23 November 1923. Garda Quinn was a native of Mountgordon, Castlebar, County Mayo, where he was born on 20 March 1904; he also had worked in farming before becoming a Guard on 1 June 1922.

All three men were conferring at Balbriggan Station shortly after 10 a.m. on

20 October 1934 following a report by a Mr Finnegan who claimed that he had been kidnapped and had just escaped. Garda Mahony noticed two suspicious-looking men passing by immediately outside the Station. Following a brief exchange of words with Garda Quinn, driver to the Chief Superintendent who was waiting outside, it was decided to keep the two men under observation. Garda Laurence joined Mahony and Quinn and the three set off in the Chief Superintendent's car to overtake the men, by now some 300 yards off. Clearly alarmed by the arrival of the car abreast of them moments later, the two men simultaneously reached into their pockets with their right hands. As Mahony and Neill emerged from the car and began to question them one of the men made a nervous gesture with his concealed hand. Realizing that the man was about to draw a gun Mahony seized him. A fierce struggle ensued as the two combatants wrestled each other across the road. At this point Mahony's foot jarred against the kerbstone, off-balancing him momentarily and causing his grip to slacken. His assailant then drew the revolver from his pocket and was attempting to aim at Mahony when the latter, recovering himself, drove his knee into the man's stomach causing the shot to miss. Mahony now hurled himself at the man, bearing him to the ground. In the meantime Garda Neill had seized hold of the second man who, like his partner, seemed intent on with-drawing something from his coat pocket. Gripping the man's concealed hand with his left hand Neill worked his right arm around the man's neck, forcing him against an adjacent wall. The man managed to get the revolver (later found to be fully loaded) out of his pocket, but the pressure of Neill's arm-lock made it impossible to aim or even point the weapon. Soon the man was too exhausted to continue the struggle and dropped the revolver. Both men were then arrested. The two struggles took place simultaneously and probably were over in under a minute. The moment they began Garda Quinn had sprung from the car and had raced to the aid, first of Garda Neill who had just succeeded in shaking the gun from his prisoner's grasp, and then to that of Garda Mahony, only to narrowly avoid being shot when the assailant's gun went off. Garda Quinn then went forward and tore the gun from the grasp of the man strug-gling with Mahony. Both guns were found to be loaded, and the two men were in possession also of pairs of handcuffs. These were the men who had kidnapped Mr Finnegan and from whom he had escaped. They had approached Balbriggan Station in pursuit of Finnegan and with the intention of using their guns to recapture him from the Station.

Mahony and Neill received their Scott Gold Medals, and Quinn his Scott Bronze Medal, from Justice Minister Patrick J. Ruttledge immediately before the opening of the Garda Aeridheacht at the Depot on 25 August 1935. Garda

Mahony went on to work in the Special Branch in the Waterford/Kilkenny Division; he died, still serving, on 23 October 1948, after a career spanning 25 years and 344 days. Garda Neill remained in the Dublin/Wicklow Division; like Mahony he was still in the force when he died on New Year's Day 1945, having served 20 years and 99 days. Soon after the incident Garda Quinn moved on to the Longford/Westmeath Division, where he was promoted to Sergeant in July 1936. He retired on 19 March 1967 after 44 years and 292 days service, and died on 4 December 1976.[29]

John Ellis, Garda 462

John Ellis, born on 20 November 1900 at Mohill, County Leitrim, had been a farmer before becoming one of the early members of the force on 24 March 1922.

Normally based at Skibbereen in the Cork West Riding Division, he was on temporary duty at a sports meeting, organized by the League of Youth, at Drimoleague, County Cork, on 12 August 1934. During the evening a party of men, who had arrived in two cars and were in an inebriated and excited state following a football match at Skibbereen, approached Garda Johnston (who was on duty with Ellis) and demanded that the two Gardaí clear the village of Blueshirts. Despite being advised by both Johnston and Ellis to go home quietly the men threatened to create disorder; already their raised voices had attracted a large crowd in which League of Youth members featured prominently. Two members of the League were then seen to draw pistols and fire towards the crowd, causing an immediate stampede. Ellis, Johnston and other Gardaí rushed to apprehend the men, who were still facing the crowd. One of them, named O'Leary, turned to see Garda Ellis making straight for him and fired his pistol at the Guard from a distance of five or six yards, narrowly missing him. Ellis, undaunted, seized O'Leary without even breaking his stride. The second gunman then turned and fired at Garda Ellis, who again had a lucky escape. For a few tense moments, while his colleagues closed in on the second gunman, Ellis kept the captured O'Leary between him and the second man. As the second man seemed about to fire again Ellis flung himself and O'Leary to the ground. The second gunman then fled along the street firing as he went at the Gardaí who continued to pursue him, and finally escaped (though he was later identified). Assisted by Garda Stevenson, Ellis disarmed and secured O'Leary who was later found to be in possession of further ammunition as well as the loaded pistol. But Ellis's ordeal was not yet over. As he and Stevenson marched O'Leary to the Station they were forced to beat off a spirited and violent attempt by a number of men to rescue the gunman.

Garda Ellis received his Scott Silver Medal from Patrick J. Ruttledge, Minister for Justice, at the Depot on 25 August 1935. He continued in the Cork West Riding Division, being promoted Sergeant in October 1954. When he retired on 24 March 1965 he had served 43 years and 1 day. John Ellis died on 24 January 1980.[30]

Joseph Egan, Sergeant 8532

Born on 19 February 1913 at The Square, Kilcormac, County Offaly, Joseph Egan had been a student until he joined the Guards on 14 December 1933.

Garda Egan was on duty on the night of 11 May 1935 at Earlsfort Terrace, Dublin, when he noticed four men behaving suspiciously. As he caught up with them near St Vincent's Hospital he saw that they had defaced the pavement with a painted political slogan. They refused to give their names and, as Garda Egan seized the man carrying the paint can, the others withdrew a short distance and one of them shouted a threat at Egan. They then fired several shots, wounding the Guard in the right arm and narrowly missing a pair of nearby strollers. The men then tried to wrest their comrade from Egan's grasp but the Guard, lashing out at them with his free hand, maintained his grip on his prisoner. The men again opened fire, this time wounding Egan in the left thigh. Then, perhaps unnerved by the piercing blasts issuing from the Guard's whistle, they fled. Egan managed to flag down a passing car, the driver of which then helped him to get his captive to Lad Lane Station. Only at this point did Garda Egan seek treatment for his injuries, which were discovered to be so serious that he was unfit for duty for three months. His other assailants were later arrested.

Egan was immediately promoted to Sergeant, and received his Scott Gold Medal from the Commissioner, Colonel Eamonn Broy, at a special parade in the Depot's Recreation Hall on 8 November 1937. Sergeant Egan continued his career in the Dublin Metropolitan Division, retiring on 30 August 1973 having served 38 years and 230 days. He died on 22 April 1976.[31]

Patrick Malone, Garda 1729

Garda Malone was born on 10 January 1902 at Dangean, County Offaly, and worked as a farmer before joining the force on 27 June 1922.

Based in the Cork East Riding Division, he was off duty and at home on the night of 18 September 1935 when he heard a loud altercation begin almost at his front door. He emerged to see a man sprawled on the pavement as two other men beat and kicked him whilst another man looked on. As Malone rushed forward to assist the man on the ground the on-looker (whom Malone now recognized as a member of an illegal organization) arrogantly ordered him to stay back. Malone then identified himself as a Garda but the man, undeterred, merely repeated the warning. When Malone thrust him aside and went to assist the injured man the spectator drew a revolver, pointed it at the Guard, and threatened to shoot him if he didn't desist. Instantly Garda Malone seized the gun-barrel in one hand, using the other to grab his assailant's collar, and the two grappled for the gun. At this point one of those who had been attacking the man on the ground came to the aid of his armed comrade, wrested the gun from the struggling pair and made off with it. The third man then abandoned his assault on the injured man and transferred his attention to Garda Malone in a prolonged effort to rescue his colleague from the Guard's grasp. Malone, however, held on doggedly to his prisoner and eventually succeeded in marching him to the Station.

Garda Malone received his Scott Silver Medal from Commissioner Eamonn Broy at the Depot on 8 November 1937. He continued to serve in Cork, and was promoted to Sergeant in 1955. On his retirement on 4 November 1961 he had served 39 years and 131 days. Sergeant Malone died on 28 March 1979.[32]

Joseph Scott, Sergeant 679

Joseph Scott, born on 4 March 1901 at Leahive, Creggs, County Galway, had worked in farming before becoming an early member of the force on 1 April 1922.

He was stationed at Manorhamilton, County Leitrim, on 22 September 1935, when he set out with a group of Gardaí to rescue a girl who, it was reported, had fallen down a narrow chasm while exploring a cave at Glencar. The actual depth of the chasm was unknown, though the Gardaí were aware of local beliefs that it was considerable and that it might contain noxious gases. Aware that each wasted moment might mean the girl's life, Sergeant Scott immediately had himself lowered into the chasm. He was lowered some ninety feet before he reached the bottom of the chasm. On touching the bottom he made the sad discovery of the girl's dead body lying in a pool of water. Remaining at the bottom in pitch darkness and crouched in almost three feet of water, he tied the rope to the body and had it brought to the surface. By the time this had been accomplished and the rope returned to him, some 2.5 hours had elapsed since Sergeant Scott had first been lowered into the narrow, deep chasm. When he finally emerged again into the open air he was in urgent need of treatment for a catalogue of severe bruises, abrasions and cuts which he had received on his round trip to the bottom of the chasm.

Sergeant Malone was presented with his Scott Bronze Medal by Commissioner Eamonn Broy at the Depot on 8 November 1937. Thereafter he continued his career in the Sligo/Leitrim Division, dying in harness on 20 August 1962 having served 40 years and 129 days.[33]

Michael P. Field, Garda 7718

Michael P. Field was born on 2 April 1906 at Ballydehob, County Cork, and had been a farmer before entering the Guards on 12 January 1928.

He was stationed at Castleisland, County Kerry, and was one of a party of three Gardaí detailed to arrest at his house one Mr Keane who was believed to be insane and dangerous. When they arrived at the house the three Guards discovered that Keane, a huge and violent man, had prepared for a siege. He had barricaded the house and locked his mother into a ground-floor room, threatening to kill her should she attempt to escape. He himself had then retreated to the loft, pulling the ladder up after him, and waited amid an assortment of hay forks, turf spades, a collection of heavy stones, and a long-handled slasher. All attempts by the Guards to reason with him came to nothing, and they were eventually obliged to force their way into the ground floor of the house, only to be driven back by a hail of missiles from the loft. An attempt to storm the loft itself via the window was also repulsed, and, at length, the assistance of the army was sought. When the soldiers arrived on the scene it was decided to drive Keane from the loft and rescue his mother by using tear-gas. From the top of a ladder Garda Field lobbed a tear-gas bomb into the loft while another Garda crashed through the locked door of the room in which Keane's mother lay imprisoned. But Keane, moving just as swiftly, seized the bomb and hurled it out of the loft into the kitchen below, where it exploded. Ignoring the fumes, Garda Field ran through and into the room where Keane's mother had now become hysterical. He lifted and carried her, struggling and screaming, back through the kitchen into the yard. He was now followed by an enraged Keane, slasher in hand. Placing the elderly woman on the ground, Garda Field turned and, ducking under the flailing slasher, grabbed him round the waist, bearing the powerful man to the ground where he was eventually secured with the help of the other Guards. On regaining his feet Garda Field found that, in the course of the short but frenzied struggle, he had received some severe injuries.

He received his Scott Silver Medal from the Commissioner, Eamonn Broy, at the Depot on 8 November 1937. Garda Field continued to serve in the Kerry Division until his death on 24 March 1961, a career of 33 years and 71 days.[34]

Hugh P. Barrett, Detective Garda 4996

Hugh Barrett, born at Emo House, Howth, Dublin, on 21 February 1900, had been a painter before joining the force on 3 August 1923.

He was on duty at Union Quay Station, Cork, on the night of 26 May 1936 when word reached him that a man had fallen into the river at Parnell Bridge, some 200 yards away, that another man had attempted to rescue him, and that now both looked likely to drown. Rushing to the spot Barrett paused only to remove his coat before diving in. When he reached the two struggling men he found that the man's original rescuer, named MacSweeney, was on the point of exhaustion. After some delay a buoy was thrown to them. Barrett grasped the buoy with one arm whilst maintaining his grip on both drowning men with the other. As they were drawn towards the bridge MacSweeney became unconscious, making it doubly difficult for Barrett to keep all three of them above water. At the bridge the original drowning man was lifted from the water by spectators, but Barrett was obliged to remain in order to support the senseless MacSweeney until a boat could be sent out to them. All three men recovered from their ordeal.

Barrett, whose rescue of another man from drowning in 1932 had already brought him to the attention of the Royal Humane Society, received his Scott Bronze Medal from Commissioner Eamonn Broy at the Depot on 8 November 1937. Hugh Barrett continued in the Special Branch in Cork and was promoted to Sergeant in July 1952. He retired on 20 February 1963 having served 39 years and 202 days, and died on 27 January 1973.[35]

Thomas P. Rowan, Garda 8089

Thomas P. Rowan, born at 13 Oakley Road, Ranelagh, County Dublin, on 10 November 1907, had worked as a wireless operator and a seaman before becoming a Guard on 8 October 1931.

He was emerging from Ennis Barracks, where he was stationed, on the afternoon of 12 September 1936, when screams of onlookers alerted him to the plight of a four-year-old girl who had fallen into the swollen river and was being swept downstream very rapidly. Without hesitating Garda Rowan dived into the swirling twelve-foot-deep water. The conditions were such that he reached the child and got them both to safety only with the greatest difficulty. The child later made a full recovery.

Garda Rowan received his Scott Bronze Medal from Commissioner Eamonn Broy at the Depot on 8 November 1937. He continued to serve in Clare, being promoted to Sergeant in March 1960, and retiring after a career of 35 years and 68 days on 14 December 1966. Sergeant Rowan died on 5 February 1985.[36]

Manus Patten, Garda 4576

Garda Patten, who came from Derreans, Achill Sound, County Mayo, was born on 12 August 1902 and had worked in farming before joining the force on 31 May 1923.

He was on duty in the early hours of 26 December 1938 at Pearse Street, Ballina, County Mayo, when he became aware that a fire had broken out in the building used both as home and business premises by Mr J.J. Duncan. Having immediately alerted those living in neighbouring houses, he entered Mr Duncan's house and made his way to the upper floor from which smoke was billowing. There he found four members of the household in a distressed state, confused and disoriented by the smoke. Garda Patten instantly urged all four of them down the stairs and out of the building, which was now well and truly ablaze. Both they and their Garda rescuer were exhausted and suffering from smoke inhalation. However, on learning that there were still persons trapped in the house, Patten rushed back into the inferno and up the stairs where he found the barely-conscious figures of a husband and wife. Again Patten made the terrifying journey downstairs, conveying the distressed couple to safety. On emerging from the building he was then informed that Mr J.J. Duncan himself was not accounted for. From the others Patten learned the location of Duncan's bedroom and, despite the evident hopelessness of the endeavour, plunged yet again into the building. When he reached the bedroom Duncan was nowhere to be seen, nor did he respond to Garda Patten's repeated shouts. By now various celluloid and stationery materials stored beneath the stairway had caught fire and were giving off a noxious cocktail of gases. After a few tense minutes Patten himself had to be dragged to safety by several of his colleagues who became alarmed at his failure to return. As he was helped from the building the stairway and ceiling collapsed. Mr Duncan's remains were later found among the ruins.

Garda Patten received his Scott Silver Medal from the Minister for Justice, Gerald Boland, at a ceremony in the Depot Library on 11 December 1939. Thereafter he continued to serve in the Mayo Division, retiring on 20 July 1965 after a career of 42 years and 51 days. Garda Patten died on 20 June 1977.[37]

Michael McGillion, Garda 11411 (Dublin Metropolitan Police)
Born on 24 August 1896 at Sixmilecross, County Tyrone, Garda McGillion had been a railway porter before joining the Dublin Metropolitan Police on 29 June 1917.

He had only just come on duty at Rathmines on the afternoon of 2 January 1938 when, as he left the Station, he was greeted by the alarming sight of a man approaching with a rifle and apparently about to use it. Having had hardly a moment to warn his colleagues still within the Station, Garda McGillion confronted the man, whom he recognized as a local resident, and sharply ordered him to drop the weapon. The man, who was to Garda McGillion's mind behaving very oddly and out of character, dropped the rifle and then came smartly to attention. McGillion lost no time in grabbing the rifle and securing the clearly deranged assailant – who, it later emerged, had just shot his brother.

Michael McGillion was presented with his Scott Silver Medal in the Depot Library by Justice Minister Gerald Boland on 11 December 1939. He continued his career in the Dublin Metropolitan Division until his retirement on 13 November 1958, having then served 39 years and 11 days. He died on 18 August 1969.[38]

John J. Conway, Garda 11965 (Dublin Metropolitan Police)
A native of Dublin, where he was born at 20 Henry Street on 12 September 1905, John J. Conway left his job as a labourer to join the Dublin Metropolitan Police on 19 October 1923.

He was on the point of going off duty on the evening of 18 August 1938 at Irishtown Station when word reached him that two boys of 11 and 12 years of age had been trapped by the rising tide on an island at Cockle Lake, Merrion Strand, an island which would be completely covered at high tide. Garda Conway, who had for two years been captain of the Garda swimming club, ran with a Mr Keogh to the spot on Merrion Strand, over a mile away. When they arrived they found that very little time remained if they were to bring the boys to safety. Conway and Keogh borrowed swimming costumes and swam through the quarter-mile of rising water until they reached the frozen and terrified youths. The boys were then persuaded to remove their clothing and to roll them into separate bundles. The return journey began, Conway and Keogh each towing one of the boys. Soon Keogh, who clearly lacked Conway's stamina, began to lag behind. As Conway neared safety a few men from the large crowd of onlookers, who until now had taken no part in the rescue, swam out and relieved Garda Conway of the boy he was towing.

This allowed Conway to swim back and relieve the exhausted Keogh of the second youth. Neither Keogh nor either of the two boys suffered any long-term effects from the incident.

Garda Conway received his Scott Bronze Medal from Gerald Boland, Minister for Justice, at a ceremony in the Depot Library on 11 December 1939. Conway continued to serve in the Dublin Metropolitan Division thereafter, retiring on 7 June 1960, after a career spanning 36 years and 220 days. He died on 6 April 1981.[39]

Daniel J. Manley, Garda 7628

Garda Manley, born on 1 March 1903 at Grevagh, Blarney, County Cork, had been a farmer before entering the Guards on 11 August 1927.

He was on duty in Tuam together with a colleague Garda Patrick Curran, after midnight on 27 August 1938, when they had occasion to advise a noisy party of men who were shouting and singing in the street to go home. All went quietly except for one truculent man who took further persuading. The two Gardaí, continuing their patrol, came across the man again half-an-hour later and again advised him to go home. Later still the man appeared again, this time brandishing a shotgun at the policemen and aggressively ordering them to 'Get back'. Momentarily blinding their assailant in the glare of his torch, Garda Manley sprang forward and wrenched the shotgun from his grasp. Both Gardaí then seized and secured the man. The gun was, it turned out, not loaded, but the prisoner was in possession of two live cartridges.

The Minister for Justice, Gerald Boland, presented Garda Manley with his Scott Bronze Medal in the Depot's Library on 11 December 1939. Manley continued thereafter with his career in the Galway East Division until his death on 29 November 1958. He had served the community for 31 years and 29 days.[40]

William Shanahan, Detective Sergeant 12016 (Dublin Metropolitan Police)
James William McSweeney, Detective Sergeant 12543 (Dublin Metropolitan Police)

Born at Ballinure, Thurles, County Tipperary, on 22 March 1897, William Shanahan left farming for the DMP on 13 November 1923. James McSweeney was a Dubliner, born at 16 Fitzroy Avenue on 26 August 1902, who had been a plumber before joining the DMP on 1 December 1924.

The two detectives were tasked on 7 May 1940 with accompanying state mails from the sorting office at Pearse Street, Dublin, to Government

Buildings in Merrion Square. Having collected the mail they had driven in a motor cycle and sidecar as far as Holles Street, almost within sight of their destination, when they were forced to a halt by a car carrying four men. As the detectives stopped, the windows of the car which had pulled in front of them were seen to open and the muzzles of two Thompson sub-machine guns protruded. One of the gunmen within the car immediately opened fire severely wounding both Gardaí. Both, however, then quickly took cover behind the motor-cycle combination. One of their assailants then emerged from the car, armed with a revolver, and made towards the motor-cycle with the clear objective of seizing the mail. The two detectives fired on the approaching gunman with their service revolvers. The man fell and was instantly dragged by his confederates back into the car which then sped away, leaving the mail still in the hands of the Gardaí. Detective Garda McSwiney continued to fire on the car as it disappeared (Detective Garda Shanahan's gun had jammed at this point). On examination soon after at Sir Patrick's Dun's Hospital it was found that both detectives were indeed very badly injured. Shanahan had sustained two separate bullet wounds one of which was affecting his left lung, and McSweeney had a bullet lodged dangerously close to his spine. For an interval the two men were in a critical condition, but in the course of time both made a good recovery.

Effective from the day of the incident, they were promoted to Detective Sergeant. Later, on 9 October 1941, they received their Scott Gold Medals from Gerald Boland, Minister for Justice, in a ceremony at the Depot Library. Afterwards the two men continued their careers at Dublin Castle. James McSweeney eventually retired after 30 years and 89 days on 27 February 1955, and died on 5 May 1971. Sadly, William Shanahan, whose career of 30 years and 6 months had been slightly longer than that of his colleague, did not see retirement but died still serving the public on 29 May 1954.[41]

John Collins, Detective Sergeant 2226
Denis Teahan, Detective Garda 6169
John Collins, born at Abbeyfeale, County Limerick, on 6 September 1905, left his previous occupation as a farmer to become one of the new police force's youngest recruits on 7 November 1922. Denis Teahan, a native of Waterville, County Kerry where he was born on 10 April 1901, had been a labourer before entering the force on 9 October 1924.

It was Teahan, on duty in Cork City on 3 January 1940, who first spotted Thomas McCurtain (son of the lord mayor murdered in 1920 and now a prominent IRA activist), whose arrest had been ordered earlier that day, as he walked along Patrick Street. He phoned the sighting to his colleagues at Union Quay Station and, in a matter of minutes the wanted man found himself confronted by Detective Sergeant Collins accompanied by Detective Gardaí John Roche and Nicholas Quinlan, with Detective Garda Teahan approaching from a short distance. As the first of the detectives spoke to him McCurtain moved as if to draw a firearm from under his coat. Collins and Roche immediately seized an arm each, but McCurtain suddenly threw himself backwards freeing his right hand, in which a revolver was now clearly visible, from Collins's grip. Before Collins could re-establish his hold or seize the gun, McCurtain had shot and fatally wounded Detective Garda Roche. Teahan, who had still been a short distance from the assembled men, rushed forward and grabbed McCurtain's left arm, now relinquished by the stricken Roche. As McCurtain, gun still in hand, tried to aim at Collins, Teahan placed his free arm under the assailant's chin and forced his head back, allowing Collins the opportunity to again grasp the gunman's right arm. As the three struggling men crashed to the ground Detective Garda Quinlan, who had remained with the Detective Branch car, now ran forward, presented his revolver at McCurtain and warned him that, should he attempt to fire again, he (Quinlan) would shoot him. This effectively ended the struggle.

John Collins and Denis Teahan received their Scott Gold Medals from Justice Minister Gerald Boland at the Depot Library on 9 October 1941. Detective Sergeant Collins continued his distinguished career in Cork Division, becoming successively Inspector (1952), Superintendent (1957), and Chief Superintendent (1963), as well as the first Guard to win the Scott Medal a second time (see below pp 58–9). He retired on 5 September 1968 having spent 45 years and 304 days a policeman, and died on 14 December 1990. Denis Teahan also continued on in Cork's Union Quay Station, retiring on 9 April 1966 after 41 years and 183 days. He died on 20 August 1970.[42]

Robert Mullally, Detective Garda 8269
Richard Wilmot, Detective Garda 8336
Detective Garda Mullally was born at Old Bawn Road, Tallaght, County Dublin, on 30 August 1904, and had been a labourer before joining the Guards on 5 August 1933. Richard Wilmot, a former teacher, who had been born at Croom, County Limerick, on 6 November 1898, entered the force on 9 September 1933.

On the morning of 16 August 1940 a party of five detectives went forth from Dublin Castle to conduct a planned search of 98a Rathgar Road in the belief that it was being used as a safe-house by members of the IRA. When they arrived Detective Sergeant McKeown and Detective Gardaí Hyland and Brady took up positions at the front of the house with a view to gaining an entrance. Meanwhile Detective Gardaí Mullally and Wilmot moved to the rear of the building to cut off any attempt at escape by persons inside the house. A delay of perhaps a quarter of an hour ensued, but when the door was opened and the detectives stepped inside they were met by a hail of revolver and machine-gun fire. McKeown and Hyland were killed, and Brady very badly wounded. Hearing the burst of fire, Mullally and Wilmot ran round to the front of the house only to see three men, one armed with a sub-machine gun and another with a revolver, already in the street and attempting to make good their escape. The two detectives shouted at the men to halt and opened fire when they continued to run from the scene. Mullally and Wilmot gave chase. Mullally, some distance ahead of his colleague, but with a now-empty revolver, watched two of the men (the third had vanished) take refuge in 56 Rathgar Avenue. The detective continued the pursuit, at great personal risk, through the front door and out the back of number 56, and at last ran the men to earth in the lane behind Rathgar Avenue. Brandishing his empty gun Mullally demanded their surrender. Winded and cornered, the two remaining gunmen raised their hands. He then shouted to indicate his location to Wilmot, who arrived very quickly and proceeded to disarm the prisoners. The Thompson sub-machine gun, with which the other detectives had been killed and injured, apparently had been abandoned by one of the men as he ran. But Wilmot discovered a fully-loaded revolver and spare ammunition on the other captive. Mullally took it in place of his own empty weapon and used it to secure the arrest of the men.

Robert Mullally was presented with his gold, and Richard Wilmot with his silver Scott Medal, by Justice Minister Gerald Boland, in the Depot's Library on 9 October 1941. Both men continued to serve at Dublin Castle, Mullally retiring after 34 years and 25 days on 29 August 1967. He died on 22 October 1973. Wilmot retired on 5 November 1961 having served 28 years and 58 days; he died on 27 September 1974.[43]

John Collins, Detective Sergeant 2226
John Driscoll, Garda Sergeant 3505
(For background details on John Collins see above p. 56). John Driscoll, born at Whiddy, Bantry, County Cork on 12 June 1894, had worked in farming before joining the force on 22 February 1923.

A Local Defence Force dance was being held at Cork's City Hall on the evening of 23 March 1941, and some of those attending had parked their bicycles for safety in the forecourt of the nearby Garda Station at Union Quay. As Detective Sergeant Collins left the Station at 10.15 p.m. he noticed smoke drifting from the saddlebag of one of the bicycles. Fearing that a bomb of some description was concealed in the bag he tried to remove the fuse. But by now the fuse was too short and had already begun to smoulder within the bag. Collins rushed the bicycle away from the Station and flung it into the roadway outside. He then ran back through the Station to warn both his detective and uniformed colleagues of a possibly-imminent explosion. Before he could reach the Uniformed Branch offices, however, Sergeant Driscoll had emerged from the doorway of those offices and spotted the smoking bicycle in the roadway. Drawing the same conclusions as his detective colleague, Driscoll lifted it and ran to the quayside opposite intending to throw it in the river. A vessel moored at the quayside obstructed him and he was forced to push the bicycle further down the road, where he worked to separate the still-burning fuse from the 30 sticks of gelignite to which it was attached. He had barely abandoned the bicycle when the detonator exploded harmlessly, as the connection between detonator and priming stick had been broken. A search of the Station yard then revealed the presence of a second saddlebag 'bomb' the fuse of which had failed to ignite properly. This second bicycle had been positioned under the window of the Sergeant's office. Efforts to locate the Command Ordnance Officer were unsuccessful, and for safety's sake Sergeant Driscoll personally threw the bicycle in the river. The gelignite from the first bicycle, when later examined, was found to be damp and extremely unstable. Detective Sergeant Collins and Sergeant Driscoll both received their Scott Bronze Medals from Gerald Boland, Minister for Justice, in the Depot's Recreation Hall on 2 November 1942. John Collins was the first Garda to win the Scott Medal a second time. John Driscoll continued on at Union Quay, retiring on 11 June 1954 after 31 years and 110 days. The date of his death is not known.[44]

Bernard Forde, Garda 7969

Garda Forde, a native of County Longford, where he was born at Derawley, Drumlish, on New Year's Day 1909, had been a labourer before entering the Guards on 7 May 1931.

He was on duty at Wexford Garda Station on the evening of 16 November 1941 when word came that a cinema operator had just been robbed of an Irish Movietone News Reel by two armed men who had seized the black bag in which it was being carried. Garda Forde was one of those who jumped on board the Detective Branch car which immediately set off in pursuit of the robbers. Before long the robbers, who had fled the scene on foot, came into view. Seeing their pursuers about to close in, the two men ran into a nearby yard where one of them managed to escape in the darkness. The other, however, got into difficulties as he tried to negotiate a galvanized fence. This allowed Garda Forde to seize him in a bear-hug, immobilizing the man's arms and preventing his escape. A search of the yard revealed a loaded revolver dropped by the prisoner in his flight and which he later admitted was his.

Garda Forde was presented with his Scott Bronze Medal by Justice Minister Gerald Boland at the Depot on 2 November 1942. He remained in the Wexford Division where he was promoted Sergeant in 1952. Bernard Forde retired on 31 August 1971 and died, sadly, a mere fortnight later on 13 September.[45]

Michael Comyns, Detective Sergeant 1233
Thomas Kavanagh, Detective Garda 3303
John Kennedy, Garda 3782

Detective Sergeant Comyns, born at Ballyhatt, Kilrush, County Clare, on 3 July 1896, was one of the earliest recruits, having left farming to join the force on 15 May 1922. Thomas Kavanagh was born on 1 October 1904 at Inch, County Wexford, and was a creamery worker before joining the Gardaí on 1 February 1923. John Kennedy, a former labourer from Ballyvary, Foxford, County Mayo, where he was born on 25 June 1901, entered the Guards on 23 March 1923.

On 16 May 1943 James Smith (aka Brennan), on the run following his escape from Mountjoy Prison where he had been serving a lengthy sentence for firearms offences, was spotted cycling through Drogheda by a vigilant Garda. Smith was known to be a particularly determined and dangerous man. After his escape he had been appointed the IRA Divisional Officer for Leinster; he had sworn never to be recaptured alive. On being informed of the sighting Detective Sergeant Comyns and Detective Garada Kavanagh armed themselves with revolvers and a sub-machine gun, and, together with Garda Kennedy who was unarmed, set out by car in pursuit of Smith who was reportedly cycling towards Dublin. They overtook their quarry at the village of Bryanstown, two miles south of Drogheda. Smith ignored two calls to halt but, on the firing of a warning shot by Detective Kavanagh, he flung himself from his bicycle and turned to confront the three Gardaí. As Detective Comyns, armed with the sub-machine gun, approached him Smith opened fire with a revolver hitting the Garda in the stomach. Abandoning the machine gun, the effects of which could not have been other than fatal at such close quarters, Comyn closed with Smith wrestling him to the ground and trapping the gunman's right hand underneath the latter's body. Comyn also seized Smith's left hand while he (Comyn) tried to draw his own revolver. Kavanagh and Kennedy, who had immediately gone to Comyn's assistance, also attempted to separate Smith from his weapon which was likewise trapped underneath the gunman's body. Unable to reach the weapon and unwilling to take the chance of lifting Smith and thereby free his right hand the three Gardaí continued to struggle with the prone gunman who resisted violently. The very nature of the conflict was now exposing all parties to an accidental if not deliberate discharge of the gun. This, in effect, was what happened. A second shot rang out, and Detective Comyn again was the victim. Redoubling his efforts, Detective Kennedy, who had had an ineffective hold of Smith's right wrist, now succeeded in tearing the gun from his grasp. Smith immediately gave up the struggle. When the gun came to be examined it was clear that two further shots had been attempted but the weapon (fully loaded) had failed to fire. Smith was found to have 54 rounds of ammunition in his possession. Comyn's escape from death and serious injury had been nothing short of miraculous. The first bullet had been obstructed by his watch and chain and had done him only minimal damage. The second bullet, fired from an awkward position beneath Smith, had grazed about a foot of skin across Comyn's lower back barely missing his spinal column.

At a presentation ceremony in the Depot's Recreation Hall on 21 November 1944 Detective Sergeant Comyn received his Scott Gold Medal, and Kavanagh and Kennedy their silver medals, from the Minister for Justice, Gerald Boland. All three men continued in the Louth/Meath Division, John Kennedy being promoted Sergeant in 1945. Comyn retired on 2 July 1959 having served 37 years and 40 days; he died on 7 December 1960. Kavanagh retired on 30 September 1954 after 31 years and 242 days; the date of his death is not known. Kennedy died in service on 12 November 1963 after a career spanning 40 years and 204 days.[46]

Michael Flynn, Garda 8002
John P. Tighe, Garda 9209
Michael Flynn, born on 3 June 1912 at Kilmurray, Aherla, Cork, had worked on farming before joining the Guards on 18 June 1931. John P. Tighe came from Mullacur, Ballymote, County Sligo, where he was born on 10 September 1919. He had been a soldier before joining the Guards on 3 June 1943.

In the early hours of 6 January 1947 the proprietor of a public house known as 'The Yellow House' in Dublin's Rathfarnham district reported a break-in.

Realizing that the alarm had been raised, the thieves fled the premises and no trace could be found of them by the first policeman on the scene, Garda O'Meara. Garda Flynn and Garda Tighe were among those detailed to make a more thorough search of the area. Two men, sighted by the Guards at the end of a sunken, enclosed garden, fled towards the river at their approach. Unwilling to attempt the river the two men then ran towards the opposite corner of the garden, pursued by Garda Flynn who tried to cut off their escape. The fleeing suspects, one of them armed, came up against a laurel hedge and, finding themselves about to be cornered by the two Gardaí, one of them turned and fired at Garda Flynn hitting him in the stomach. Flynn did not falter in his pursuit but flung himself headlong at the unarmed suspect, knocking the man into the hedge. As Flynn continued to struggle with the man the armed assailant circled around behind the Garda and shot him in the head at point-blank range. One or both men then rained blows on the injured Guard until the arrival, moments later, of Garda Tighe. With one hand Tighe seized the gunman's hand and pinned it to his side; with the other he imposed a pincer grip on the man's neck and shoulder, forcing him onto his knees. His unarmed comrade, however, having pulled himself from beneath the wounded Garda Flynn, then proceeded to attack Garda Tighe who made desperate efforts to maintain his grip on the armed suspect. Tighe was eventually knocked unconscious and the two suspects made good their escape. Incredibly, despite their horrific injuries, both Gardaí managed to make their way back to Rathfarnham Station. The bullet which wounded Garda Flynn in the stomach ultimately could not be removed and he carried it inside him for the rest of his life. By an extraordinary stroke of luck the second bullet, which struck Flynn in the back of the head and would ordinarily have proved fatal, had lodged against the occipital bone at the junction of the head and neck, and so did not penetrate Flynn's brain. Both Gardaí had suffered numerous savage cuts, abrasions and bruises. It was a small satisfaction that the thieves had left at the scene of the struggle not only their house-breaking tools, pistol and ammunition (filed into dum–dum bullets), but also the £25 in coins which they had stolen from the 'Yellow House'. Both assailants were eventually arrested; one was acquitted and the other sentenced to 21 years penal servitude.

At the Depot on 20 May 1948 Michael Flynn and John Tighe received their Gold Scott Medals from the Minister for Justice, Sean McEoin. Garda Flynn (later promoted to Sergeant) continued his career at Garda Headquarters, retiring on 1 October 1972 after 41 years and 105 days. He died on 15 December 1991. Garda Tighe, promoted Sergeant in April 1948, later served in the Clare Division. He retired on 1 October 1982 after 39 years and 121 days.[47]

Patrick J. Ryan, Garda 12654

Born on 28 July 1934 in Kerry, the son of a serving Garda, Patrick J. Ryan (known to many as 'Eric Ryan the footballer') left teaching to join the force on 10 May 1955.

On a cold afternoon, 14 January 1958, two passers-by near the River Bandon in the west Cork town of the same name observed an elderly man lose his balance on a footbridge and fall into the river. At this point the river is some 140 feet wide and over a dozen feet deep. They alerted Garda Patrick J. Ryan and his colleague Garda P.J. O'Sullivan who were patrolling nearby. Garda Ryan, whose athletic accomplishments included swimming, hesitated only to remove his tunic before diving into the river. When Ryan reached the hapless man the latter, encumbered by an overcoat, had been carried some 75 yards downriver and was on the point of drowning. Panic stricken, he seized hold of Ryan's clothing at chest level, making it almost impossible for the Guard to swim to safety. Soon the intense cold began to take effect. Ryan felt his arms and legs begin to stiffen and he feared the onset of a cramp. Keeping a tight hold on the distressed man, Ryan, exhausted and nearing collapse, managed to reach the river bank where both men were assisted by a crowd which had gathered there. It was some time before Garda Ryan was fit to return to duty.

He received his Scott Bronze Medal at the Depot in May 1960 from the Minister for Justice, Oscar Traynor. Thereafter Patrick Ryan continued his career in the West Cork Division, being promoted Sergeant in August 1962 and Inspector in February 1973. He retired on 2 May 1986 having served 30 years and 358 days, and died on 9 September 2001.[48]

John B. Moynihan, Garda 13259D
Matthew J.V. Nolan, Garda 13349
Thomas J. Slattery, Garda 13067

John Moynihan, born on 18 April 1933 at 2 Orchard Terrace off Dublin's North Circular Road, had been a carpenter and joiner before joining the force on 3 October 1957. Thomas Slattery was born in Sligo on 24 November 1935 and had worked as a clerk before entering the Guards on 20 June 1956. Vincent Nolan, born at The Square, Ardrahan, County Galway on 27 August 1936, had been a boiler attendent before becoming a Guard on 24 January 1958.

In the early hours of 17 December 1958 the three Gardaí were on their way to their beats when heavy smoke from the chimney of 603 North Circular Road, Dublin, alerted them that the house was on fire. While Garda Slattery called the fire brigade from a nearby telephone box Garda Moynihan and Garda Nolan roused the occupants of the house. Moynihan checked the second floor for occupants and on his return to the first floor he found a five-year-old child in a bedroom. Rolling the child in a blanket, he carried it outside before returning to rouse a man still asleep on the first floor. He then became aware that there was a baby in a cot still on the first floor. This child also he rolled in a blanket and carried it downstairs to be handed to its father. Despite clear evidence that it was now entirely unsafe to do so Garda Moynihan again returned to the first floor to check for any remaining occupants. When he tried to regain the ground floor he was cut off by the fire, the intense heat of which forced him to retreat to the second floor. The second-floor landing was now also gripped by the flames and the floors below were quite impassable. Heat, flames and smoke soon forced Moynihan first into the second-floor front room and thence onto the window sill outside this room. As he stood there flames from below licked at the sill and consumed the floor-boards of the room in which he had been standing a moment before. No other option being open to him, Moynihan jumped, clearing the area railings and landing on the footpath on his hands and knees. Despite his cut hands and painful injuries to his thumbs which would later keep him from duty for a month, Garda Moynihan then helped to clear cars away from the vicinity of the inferno. But Moynihan had not been the only Garda busy on the first floor. When Garda Slattery returned from summoning the fire brigade he also entered the blazing house and on the first floor landing came on a woman holding a terrified child. When the trio reached the ground floor the hallway was ablaze. Slattery, with the child in his arms and the woman following, dashed through the veritable tunnel of flames and emerged into the street where he left the pair wrapped in his greatcoat. The front entrance now being impassible, Garda Slattery re-entered the house through the back door and climbed the stairs. On the second floor he met a teenage boy and brought him out safely through the rear entrance. Slattery then joined Garda Moynihan and other of his colleagues in the task of clearing adjacent cars to make room for the fire brigade. Meanwhile Garda Nolan was endeavouring to reach a woman reportedly asleep in the basement. He eventually found her, alive, in a room filled with dense smoke and brought her to safety as the ceiling above them collapsed into burning fragments.

All three men received their Scott Bronze Medals from the Minister for

Justice, Oscar Traynor, at the Depot in May 1960, and all afterwards continued their careers in the Dublin Metropolitan Division. John Moynihan was promoted Sergeant in August 1966 and Inspector in January 1981. He retired on 12 September 1989 having served 31 years and 345 days. Sadly he died little more than a year later on 5 October 1990. Thomas Slattery also saw promotion to Sergeant. He retired on 22 June 1994 after 38 years and 2 days. Vincent Nolan died in service at the age of 43 on 25 January 1980; he had served for 22 years and 2 days.[49]

John James Casey, Garda 10573B

John James Casey, born at Monasteraden, County Sligo, on 7 May 1933, had been a farmer before joining the Guards on 13 November 1953.

Garda Casey was on duty at Ballydesmond Station in west Cork on 21 March 1960 when a local dispensary doctor phoned him for assistance in securing a violent mentally ill patient. When both Guard and doctor arrived at the patient's residence they found the powerfully-built middle-aged man in the yard prepared to fend them off with a pitchfork. While the doctor attempted to reason with and calm the disturbed man Garda Casey moved to cut off any possible escape route. At a moment when the man's attention had been distracted by the doctor Garda Casey seized him from behind and managed to grab the huge hands which still brandished the pitchfork. The doctor, who suffered from a physical disability, could not intervene, and Casey found himself struggling alone with the deranged man. In the minutes that followed the man sank his teeth into Casey's thumb and gnawed frenziedly at the back of both the Guard's hands stripping away the skin. Only barely did Casey prevent his assailant from reaching a nearby hay-knife. Having been butted savagely in the face several times Garda Casey finally succeeded in pinning the man down on a pile of manure. Two more men now arrived in the yard and, with the doctor's assistance, they managed to tie the man up and drive him to the local mental hospital.

John James Casey was presented with his Scott Silver Medal at the Depot on 5 May 1961 by Oscar Traynor, Minister for Justice. Promoted Sergeant in November 1970, J.J. Casey continued to serve in west Cork, retiring after 39 years and 175 days on 6 May 1993.[50]

John James Acton, Garda 12785L

Born at Main Street, Glin, County Limerick, on 3 November 1934, John James Acton had been a hackney driver before entering the Guards on 12 May 1955.

He was off duty and returning from a swim at Bray, County Wicklow, on the early afternoon of 10 July 1960, when his attention was drawn to a developing tragedy some fifty yards from him. A 13-year-old girl had got out of her depth as the tide rose and had been swept about forty yards from the sea-wall. Two fully-dressed elderly men attempted to save her only to get into difficulties and found themselves in need of rescue. A further effort by two young men had to be abandoned. Garda Acton, having dashed to the scene, seized a lifebuoy and, leaving its rope in the hands of a man on the shore, ignored warnings that the waves were too strong and swam gamely towards the drowning trio. On reaching them he found that one of the elderly men, though exhausted, had managed to keep the girl's head above water. In the midst of the thrashing waves Acton enabled one elderly rescuer to take a firmer hold of the girl and, placing the other man's arm round his neck, he put all three into contact with the lifebuoy. On Acton's shouted directions the man at the water's edge then pulled the lifebuoy towards the shore. All were brought to safety.

Garda Acton received his Scott Silver Medal from Justice Minister Oscar Traynor at the Depot on 5 May 1961. He continued thereafter in the Dublin/ Wicklow Division, retiring on 2 November 1994 having served 39 years and 175 days. John Acton died on 16 March 2005.[51]

James Doddy, Garda Sergeant 1142
Patrick Mullaney, Garda Inspector 7963
William H. Thorne, Garda Sergeant 2311
James Doddy, born on 15 February 1901 at Clonkeary, Ballymote, County Sligo, had been a labourer before joining the force on 10 May 1922. Patrick Mullaney was born at Enniscrone, County Sligo, on 31 August 1907, and had left farming for a career in the Gardaí on 7 May 1931. William H. Thorne, a native of Cork City where he was born on 27 July 1902, had been a fireman on the Great Southern and Western Railway before entering the Guards on 11 November 1922.

These three men were the senior officers amongst a party of Gardaí who late on the afternoon of 26 December 1961 responded to a report that a Longford farmer was firing his rifle at persons who ventured anywhere near his property. In two separate incidents that afternoon a neighbouring farmer had been wounded and three women walking along an adjacent road were put in fear of their lives. On arrival at the farm the Gardaí learned from neighbours that the middle-aged man, who was the owner of a shotgun as well as the rifle, had been behaving oddly for the previous few days and had been shooting apparently at random at all hours. The house, when approached by the Gardaí, was locked, shuttered and in darkness. A search of the outhouses revealed nothing and it was only with perseverence that Sergeant Doddy elicited a reply from the man who had shut himself up inside the farmhouse. After considerable persuasion the farmer, who had threatened to shoot anybody who would attempt an entry, agreed to open the door a fraction provided any approach was kept to one person at a time. When he opened the door, rifle in hand, Doddy, Mullaney and Thorne rushed the doorway. Sergeant Doddy seized the rifle whilst his two colleagues laid hold of the farmer. A short struggle followed during which, having lost the rifle to Sergeant Doddy, the demented man tried in vain to grab the shotgun positioned nearby. As other Gardaí poured through the doorway the farmer was eventually subdued. The man, who had lived alone, seemed prepared for a siege. Aside from the loaded rifle and shotgun he carried a haversack containing almost 600 rifle bullets and some three dozen shotgun cartridges. A search of the house later revealed a further 400 rifle bullets and 125 shotgun cartridges.

At a ceremony at Garda Headquarters in May 1962 Sergeant Doddy received his Scott Gold Medal, and Inspector Mullaney and Sergeant Thorne their Scott Silver Medals. James Doddy continued in the Longford/Westmeath Division until he died in service after 40 years and 300 days on 24 July 1963. Inspector Mullaney later transferred to the Dublin Metropolitan Area, rising to Superintendent in June 1962 and to Chief Superintendent in June 1968. He retired after a career of 39 years and 116 days on 30 August 1970, and died on 12 May 1973. William Thorne also continued to serve in the Longford/Westmeath Division, retiring after 42 years and 258 days on 26 July 1965; he died on 7 January 1989.[52]

John O'Connor, Garda 10776

John O'Connor was born at Kenmare, County Kerry, on 9 July 1929, and worked as a motor mechanic before joining the Guards on 26 May 1954.

He and a colleague were travelling in a patrol car late on the freezing night of 19 January 1961 when bystanders at Dublin's Bachelor's Walk alerted them to the plight of a woman who, seemingly bent on suicide, had thrown herself into the river. Pausing only to divest himself of his cap, greatcoat and tunic, Garda O'Connor, who was not a very strong swimmer, leaped the fourteen feet from the quayside to the icy water, seized the woman and swam with her to the wall. Once there he used the lifebuoy thrown to him by his colleague to keep both himself and the woman afloat until the arrival of the fire brigade some minutes later.

Garda O'Connor received his Scott Bronze Medal at a Depot ceremony in

May 1962. He continued thereafter in the Dublin Metropolitan Division, being promoted Sergeant in April 1962. Sadly, John O'Connor died at the age of 36 after 11 years and 106 days service, on 8 September 1965.[53]

Jeremiah Connolly, Garda 12663

Born at Lissanuhig, Skibbereen, County Cork, on 7 November 1932, Jeremiah Connolly had worked in farming before joining the force on 10 May 1955.

Garda Connolly was one of four Gardaí who, on 22 May 1961, responded to a phone message from a frightened farmer at Clondalkin, County Dublin, that one of his workmen had apparently lost his reason and was threatening him and his family with a pitchfork, forcing them to take refuge in the farm-house. On arrival at the farm they found the workman pacing up and down in front of the farmhouse, pitchfork on shoulder. But when the Guards left the safety of their patrol car and approached, the man menaced them with the pitchfork and threatened to impale anyone who came too close. Efforts to reason with him or to outflank him had come to nothing when Garda Connolly volunteered to enter the farmhouse by the back door and then to emerge by the front door and seize the man from behind. By some uncanny instinct, however, the assailant seemed to sense the impending tactic and screamed that he would kill anyone coming through the front door. Garda Connolly, undaunted, came through the house as planned and flung himself towards the man standing some twenty feet from the front door. When he turned to stab Garda Connolly, the latter, with the help of three colleagues who then closed in, managed to disarm and subdue the man.

Garda Connolly received his Scott Bronze Medal at the Depot in May 1962. Jeremiah Connolly later transferred from Rathfarnham Station to Garda Headquarters and was promoted Sergeant in July 1976. He retired on 6 November 1989 after 34 years and 181 days.[54]

Daniel Kennedy, Garda Inspector 10135D
Jeremiah Clifford, Garda 14685D

Daniel Kennedy, born on 16 November 1926 at Midleton, County Cork, son of a Guard and one of four brothers all of whom became Guards, had been a gardener before he himself joined the force on 29 April 1948. Jeremiah Clifford was born at Ballyhindon, Fermoy, County Cork, and had worked in a factory before becoming a Guard on 19 April 1961.

Inspector Kennedy and Garda Clifford were among a party of Gardaí who engaged in protracted efforts to disarm and apprehend an armed farmer in the Louth/Meath Division who had become insane, violent and dangerous in the course of the afternoon of 14 April 1962. According to his terrified sister, who had fled the house, he had put his two dogs into a sack and then shot them. Approaches during the evening from friends of the man and his sister as well as from the local doctor drew only warnings from the man in the locked house that everyone should keep away, and at one point, a single shot. Gardaí had been in position near the house for above an hour when Inspector Kennedy arrived towards midnight. He and several other Guards managed to slip into the house via the scullery, and it soon became plain that the unfortunate man was hiding in a locked ground-floor bedroom. As Kennedy and another Guard tried with the aid of a torch from outside the window to view the inside of the bedroom the man took fright and fired seven shots, forcing the Gardaí nearby to scatter in search of cover. This enabled him to make good his escape through the window and into the dark countryside. Spotted some time later by a patrol car about a mile from the farmhouse, he again opened fire shattering one of the car's headlights and damaging its radiator. It was noticed that he paused to reload his gun before again vanishing into the night. When the Gardaí cornered him around dawn, he took refuge in a nearby farmhouse from the doorway of which he stood brandishing his gun at the approaching Gardaí. The elderly brother and sister who lived in the house appealed to him in vain to give up, as did a local priest summoned to the scene by the Guards. When a further hour passed without result, Inspector Kennedy, accompanied by Garda Clifford, managed to enter the house through a small first-floor gable window. The two men, unarmed, crept downstairs and, bursting into the room in which the assailant was standing, they both seized him. After a desperate struggle they succeeded in wresting the gun from his grasp.

Inspector Kennedy and Garda Clifford were presented with their Scott Silver Medals by the Minister for Justice, Charles J. Haughey, at Garda Headquarters on 26 April 1963. Daniel Kennedy had already moved to the Dublin/Wicklow Division, becoming Superintendent in January 1965 and Chief Superintendent in January 1973. He retired on 15 November 1989, having served 41 years and 201 days. Jeremiah Clifford continued on in the Louth/Meath Division; he was promoted Sergeant in October 1972, Inspector in May 1984, and Superintendent in January 1991. On his retirement on 14 January 2000 he had served 38 years and 271 days.[55]

Aidan Murray, Garda 13829M

Born at Belgium Park, Monaghan, on 21 February 1938, Aidan Murray had been a bus/taxi driver before joining the Guards on 3 April 1959.

Garda Murray was one of a party of eight Gardaí and two mental hospital attendants who, on 28 May 1962, went to a house in a rural part of the Waterford/Kilkenny Division to secure a mentally-unstable man for transport to the district mental hospital. Garda assistance had been sought after an earlier attempt by the hospital attendants to take the man had failed, the patient having threatened them with a manure sprong. On the second attempt the man fled across the fields at the Gardaí's approach, a knife as well as the sprong now visible. When finally run to ground in a corner of a field he was impervious to reason and held the Guards at bay. Garda Murray, separated from the man by a fence, armed himself with a beet sprong and, stepping over the fence, moved towards him. The deranged man, now totally out of control, used his manure sprong to knock the beet sprong from Garda Murray's grasp. Murray instantly flung himself at his assailant, seizing him and tearing the manure sprong from him. For a long moment the two combatants struggled for possession of the knife gripped in the madman's other hand, before two other Guards intervened and wrenched away the knife.

Garda Murray received his Scott Bronze Medal from Justice Minister Charles J. Haughey at the Depot on 26 April 1963. Aidan Murray served also in the Donegal Division, was promoted Sergeant in March 1972, and retired on 20 February 1995 having served 35 years and 324 days.[56]

John Hennessy, Garda Sergeant 10108

A native of Templemore, County Tipperary, John Hennessy was born on 4 July 1926 and had been a farmer before joining the Guards on 23 April 1948.

A few hours after receiving a report on 5 June 1963 that a farmer from the Drinaghen area of County Sligo was missing and that efforts by his relatives and neighbours to locate him had failed, Sergeant Hennessy orchestrated a series of systematic searches of the mountain and bogs surrounding the man's home. Some hours into the search attention became concentrated on some freshly disturbed bushes adjacent to a pothole, and, from the bottom of the 120-foot hole, faint moans indicated that the missing man was not only there but alive also. An initial rescue attempt by a local farmer ended when the man became trapped on a ledge forty feet inside the hole and had himself to be rescued after a lapse of some four hours. While this volunteer remained trapped on the ledge Sergeant Hennessy and the local doctor arrived on the scene with a stretcher. The Sergeant then had fresh ropes lowered to the man on the ledge directing him to lower them down to the missing farmer with instructions to fasten them around his body. This gambit failed, however, when it became clear that the missing man was stuck at the bottom and could not be moved. Aware that time might be running out for the man, Sergeant

Hennessy volunteered to go down and try to bring him up himself. As he descended, devoid of protective clothing or headgear, he was struck repeatedly by showers of debris unavoidably dislodged from the sides of the hole. On reaching the bottom of the hole Hennessy tied the ropes around the missing farmer, a middle-aged man some 16 stone in weight. The original would-be rescuer, still on the ledge, was instrumental in the successful lifting of the man to safety by those at the opening of the hole. The hole was just wide enough to permit Sergeant Hennessy to be lifted simultaneously on a separate set of ropes. This enabled him to guide the progress of the missing man up through the hole, preventing him from snagging on protruding rocks and, insofar as was possible, to save him from further injury from dislodged stones and clay. When Sergeant Hennessy had been pulled level with the man on the ledge he stayed with him and allowed the missing farmer to be raised the remaining forty feet on his own. This enabled the Sergeant, as soon as the missing man had been pulled to safety, to arrange and oversee the rescue of the man on the ledge. Only then did Hennessy allow himself to be lifted to safety.

John Hennessy received his Scott Silver Medal at the Garda Training Centre, Templemore, on 5 November 1965, from Justice Minister Brian Lenihan. Thereafter he continued his career in the Sligo/Leitrim Division, retiring on 20 January 1987 after 38 years and 273 days.[57]

James Galvin, Detective Sergeant 7331
William Blackwell, Garda 7874
Born on 25 July 1905 at Raheny, County Dublin, James Galvin had been a clerk before entering the Guards on 7 May 1926. William Blackwell, a native of Athlone, County Westmeath, born on 13 November 1907, had worked as a shop assistant before joining the force on 10 October 1928.

They were in a party of four Guards responding to a report, on the night of 6 February 1963, that a farmer from the Portlaoise area had assaulted his daughter, broken into a house, and fired a shotgun causing damage to windows and a television set. The four Gardaí arrived in a patrol car to find the man, still armed, attempting to break into yet another house. Fearing the possible effect on the man of too sudden an appearance of uniformed Guards, Garda Blackwell donned a garage overall while Detective Sergeant Galvin told the two other uniformed men not to leave the car until a whistle was given. Blackwell and Galvin then crept towards the man who, intent on gaining entry to a house, did not notice them until they leaped at him from a distance of ten feet. Detective Sergeant Galvin, who was first to reach the man, seized the gunbarrel and forced the weapon upwards while Garda Blackwell flung his arms around the man's middle. In the course of the fearsome struggle a shot was fired, but, galvanized into action by the sound of Blackwell's whistle, the two uniformed Guards were quickly on the scene and the man was disarmed and secured. A few hours later, on medical advice, he was removed to a mental hospital. The incident had been triggered by a domestic dispute involving the man's daughter.

James Galvin and William Blackwell were presented with their Scott Silver Medals by the Minister for Justice, Brian Lenihan, at the Garda Training Centre, Templemore, on 5 November 1965. Both men continued thereafter in the Leix/Offaly Division. Detective Sergeant Galvin retired on 24 July 1968 after 42 years and 79 days, and died on 16 June 1980. Garda Blackwell retired on 1 January 1971 having served 42 years and 2 days; he died on 30 August 1986.[58]

William McCarthy, Garda Sergeant 7932
Born on 27 February 1908 at Farranacoush, west Cork, William McCarthy had worked in farming before becoming a Guard on 27 March 1930.

Sergeant McCarthy was on duty on the morning of 29 June 1964 at Ballyheigue Station, County Kerry, when word reached him that two survivors from a badly-damaged trawler were adrift in a wild sea, each man clinging precariously to a lifebuoy. They had set sail the previous morning from the Aran Islands but their engine failed opposite Loop Head, County Clare. They had no radio. Distress flag, flares and burning rubber tyres had failed to call attention to their plight and they had drifted south until, caught in heavy seas, their boat hit a tall structure known as Bird Rock some 200 yards off-shore at Castleshannon, Ballyheigue. Fearful of sinking but feeling that no secure foothold was to be had on Bird Rock itself, the two crewmen, wearing lifejackets and carrying a lifebuoy each, jumped into the water. They managed to keep together by linking their arms through the buoys, but were soon carried further out to sea. When Sergeant McCarthy arrived on the shoreline he joined forces with the owner of a currach, Patrick O'Connor, who until that moment had been unable to find anyone willing to accompany him in a rescue attempt. The currach was of uncertain sea-worthyness but, undaunted by this circumstance, by the wildness of the sea or by a succession of dangerous rocks, both men set out guided only by frantic signals from onlookers positioned on the clifftop. After an hour's search they came upon the two unfortunate crewmen, now slumped across their lifebuoys, and with great difficulty and not a little daring managed to get them on board the currach.

One of the crewmen, sadly, was beyond help despite valiant attempts by Sergeant McCarthy to resusitate him.

William McCarthy received his Scott Gold Medal from Justice Minister Brian Lenihan at the Garda Training Centre at Templemore on 5 November 1965. He continued with his career in the Kerry Division until his retirement, after 40 years and 337 days, on 26 February 1971. The date of his death is not known.[59]

William A. Barrett, Garda 10974F
Patrick J. McIntyre, Garda 16042C

Born at Ardagh, Causeway, County Kerry on 1 August 1929, William A. Barrett left farming for a career in the Guards on 2 November 1954. Patrick McIntyre was born on 9 September 1944 at Banagher, County Offaly; he likewise had worked in farming before joining the force on 7 January 1965.

Garda McIntyre had been a serving Guard for barely seven months when he won his Scott Medal. Both men were on duty on the evening of 6 August 1965 at Rathmore Station, County Kerry, when they were alerted to the presence of an armed man behaving suspiciously on a nearby river bank. On arrival at the scene they noticed at the far end of a field a man apparently carrying a shotgun. The man took to his heels on sighting the Guards, running into a grove of trees as Barrett and McIntyre closed in on him from two sides. Keeping some hay-cocks between them and the gunman the Guards called on him from a distance of forty yards to stay put. The man, who had now mounted a fence at the field's edge, pointed his gun at them and explicitly threatened to kill them. He followed this by firing directly at Garda McIntyre who remained prone on the ground behind a hay-cock, and then at Garda Barrett who had taken similar cover. Anxious to avoid giving him a chance to re-load, the two Guards chased him across a stream into another field, the gunman's vain efforts to re-load slowing him as he ran. Within seconds the man was seized and disarmed; he had eight live cartridges in his possession and had managed to get a further two into the gun's breech. Medical examination eventually confirmed that the gunman was insane.

Garda Barrett and Garda McIntyre were presented with their Scott Silver Medals by Justice Minister Brian Lenihan at the Depot in November 1966. William Barrett later moved to the Dublin Metropolitan Area. He was promoted Sergeant in November 1976 and retired on 7 August 1979 having served 24 years and 279 days. Patrick McIntyre remained in the Kerry Division, retiring on 8 September 2001 after 36 years and 245 days.[60]

Patrick Farrell, Garda 8232

Patrick Farrell was born at Doon, Loughrea, County Galway, on 6 June 1909, and had worked in farming before joining the Guards on 8 March 1932.

Garda Farrell was the only person on duty at Kilsheelan Station, County Tipperary, on the morning of 12 June 1965, when a man arrived on a bicycle with a message that a neighbour of his had gone berserk and was threatening his (the neighbour's) widowed sister and a workman with a shotgun. Taking his own car, Garda Farrell drove the three miles to the farmhouse where he found the man's sister standing fearfully with the workman at some distance from the building. Using such natural cover as was afforded by the farmyard the Garda approached the house and found it locked. Windows were likewise secured and appeared to have been barricaded. From within came the sounds of muttering and of furniture being moved about. When Farrell asked for the door to be opened and for an opportunity to talk, the man demanded to know what business the Guard had with him and eventually told him to clear off. After a silence lasting some 15 minutes Garda Farrell, who had stayed near the front door, heard the sound of the bolt being drawn. As the door began to open the Garda rushed forward pushing the door further back and in the process trapping the gunman against the adjacent wall. After a violent struggle Farrell succeeded in disarming his assailant. Subdued, the man allowed himself to be placed sitting in a kitchen chair while Garda Farrell unloaded the single cartridge from the gun. He then diverted the man's attention with a game of cards until his sister and the workman, hearing or seeing no further disturbance from the open doorway, ventured back into the house. This had the effect of again arousing the man's passions and it became necessary to send for a doctor. The unfortunate man was later taken to a private mental home where, some time afterwards, he died.

Patrick Farrell received his Scott Bronze Medal at the Depot from the Minister for Justice, Brian Lenihan, in November 1966. Garda Farrell continued his career in the Tipperary Division until his retirement on 5 June 1972; he had served 40 years and 90 days.[61]

Timothy J. Mahony, Garda 13944

Born on 15 August 1938 in County Kerry, Timothy J. Mahony had been a fitness and sports instructor before joining the Guards on 9 July 1959.

Garda Mahony was one of a party of three Guards in a patrol car summoned from Pearse Street Station, Dublin, in the early hours of 20 January 1965 in response to a report that a firearms shop in Parliament Street was being burgled. On arrival at the shop O'Mahony, who was first out of the car, sighted the man helping himself to goods from the shelves within, and called on him to come out. In response the man turned and appeared to take aim at Garda O'Mahony with a double-barrelled shotgun, and shouted threats when called on repeatedly to drop the weapon. Ignoring the levelled gun, O'Mahony broke the remaining glass in the shattered door and stepped through into the shop, coming within eight feet of the burglar who then backed away nervously towards the rear of the premises. Garda Mahony was followed into the shop by his two colleagues, Garda Carey and Garda Wallace, who also called on the man to drop the gun while moving simultaneously so as to distract his attention from Garda Mahony. Now within three feet of his quarry and aware that the man's nervousness and excitement were increasing, he lunged forward. The man reacted by hurling the gun to the floor, pulling a hatchet from his coat pocket and moving towards Garda Carey. Mahony and Carey leaped on him together, grappling for the hatchet which, after a moment, fell onto the shop counter from where it was later recovered by Garda Carey. As the three men struggled, Garda Wallace seized the prone shotgun and, on checking its breech, found it to be loaded with two cartridges. The weapon's safety catch was found to be in the 'on' position, and, from a remark made later by their captive, it seemed clear that this one circumstance prevented the man from shooting Garda Mahony.

The Minister for Justice, Brian Lenihan, presented Garda Mahony with his Scott Bronze Medal at the Depot in November 1966. Timothy J. Mahony continued in the Dublin Metropolitan Division until he retired on 8 July 1989, having served exactly 30 years to the day.[62]

Michael C. Collins, Garda 13998

Born in Newcastlewest, County Limerick, on 12 March 1938, Michael Collins had been a nurse before joining the Guards on 20 August 1959.

A few minutes before ten o'clock on the evening of 5 July 1966 Garda Collins was resident in charge of Mulranny Station in the Mayo Division when word reached him of a man possibly drowning near the pier. On arrival he was met by the alarming sight of an upturned boat several hundred yards away to which a young man was clinging in distress. Amongst a crowd of concerned onlookers was the man's mother who made an anguished plea to the Guard to save him. Collins was informed that a boat was on its way to rescue the man but that it had to make a four-mile journey across the bay and, as yet, there was no sign of it. The Guard, who was not a good swimmer and who had no life-saving skills, had nonetheless decided to go to the stricken man and stay with him until the arrival of the boat. Except for the occasional wave the sea was fairly calm and Collins felt that he could rely on the strong ebb tide and currents to help carry him to the boat. By the time he reached his objective the boat itself had been carried a further hundred or so yards out to sea. The man clinging fitfully to it fully dressed and in Wellington boots told Collins that he was unable to swim and was suffering severely from the cold. Since it was clear that the young man was nearing exhaustion, Collins determined to swim back to the shore towing the boat and man behind him by means of a short piece of attached rope. But as soon as he began to do so the man panicked and seized hold of the Guard, dragging them both momentarily beneath the surface and separating them from the boat. Realizing that to attempt to bring the distraught man across five hundred yards of water to safety solely by his own strength would merely risk both their lives, Collins swam with him back to the boat and told him to hang on to it. Collins then resumed towing but they had covered no more than a hundred yards when a wave washed the young man from the boat. The Guard dived beneath the surface, found and returned the man to the boat. Over half the distance had been covered when Collins heard a cry from the now-dazed and freezing man and looked round just in time to see him again slide under the surface. Again he dived and searched but without success until an underwater current carried him, incredibly, into contact with the young man who, no less miraculously, was still alive. Again the two returned to the boat, though this time Collins himself had to rest and support the young man while he recovered sufficiently to maintain his grasp on the boat. Fortunately by this time several of the onlookers had stirred themselves to go to the Guard's assistance, and their arrival at the boat spared the near-exhausted Collins the need to endure further towing. The shore having at last been reached, though not without further difficulty, the young man was passed into the care of a doctor, while Garda Collins quietly went home. It was some time before the doctor was able to check on him, and he found the Guard, who had been over an hour in the water, suffering from exposure and shock. He was also covered with minor cuts and abrasions sustained through contact with rocks and with nails protruding from the boat. It later emerged that the rescue vessel from across the bay had suffered an engine failure and would never have come to the young man's aid.

The Garda Commissioner, P.J. Carroll, presented the newly-promoted Sergeant Michael Collins with his Scott Gold Medal at Templemore Training Depot on 24 May 1967. Sergeant Collins continued to serve in the Mayo Division, retiring on 11 March 1995 after 35 years and 204 days. (Sergeant Collins was to win the Scott Bronze Medal in 1975; see p. 95 below).[63]

William Ronayne, Detective Garda 9188
James P. Liston, Sergeant 10148F

Detective Ronayne, born at Ballinacurra, near Midleton, County Cork, on 12 January 1923, had spent time in charge of a Fermoy cargo boat before becoming a Guard on 2 June 1943. Sergeant Liston was born at Knockaderry, near Newcastlewest, County Limerick, on 22 August 1932; he joined the force on 18 November 1952.

Sergeant Liston, in uniform, was driving the patrol car with his plain-clothes colleagues Detective Ronayne and Garda Patrick Garvey 13525 on board as all three responded to a '999' call on the morning of 2 March 1966. The caller claimed that a man had been shot at the Banba Café in Dublin's Talbot Street. The three Guards arrived five minutes later at 9.10 a.m. to find a man with gunshot wounds lying in the hallway face down and almost unconscious. As they approached him the café's owner, who was hiding on an upper landing, called out a warning that the gunman was in a room immediately to their rear. Through a broken pane of glass in the door of the room Ronayne saw a man facing him at close quarters pointing a single-barrelled shotgun, his finger on the trigger. Ronayne identified himself and his colleagues as Gardaí and demanded entrance. The man moved briefly out of sight and there was the sound of a bolt being drawn. As the door began to open Ronayne, closely followed by Liston, rushed in. Ronayne seized the weapon and directed its barrel away from himself while Liston grabbed the gunman. A short struggle ensued during which Ronayne succeeded in breaking the gun open and ejecting its live cartridge from the breech. The injured man died several days later and his assailant, initially charged with murder, was found to be unfit to plead due to insanity and was duly detained at the government's pleasure.

Detective Garda Ronayne received his Scott Silver Medal and Sergeant Liston his Scott Bronze Medal from Commissioner P.J. Carroll at Templemore Training Depot on 24 May 1967. Both men continued their careers in the Dublin Metropolitan Area thereafter, Detective Ronayne being promoted to Sergeant in 1969 and to Inspector in 1973. He retired on 2 September 1983 having served 40 years and 93 days. Sergeant Liston retired on 30 June 1984 after 31 years and 226 days.[64]

Martin Walsh, Sergeant 16180

Born at Gurteen, Ballinasloe, County Galway, on 25 May 1945, Martin K. Walsh worked as a film setter before joining the Guards on 21 April 1965.

He was attached to Dublin's Cabinteely Station on 11 July 1967 when at 2.45 a.m. he stopped his patrol motor cycle at a junction and noticed a car parked at a nearby filling station. As he approached to investigate the car made off at high speed. Following a two-and-a-half mile chase at speeds of up to sixty-miles per hour through the suburbs the car crashed into a high wall. Garda Walsh arrived in time to see a man armed with a narrow foot-long metal tool abandon the car and attempt to flee the scene. After a short pursuit on foot the man fell. But on pouncing on him Walsh found that his quarry was bigger than him and many times his weight. In the course of the struggle which ensued the assailant caught the Guard a severe blow in the left eye with the implement, forcing him to retreat using his crash helmet and gloves to ward off a succession of heavy strokes. Seizing an opportunity the Garda aimed a kick at the man's stomach, causing him to bend forward and allowing Walsh to hit him in the chest. Walsh was then also able to grab the implement which broke and fell to the ground. When the struggle was renewed, however, Walsh saw that the man now had a screwdriver. He pounded the assailant with his fists and eventually managed to wind him. Seizing him, he dragged the man into a doorway and rang the doorbell, noticing as he did so that a light had been switched on in another house nearby. But the assailant then made a frantic effort to free himself. In the course of this he managed to pin the increasingly faint and exhausted Garda to the ground and proceeded to stab him round the eyes with the screwdriver, seemingly intent on killing him. With a herculean effort Guard Walsh threw the man off and, as he attempted again to flee, brought him to the ground and disarmed him. He then grasped the man's hair and struck his head several times against the footpath, weakening him and finally gaining the upper hand. A patrol car arrived at this point and took the young Guard, who was unable to rise and almost blind, to a hospital where he spent he next two days.

While in hospital Martin Walsh was promoted to Sergeant. His assailant was later sentenced to three years penal servitude. Sergeant Walsh received his Scott Silver Medal at the Training Centre, Templemore, on 2 May 1968, from the Minister for Justice, Mr Michael Moran. He served thereafter in the Limerick Division, retiring on 23 May 2002 after 37 years and 33 days.[65]

Philip Brady, Garda 10091
Philip Brady was born on 28 February 1925 at Middletown, Lough Duff, County Cavan, and had been a porter for Coras Iompair Eireann (CIE) before becoming a Guard on 23 April 1948.

He was on duty close to midnight on 8 August 1969 at Castleblaney Station, County Monaghan, when a man asked for Garda assistance with his son who was causing trouble at home. Accompanied by a fellow Guard, Brady arrived at the house and waited a short distance from the front door while the complainant went inside. The man reappeared almost at once and warned the two Guards that his son had armed himself with a rifle. Brady called in at the doorway that they were Gardaí but the young man threatened to shoot them if they did not withdraw. A few minutes later the gunman emerged from the rear of the house brandishing the rifle and repeated his threat when the two Guards made a move to approach. He then tried to retrieve from a car parked in front of the house a box of bullets which he claimed was within. A further attempt by the Guards at this point to approach him led to further brandishing and threats. After a few minutes Garda Brady succeeded in getting the young man's agreement to talk with him alone in the kitchen. Brady was forced to lock both of them in the kitchen before listening to the gunman's account of the domestic quarrel which had led to the incident. While he listened, the Guard cleared from the area around his feet the broken delph which littered the kitchen and waited for the moment when the man, distracted with his story, moved his finger off the trigger. Brady seized the moment and leaped on the gunman, quickly overpowering and disarming him. Still gripping his quarry the Guard managed to unlock the kitchen door and admit his colleague. It was discovered that the rifle was loaded. The two Guards then took the man, who was greatly agitated and, it seemed, rather drunk, to the station.

Philip Brady received his Scott Silver Medal at the Training Centre, Templemore, on 10 September 1970 from Desmond O'Malley, Minister for Justice. Garda Brady continued to serve in the Cavan/Monaghan Division until his death, in service, on 8 May 1980. He had been a Guard for 32 years and 16 days.[66]

James Callaghan, Garda 11011F
Mark Fitzgerald, Garda 16815G
James Callaghan was born at Anglosboro, Mitchelstown, County Cork, on 29 May 1931, and had farmed until his appointment to the Force on 3 November 1954. Mark Fitzgerald , born at Tullakeel, Sneem, County Kerry, on 2 November 1945, had likewise worked in farming before joining the Guards on 18 January 1967.

Following extensive damage to Bridgetown National School, County Clare, resulting from an arson attack in December 1969, Gardaí from Killaloe Station, some six miles away, were regularly detailed for protection duty at the building. Gardaí James Callaghan and Mark Fitzgerald drew the midnight to 8 a.m. shift on 4 July 1970, Garda Fitzgerald patrolling the grounds outside the school. Both men had just finished a meal-break inside the hallway of the prefabricated schoolroom at 3 a.m. when they heard the classroom door being opened. As Garda Fitzgerald approached the door suddenly burst open and five men appeared, one of whom brandished a gun and ordered the two Gardaí to stand against the wall. As the men entered the room proper it was clear that another of them was also armed with a revolver. In addition they carried an iron bar and pieces of timber shaped into weapons as well as a lengths of rope measuring some twelve feet, and thirty-six feet of plastic-covered wire. All five were masked. Despite the fact that a revolver remained trained on them Callaghan and Fitzgerald refused all orders to stand against the wall or to lie on the floor, and resisted attempts to secure their hands. A struggle developed in which Garda Fitzgerald was severely gashed on the head and wrist while Garda Callaghan received arm injuries. Despite uttering a series of lurid threats, the men with revolvers did not dare open fire and, gradually, the assailants began to retreat towards the doorway. With grim determination and perseverence the two Guards forced their five attackers out of the room and into the school yard and slammed the door shut. Garda Fitzgerald then blew his whistle repeatedly and switched on the lights thereby throwing light also across the yard. Callaghan and Fitzgerald then searched the yard but the attackers had fled. The alarm was raised and cordons put in position, but the men had escaped. The two Gardaí, who were on sick leave for above a fortnight after the incident, were believed to have foiled a further attempt to destroy the school.

Both men received their Scott Silver Medals from the Minister for Justice, Desmond O'Malley, at the Training Centre, Templemore, on 14 January 1972. By the time of the presentation ceremony Garda Callaghan had departed for the Tipperary Division but Garda Fitzgerald remained in Clare. James Callaghan retired on 3 January 1988 having served 33 years and 61 days, and Mark Fitzgerald on 1 November 2002 after 35 years and 288 days.[67]

Michael B. McGann, Garda 16395C

Michael McGann, born in Ballymahon, County Longford, on 5 February 1945, worked in a garage before becoming a Guard on 17 November 1965.

He was stationed at Gort, County Galway, when in the early afternoon of 4 December 1970 he heard fire engines as they made their way to a burning public house in Church Street. He rushed to the scene to find a woman screaming that her two-year-old boy was trapped in the pub's kitchen. Despite warnings from a previous would-be rescuer that the heat and smoke of the kitchen were intolerable, Garda McGann attempted an entry. Once inside he saw that all fittings were ablaze and that the very structure of the room was disintegrating. Crawling along and feeling his way by the walls, he spotted a partly-open cupboard door. He discovered that the child had taken shelter within. The Guard pulled the child forth and, protecting him with his body from the debris now falling from all parts of the collapsing room, he dashed from the building. The child was uninjured. Garda McGann went back to re-enter the premises in the hope of saving any surviving bits of furniture, but found only a pile of smouldering masonry and blazing wood on the spot from which he had plucked the child only fifteen seconds earlier. Miraculously he himself was only slightly hurt. Two of his colleagues from Gort Station, in fact, had succeeded in the meantime in rescuing from the other ground-floor rooms virtually all the furniture therein.

Michael McGann received his Scott Bronze Medal from Desmond O'Malley, Minister for Justice, at the Templemore Training Centre, on 14 January 1972. He continued to serve in the west of Ireland, retiring on 17 November 1995 after 30 years and 1 day in the Force.[68]

Richard Fallon, Garda 9936
Paul Firth, Garda 16329E

Richard Fallon, born 18 December 1926 at Moneen, Kilrooskey, County Roscommon, left farming for a career in the Gardaí on 5 November 1947. Paul Firth, formerly a soil sampler, born at Tulla, Ennis, County Clare, on 26 June 1946, joined the Force on 22 September 1965.

On the morning of 3 April 1970 three armed men entered the Royal Bank of Ireland on Dublin's Arran Quay and indicated aggressively to the staff and the few customers present that their motive was robbery. They had taken what they believed to be the precaution of cutting one of the bank's telephone wires, not realizing that by doing so they had triggered an alert which led to the speedy arrival of a Garda mobile patrol outside the bank. The two uniformed unarmed Gardaí who alighted from the car, Richard Fallon and Paul Firth, approached the building just in time to confront the robbers near the entrance. As the Guards moved determinedly towards them all three of the raiders fired repeatedly at them. Garda Firth, who was behind Garda Fallon, called back to the patrol car driver to summon assistance before he dived to the ground. As he reached out to seize the gunman nearest to him Garda Fallon was hit by fire from one of the others and fell mortally wounded. He had been shot twice, in the shoulder and, fatally, in the neck. He died instantly. The robbers ran to their getaway car and fled the scene. Garda Fallon, married with five young children, was the first Garda to be shot dead on duty in 28 years. He was awarded posthumously the Scott Gold Medal. Garda Firth, also in the line of fire that day, received the Scott Silver Medal.

Paul Firth continued to serve in the Dublin area, but died, sadly, at the age of 45 on 16 August 1991 while still in service.[69]

James B. Griffin, Garda 15118A
John F. Murray, Garda 15608F

James B. Griffin was born at Banna South, Ardfert, County Kerry, on 14 August 1942, and worked in farming before joining the Guards on 21 November 1962. John F. Murray from Patrickswell, County Limerick, born 7 July 1943, had been a storekeeper until his appointment to the Guards on 6 May 1964.

Both men were attached to Union Quay Station in Cork City on the morning of 20 August 1971 when a 'general car and station alert' was put in hand due to a robbery then in progress at a supermarket in the suburban Togher district. Two Gardaí from Togher Station had already arrived on the scene but were forced back at gunpoint by three assailants who then drove off at speed, followed by one of the Togher-based Guards, to a premises where they abandoned the car. Gardaí Griffin and Murray arrived at that moment and immediately gave chase and maintained the pursuit despite occasional threats and even a shot fired (at Garda Murray) from a distance of twenty yards. Eventually the man who had fired at him ran into a heavily shrubberied garden and was lost to sight, and Garda Murray waited for further help to arrive. Within minutes his colleagues arrived and a search of the garden unearthed the robber from underneath a hedge; his pistol was quickly found nearby. Meanwhile Garda Griffin continued in pursuit of the other two men, one of whom was armed. With the fortuitous arrival of another patrol car Garda Griffin managed to overtake the armed man (who had momentarily disappeared), jumped from the car and charged at him. As the Garda came at him the robber levelled the gun at him. Without hesitating, Garda Griffin seized and disarmed the man, and then handed him over to his colleagues in the patrol car. Griffin then went to the aid of those Gardaí who were at the point of dislodging the other armed man from his hiding place and assisted in his arrest. The third raider was later apprehended.

James Griffin and John Murray received their Scott Gold Medals from Desmond O'Malley, Minister for Justice, at the Templemore Training Centre on 21 September 1972. Garda Murray was promoted to Sergeant in February 1973 and continued to serve in the Cork region until his retirement on 6 July 2000 after 36 years and 62 days. Garda Griffin was promoted to Sergeant in February 1972 and later, in January 1992, to Inspector. He retired on 13 August 1999, having served 36 years and 266 days.[70]

Desmond O'Kelly, Sergeant 13296K

Desmond O'Kelly, originally of Drunloonay, Killegar, County Cavan, was born on 19 February 1936 and left farming to enter the Guards on 12 December 1957.

He was stationed at Kilkelly, County Mayo, on the evening of 7 March 1972 when a disastrous fire broke out at the nearby residence of one of his police colleagues. Early attendance by a member of the local fire brigade and by a neighbour secured the rescue of two of the policeman's three children who were asleep in an upstairs back bedroom. But, despite the immediate use of a ladder and the assistance of local and other fire brigades, efforts to rescue the third child, a baby asleep in a cot in the upstairs front bedroom, came to nothing. On arriving at the scene and learning that the baby was still trapped inside the house Sergeant O'Kelly tried in vain to gain access to the room both through the hall door and by the ladder. Realizing, however, that the ladder represented the only potential means of entry to the blazing house, and heedless of pleas from concerned onlookers, the Sergeant wrapped his head in a wet towel and again scaled the ladder, this time gaining access to the front bedroom. The cot was on the other side of the room, but Sergeant O'Kelly persevered through the dense smoke, clambered over a bed, and took hold of the cot despite the fact that its plastic sides had melted from the heat. Maintaining his grip also on the bed as the floor seemed likely to collapse at any moment, O'Kelly dragged the cot and baby across the room, over the intervening bed and passed it through the window to a rescuer perched on the ladder outside. The Sergeant, almost at the point of suffocation, was helped through the window and down the ladder to safety. Sadly, the baby did not recover from the ordeal.

Sergeant O'Kelly received his Scott Silver Medal from the Minister for Justice, Patrick Cooney, at Templemore Training Centre in November 1973. He continued to serve in the Mayo Division until his retirement on 1 December 1992 after a career lasting 34 years and 52 days. He died on 13 March 2003.[71]

Thomas Stephen Walsh, Inspector 9369F

Myles Hawkshaw, Detective Sergeant 13621B

Born on 10 January 1925 near Castlebar, County Mayo, Thomas Walsh worked in farming before joining the Guards on 6 June 1944. Myles Hawkshaw was born at Castlerea, County Roscommon, on 11 July 1937, and had been a draper's assistant before becoming a Guard on 2 October 1958.

Both men were members of a party tasked with carrying out a search for firearms on a farm near Dundalk on 14 December 1972. Having opened the gate leading to the farmhouse for Inspector Walsh to follow in his car, Hawkshaw was approaching the house when a man looked out from the doorway of a shed to the right of the detective and then vanished inside slamming the door. Before Hawkshaw could make any move, four men who had been concealed inside the shed emerged suddenly. Three of them attempted to escape but only one managed to elude the pursuing Gardaí. The fourth man, however, was armed with a rifle and draped with bandoliers of ammunition. Ignoring the rifle pointed at him, Hawkshaw charged at the gunman shouting 'don't fire, don't fire'. Within seconds both Hawkshaw and Inspector Walsh, who had circled around behind the gunman, closed with him and after a brief struggle Hawkshaw managed to grab the rifle. Both officers then wrestled the man to the ground. On being examined the gun was found to be fully loaded and ready to fire. The search of the shed unearthed a further three rifles and two more bandoliers of ammunition.

Detective Sergeant Hawkshaw received his Silver Scott Medal, and Inspector Walsh his Scott Bronze Medal, from Justice Minister Patrick Cooney at Templemore Training Centre in November 1973. Myles Hawkshaw later served in the Dublin Metropolitan Area; he was promoted to Inspector in 1975 and to Superintendent in 1989. He retired after a career spanning 38 years and 282 days on 10 July 1997. Inspector Walsh, who had been on temporary assignment at Dundalk at the time of the incident, later served in the Donegal Division and was promoted to Superintendent on 2 June 1974. He retired after 40 years and 226 days on 17 January 1985. Superintendent Walsh died on 18 May 2003.[72]

Gerard O'Sullivan, Garda 14160G

Gerard O'Sullivan was born in Killarney, County Kerry, on 14 November 1939 and joined the Gardaí on 19 January 1960 after a period as a shop assistant.

On the evening of 22 April 1972 two officers based at Togher Station in Cork City were attempting to arrest a man who, the previous day, had stolen cash from a public house by keeping the barmen at bay with a bottle. When approached by the two Gardaí the man brandished a knife and threatened both officers in a particularly vicious manner. At this moment Garda O'Sullivan, also stationed at Togher, arrived and, seeing his colleagues being threatened, immediately drew his baton, rushed at the man and seized him. The knife punctured Garda O'Sullivan's left cheek and cut into the roof of his mouth, but the Guard did not slacken his grip and brought his baton into play. O'Sullivan's two colleagues then entered the fray and the man was arrested. Garda O'Sullivan was taken to hospital where the injuries to his face were found to be serious.

Patrick Cooney, Minister for Justice, presented him with his Scott Silver Medal at Templemore Training Centre in November 1973. Thereafter he continued to serve in the Cork East Riding Division until his retirement after 28 years and 318 days on 1 December 1988.[73]

John Martin Cafferky, Garda 17328C

John Cafferky came from Keel, Achill, County Mayo, where he was born on 30 July 1947. He had been a steel-fixer before joining the Guards on 26 June 1968.

He was one of several Guards summoned to the scene of a blaze at a terraced house in Ballyfermot in the early hours of 10 September 1972, where a number of persons were trapped on the upper floor. Garda Cafferky managed to enter the house by the front door, despite the fact that the front room was ablaze and the hallway and staircase beginning to catch, and made his way upstairs. A colleague who had accompanied Cafferky into the hallway had already been driven back by the heat and dense smoke. In a back bedroom Cafferky found an elderly man immobilized by shock and fear. The Guard managed to persuade him to make the desperate journey with him downstairs and out to safety. On hearing that a man was still trapped in the front bedroom Garda Cafferky immediately returned, made his way up the now-burning staircase and located the man, an invalid, who was desperately sucking in air through a part-open window. Cafferky broke open the window and, with the help of Garda Moolick who had scaled a drainpipe to reach the ledge, got the man through the window and down to safety. At this point no other escape route was left to Cafferky himself but to jump from the window. On landing he injured his right ankle.

He was presented with his Scott Silver Medal at the Templemore Training Centre in November 1973 by Justice Minister Patrick Cooney. Garda Cafferky continued in the Dublin Metropolitan Area until his retirement on 20 April 1981 having served 12 years and 10 months.[74]

William Cullen Fortune, Detective Garda 8843
John Thomas Mulderrig, Detective Garda 15007L

William Fortune was born in Ferns, County Wexford, on 18 September 1914 and left labouring for a career in the Garda Síochána on 27 September 1939. John Mulderrig, born at Althbaun, Kiltimagh, County Mayo, on 14 August 1942, had worked in farming before joining the Guards on 2 May 1962.

Both officers were in a patrol car near Beggar's Bush shortly before noon on 1 June 1972 when word reached them that the Dublin Master Stevedores Association Office had been robbed of £7,351 by two gunmen. Fortune and Mulderrig immediately made for the Liffey's cross-ferry terminal as it seemed a likely escape route for the robbers. The two detectives had few details regarding their quarry other than that both assailants had worn para-military dress. However, they were suspicious of the ferry passenger wearing a green blazer and carrying a hold-all. Their suspicions were confirmed when the man evaded Fortune's attempt to stop him and, after a brief chase, threatened the two Guards with a pistol. Mulderrig radioed for assistance and continued to pursue the man until he was eventually lost from sight. Within seconds Fortune, in the patrol car, had spotted the robber and spread the word to other nearby patrol cars. Mulderrig, picked up by one of these cars, caught up with the man as he attempted to discard his green blazer. The man then abandoned both blazer and hold-all and took to his heels only to be confronted by Detective Fortune approaching from the opposite direction. The trapped robber than made a dive for his blazer and hold-all but was tackled by Fortune and Mulderrig who, with the help of other Guards, quickly effected his arrest. The blazer pocket held the loaded pistol with which the two detectives had earlier been threatened, and the hold-all yielded up a loaded revolver together with virtually all the stolen cash.

William Fortune and John Mulderrig received their Scott Bronze Medals from Patrick Cooney, Minister for Justice, at Templemore Training Centre in November 1973. Both men continued to serve in the Dublin Metropolitan Area. William Fortune was promoted to Sergeant in 1974. He retired some three years later, after a career of 38 years and 36 days, on 1 November 1977, and died on 26 May 1999. He did, however, live to see his son awarded the Scott Bronze Medal in 1982 (see *John P. Fortune*, pp 115–16 below). John Mulderrig was promoted to Sergeant in 1978, Inspector in 1982, and Superintendent in 1994. He retired after 40 years and 104 days on 13 August 2002.[75]

Bartholomew Kevin Carty, Garda 17524B

Kevin Carty, born in Sligo on 7 June 1950, joined the force on 6 August 1969.

Garda Carty was on border patrol with Garda Joseph O'Sullivan on 8 August 1973 at Drumnart, County Monaghan, when they came upon two men in a field. The pair fled at the sight of the Gardaí, one of them pausing to pick up a rifle before he decamped in the direction of the border. Garda Carty went in pursuit. When Garda Carty had almost caught up with him the man turned, pointed his gun at Carty's stomach and pulled the trigger. The rifle, however, failed to fire. The chase then continued, Garda Carty at one point laying hands on his quarry only to receive the rifle butt heavily in his face. The Guard picked himself up and resumed the chase, eventually catching the gunman and arresting him after a violent struggle. The rifle was recovered and was found to be fully loaded but with a fault in its bolt mechanism.

Garda Carty received his Scott Gold Medal from Patrick Cooney, Minister for Justice, at the Templemore Training Centre in September 1974. He continued his distinguished career thereafter, rising to Sergeant in 1975, to Inspector in 1986, to Superintendent in 1989, to Chief Superintendent in 1993, and finally to Assistant Commissioner in 1998.[76]

Gerard M. Lovett, Garda 17653B

Gerard Lovett was born in 1950 at Ballingeary, County Cork, and was a civil servant before joining the Guards on 4 March 1970.

In the early hours of 29 April 1973 Garda Lovett and Detective Garda James Murphy challenged two men who were robbing a petrol-filling station at knife-point in Dublin's Ranelagh district. Detective Murphy pursued one of the robbers who, unfortunately, escaped in the darkness. The other robber, however, attacked Garda Lovett with a knife inflicting two stab wounds one of which was life-threatening. Despite bleeding profusely from the dangerous stomach wound Garda Lovett chased his attacker and, with the help of a civilian, arrested him. After speedy hospitalization and some skilled surgery Garda Lovett made a good recovery.

Garda Gerard Lovett received his Scott Silver Medal from the Minister for Justice, Patrick Cooney, at Templemore Training Centre in September 1973.[77]

Patrick English, Inspector 9995C
James A.D. Madigan, Detective Garda 14294M
Patrick T. McGowan, Detective Garda 14768M

Born at Corbooley, Knockcroghery, County Roscommon, on 12 September 1926, Patrick English had worked as an attendant in a mental hospital before joining the Guards on 6 November 1947. James Madegan was born on 29 July 1936 at Drimnakillen, Inver, County Donegal, and had managed a bar before his appointment to the Guards on 16 September 1960. Patrick McGowan came from Laughta, Kinlough, County Leitrim, and was born on 8 April 1941; he had worked in farming before joining the force on 5 July 1961.

The three men, under the direction of Inspector English and accompanied also by Detective Sergeant William O'Shea, arrived at Coughfin, Castlefin, a border area of County Donegal, near mid-day on 18 February 1974 to investigate a shooting incident. They spotted two men armed with rifles and pursued them across a field. As the distance between the pursuers and their quarry narrowed to about twenty yards the Inspector called on them to halt. At this one of the men turned and fired a shot over the heads of the Gardaí who, nevertheless, continued the chase. As the fleeing gunmen scrambled over a fence Inspector English seized one of them and knocked him down. The man called out a warning that his gun was loaded, but Garda Madigan now caught up with the Inspector and between them they disarmed the gunman. The pursuit of the other gunman, meanwhile, was continued by McGowan and O'Shea. As he saw McGowan closing in on him the man turned and fired, again from a distance of no more than twenty yards, over McGowan's head, this time shouting that he would kill the Garda if he didn't desist. Detective Garda McGowan, unmoved, continued the chase until the man, on reaching the main road, was picked up by a passing motorist and escaped. However, Garda McGowan arrested him next day at a border check-point.

Inspector English received his Scott Gold Medal, and Detectives Madigan and McGowan their Scott Bronze Medals in October 1975 in Templemore Training Centre from the Taoiseach, Liam Cosgrave, at a ceremony attended by several cabinet ministers. Inspector English continued in the Donegal Division, rising to Superintendent in October 1978; he retired on 6 May 1987 having served 39 years and 182 days. James Madigan also continued thereafter to serve in Donegal, retiring on 28 May 1993 after 33 years and 39 days. Detective McGowan likewise remained in Donegal, retiring on 1 February 1995 after a career of 33 years and 212 days.[78]

Dermot P. Doran, Garda 16849A
James A. Roche, Garda 17301M
Thomas M. Jones, Garda 17590M
Thomas F. Flynn, Garda 18725K
Born at Carrick-on-Shannon, County Leitrim, on 2 July 1945, Dermot Doran had been a waiter before joining the Guards on 15 February 1967. James Roche, born on 12 April 1948 at Ballina, County Mayo, had worked as a shop assistant before his appointment to the force on 18 September 1968. Thomas Jones, born 7 June 1950 at Dromard, Moyne, County Longford, entered the Guards on 12 November 1969 after working as a wool grader. Thomas Flynn was born at Nenagh, County Tipperary on 11 May 1952, and had been a labourer before becoming a Guard on 15 November 1972.

The four Gardaí were off duty and attending a dance in the Portlaoise area on 10 December 1973 when they succeeded in arresting Kevin Mallon, an

IRA escapee from Portlaoise Prison. Gardaí Doran and Roche were about to arrest Mallon when they were challenged by an armed woman whom Mallon called upon to use a gun. The woman was disarmed by Gardaí Jones and Flynn. Despite being challenged by another armed woman who was to escape in the crowd, Doran and Roche kept a firm grip on the captive.

All four men were presented with their Scott Gold Medals at the Templemore Training Centre by the Taoiseach, Liam Cosgrave, on 2 October 1975 at a ceremony attended also by several cabinet ministers. Garda Doran went on to serve in the Longford/Westmeath Division, retiring on 18 August 1997 after a career of 30 years and 185 days; he passed away in 2007. Garda Flynn continued to serve in the Laois/Offaly Division, and retired on 15 November 2002 having served 30 years and one day. Garda Roche moved to the Waterford/Kilkenny Division in 1977, becoming a Sergeant a year later; after a stint in Cambodia he rose to Inspector in 1993 and to Superintendent in July 2000. Garda Jones continued his career at Portlaoise.[79]

Thomas A. Hanahoe, Garda 10512M

Thomas Hanahoe was born on 1 September 1931 at Tullamore, County Offaly, and had been a hardware assistant before joining the Guards on 12 November 1953.

He was a customer in a bank at Clontarf, County Dublin, on 19 December 1974 when two masked men, one of them armed, entered and announced a hold-up. The armed man went behind a counter, spoke to the manager, and a shot was fired. Garda Hanahoe tackled the gunman and in the struggle for the weapon he was struck on the head with it several times, sustaining injuries which later required several stitches. The would-be robbers fled from the bank empty-handed.

Garda Hanahoe was presented with his Scott Gold Medal by the Taoiseach, Liam Cosgrave at Templemore Training Centre on 2 October 1975 at a ceremony attended also by several cabinet ministers. Promoted Sergeant in 1981, Thomas Hanohoe continued to serve at No. 3 Company Depot in Dublin until his retirement on 24 April 1988 after a career spanning 34 years and 165 days.[80]

James Kane, Garda 16946C
Patrick M. Counihan, Garda 18466G
James F. Mitchell, Recruit Garda 19721A

James Kane, born on 18 April 1947 at Drumgora, Stradone, County Cavan, had been an apprentice carpenter before joining the Gardaí on 17 May 1967.

Patrick Martin Counihan was born on 17 August 1951 at Inchicore, County Dublin, and had worked as a fitter before his appointment to the Guards on 5 July 1972. James Mitchell, born at Tuam, County Galway, on 28 October 1954, was training to work with computers but left to become a Guard on 17 July 1974.

On the evening of 4 December 1974 Garda Kane with Recruit Garda Mitchell acting as observer, left their patrol car and took from a bus at Cabinteely, Dublin, two men whom they suspected of having been involved earlier in an armed robbery at a petrol station. They were assisted by Garda Counihan on motor cycle patrol and Recruit Garda Lyons who was on the beat locally. As the men were being searched one of them produced a pistol and the Gardaí were ordered back into the patrol car. The two men got in the car also and Garda Kane was told to drive off while the gun was held to Garda Counihan's head. After travelling a short distance Kane was told to stop and the four Gardaí were forced, still at gunpoint, into a field and made to lie on the ground. The men began to tie up Garda Mitchell, threatening as they did so to cripple or mutilate their captives. Garda Kane seized an opportunity to tackle the gunman, and with help from Counihan and Mitchell, overpowered and disarmed him. A shot was fired, but without injury to anyone present. While Recruit Garda Lyons ran to the patrol car to radio for assistance, the other man attempted to flee but was quickly pursued and captured by Counihan and Mitchell.

Garda Kane received his Scott Silver Medal, and Garda Counihan and Recruit Garda Mitchell their Scott Bronze Medals from the Taoiseach, Liam Cosgrave, on 2 October 1975 at a ceremony at the Templemore Training Centre which was attended also by several other members of the cabinet. Garda Kane continued to serve in the Dublin area until his retirement on 17 May 1999 after a career lasting 31 years and one day. Garda Counihan later served in the Ros/Galway and Cavan/Monaghan regions. Garda Mitchell, promoted to Sergeant in November 1993, later served at the Garda Technical Bureau.[81]

Joseph P. Madigan, Detective Sergeant 14733H
James O'Neill, Garda Sergeant 13146G
Patrick J.L. Ahern, Detective Sergeant 14814H
Jude M.D. Murphy, Detective Garda 16170E
Joseph Madigan was born on 22 August 1941 at Ashtown, Castleknock, County Dublin, and had been a shop assistant before his appointment to the Guards on 10 May 1961. James O'Neill, born on 19 November 1935 at

Donaghpatrick, Navan, County Meath, left farming to join the force on 12 December 1956. Patrick Ahern, born at Donard, County Wicklow, on 15 April 1940, had worked as a student radio operator before joining the Guards on 23 August 1961. Jude Murphy was born on 7 November 1945 at Rialto, Dublin, and had been a clerk before beginning a career with the Gardaí on 21 April 1965.

On 26 November 1972 while the IRA leader Sean MacStiofain was under Garda escort at Dublin's Mater Hospital, an attempt was made by eight or nine armed men to remove him from police custody. The four Gardaí, including Sergeant O'Neill who was unarmed, successfully repelled the attempt during the course of which several shots were exchanged. Detective Sergeant Madigan sustained a bullet wound to the little finger of his left hand.

Joseph Madigan received his Scott Gold Medal, and James O'Neill, Patrick Ahern and Jude Murphy their Scott Silver Medals on 2 October 1975 from the Taoiseach, Liam Cosgrave, at the Templemore Training Centre during a ceremony attended also by several other members of the cabinet. Promoted to Inspector in June 1978, Detective Madigan continued to serve in Dublin until his retirement, after 34 years and 325 days, on 29 March 1996. Sergeant O'Neill was also promoted to Inspector in June 1978; he likewise continued serving in Dublin, retiring on 9 June 1989 having served 32 years and 180 days. He died on 12 July 1998. Detective Ahern also continued his career in Dublin. He was promoted to Inspector in May 1986 and to Superintendent in December 1993, retiring on 14 April 2000 after 38 years and 236 days. He was awarded a further Scott Silver Medal in 1977 (see p. 101 below). Detective Murphy continued also in Dublin, being promoted to Sergeant in October 1980. He retired on 12 October 2000 having served 35 years and 175 days.[82]

Kevin Patrick Duffin, Garda 12793M
Michael Heneghan, Garda 10307A
John O'Loughlin, Garda 13427K

Kevin Duffin came from Clonreher, Portlaoise, where he was born on 4 May 1932. He had worked as a labourer before joining the Guards on 12 May 1955. Michael Heneghan, born at Milltown, County Galway, on 15 September 1929, had been an insurance agent before his appointment to the Gardaí on 19 November 1952. John O'Loughlin was born on 22 June 1936 at Ennistymon, County Clare, and had driven a bus before joining the Guards on 17 April 1958.

The crew of a patrol car, four Gardaí which included Garda O'Loughlin who was driving, on the morning of 3 October 1968 sighted and pursued a stolen car through Dublin from Ballyfermot to Drimnagh. There were four men in the vehicle, one of whom during the chase fired two rifle shots at the pursuing patrol car. The Gardaí, however, maintained their pursuit until the stolen car crashed in a cul-de-sac. The thieves then fled through back gardens. By now all patrol cars in the area had been detailed to go to the scene. While responding to the alert Garda Duffin and Garda Heneghan encountered three men, one of them armed with a rifle, at Kilworth Road not far from the scene of the crash. When the two Guards approached to within a few feet of him the gunman took aim at them. Garda Duffin managed to distract him by shouting 'Lads, don't shoot, it's all up'. Although the gunman hadn't lowered the weapon Garda Duffin closed with him and, after a desperate struggle, succeeded in disarming him. Garda Heneghan seized and overpowered the second man while the third fled into a nearby house, but was later arrested. On examination the stolen car was found to contain two loaded pistols and a revolver. The rifle which had been levelled at Garda Duffin and Garda Heneghan was a .22 calibre fitted with a telescopic sight; one round was in the breech and three more in the magazine.

Kevin Duffin received his Scott Gold Medal, and Michael Heneghan and John O'Loughlin their silver and bronze medals respectively from the Taoiseach, Liam Cosgrave, on 2 October 1975 during a ceremony at the Templemore Training Centre attended by several other members of the cabinet also. All three Guards continued to serve in Dublin. Garda Duffin retired on 3 May 1989 after 33 years and 357 days. Garda Heneghan retired on 15 August 1986 having served the community for 33 years and 270 days; he died on 9 October 2000. Garda O'Loughlin retired on 1 September 1988 after 30 years and 138 days.[83]

Bryan Thomas Moroney, Garda 14001E

Bryan Thomas Moroney, born on 16 August 1939 at Killarney, County Kerry, had been employed as a labourer before joining the Guards on 25 August 1959.

On the night of 1 December 1972 Garda Moroney was one of a party of Gardaí from Drogheda Station investigating an attempted armed robbery when they were confronted with a man carrying a semi-automatic shotgun who threatened to shoot any Guard who tried to approach him. To reinforce his threat, after running some distance away from them, he blew several branches off a tree near where the Gardaí were standing. Undeterred by repeated threats and the experience of having the gun pointed directly at him, Garda Moroney moved in ever closer. Eventually he was near enough to risk rushing the gunman and, after a struggle, managed to pull the gun from the man's grasp.

Garda Moroney received his Scott Silver Medal from the Taoiseach, Liam Cosgrave, on 2 October 1975 at the Templemore Training Centre, during a ceremony attended also by several members of the cabinet. He continued to serve thereafter in the Louth/Meath Division, being promoted Sergeant in October 1980. Garda Moroney retired on 15 August 1996 after a career spanning 36 years and 357 days.[84]

John M.G. Cosgrove, Garda 17458H

John Cosgrove, from Clifden, County Galway, was born on 26 July 1949, and left farming for a career in the Gardaí on 25 June 1969.

He was on plainclothes duty and on attachment to Cork's Mallow Road Station in the early hours of Christmas Eve 1972 when he noticed two youths acting suspiciously. They ran off as he approached and Cosgrove set off in pursuit. As he seized one of the youths the other came back towards him brandishing a revolver and demanding that his comrade be released. Cosgrove maintained his grip on his prisoner, but suddenly the boy dropped onto one knee exposing the Guard to the line of fire. The armed youth then fired at point blank range hitting Cosgrove in the right shoulder. The two then made good their escape but were later apprehended. Garda Cosgrove, left for dead by the youths, later had the bullet removed, the surgery necessitating some seventeen stitches.

He received his Scott Bronze Medal from the Taoiseach, Liam Cosgrave, on 2 October 1975 at the Templemore Training Centre, during a ceremony attended also by several other members of the cabinet. He still serves the community.[85]

Patrick J. Morgan, Detective Sergeant 13014A
John K. Connell, Garda 17122M
Timothy A. Hickey, Detective Garda 16070K
Michael P. Bugler, Detective Garda

Patrick Morgan was born on 19 January 1933 at Inchicore, Dublin, and worked as a presser before joining the Guards on 11 April 1956. John K. Connell, born at Headford, County Galway, on 2 June 1946, had been a clerk before his appointment to the force on 28 December 1967. Timothy Hickey, from Castlemaine, Rusheen, County Kerry, was born on 6 March 1945 and left farming for a long and successful career in the Gardaí on 20 January 1965. Michael Bugler, born on 15 March 1934 at Scarriff, County Clare, had been a motor driver before joining the Guards on 9 November 1955.

On the morning of 4 February 1975 these Gardaí tackled, disarmed and arrested two men who were in the act of robbing a post office at Cabra Road, Dublin. The robbers, both members of the Irish Republican Socialist Party (IRSP), were armed with a loaded sawn-off shotgun and a loaded .45 revolver.

Scott Gold Medals were awarded to Detective Sergeant Morgan and Garda Connell, a Scott Silver Medal to Detective Hickey, and a Scott Bronze Medal to Detective Garda Bugler. The awards were presented by the Minister for Justice, Patrick Cooney, at the Templemore Training Centre on 16 July 1976. Patrick Morgan continued to serve in Dublin until his retirement on 18 January 1993 after 36 years and 283 days in the Force. John Connell likewise remained in Dublin; he was promoted to Sergeant in April 1983 and retired on 28 October 1999 having served 31 years and 305 days. Timothy Hickey later served in Castlebar, Sligo and Mullingar before returning to Dublin. He rose through the ranks, becoming Sergeant in 1980, Inspector in 1986, Superintendent in 1990, Chief Superintendent in 1993, and Assistant Commissioner in 1996. Michael Bugler continued on in Dublin, was promoted to Sergeant in April 1979, and retired after a career of 38 years and 126 days on 14 March 1994.[86]

Thomas W. Connolly, Detective Garda 12622E
Patrick J. Burke, Garda 14100C

Thomas Connolly was born on 2 August 1934 at Clonakilty, County Cork, and and been a clerk before joining the Gardaí on 10 May 1955. Patrick Burke, born on 4 April 1938 at Cloughjordan, County Tipperary, worked as a salesman until his appointment to the force on 17 November 1959.

Both Guards were on duty unarmed and in plain clothes on 1 May 1975 when, at Punchestown Races, they recognized and arrested a much-wanted criminal, a man whom they had been warned was probably armed and certainly dangerous. The man resisted arrest, drew a .22 pistol and pointed it directly at Detective Connolly. Without hesitation the detective grabbed the gun and, with help from Garda Burke, succeeded after a violent struggle in disarming the man and taking him into custody. On examination the gun's hammer was found to be cocked; one round was in the breech and a further nine in the magazine.

Detective Connolly received his Scott Gold Medal and Garda Burke his Scott Silver Medal from Patrick Cooney, Minister for Justice, on 16 July 1976 at the Templemore Training Centre. Thomas Connolly remained in the Carlow/Kildare Division, rising to Sergeant in 1979, to Inspector in 1983, and to Superintendent in 1988. He retired on 24 June 1994 after a career of 39 years and 46 days. Patrick Burke also stayed on in the Carlow/Kildare

Division until his retirement on 3 April 1995, having served 35 years and 138 days.[87]

Michael C. Collins, Garda Sergeant 13998L

Michael C. Collins, born at Newcastlewest, County Limerick, on 12 March 1938, left a career as a male nurse to join the Guards on 20 August 1959.

Sergeant Collins was one of those engaged on 4 July 1975 in an intensive search in the Ballycastle area of County Mayo for a woman and her three children who had been missing for two days. The woman's body was sighted at the foot of a set of very steep and dangerous cliffs near Downpatrick Head. This particular spot was notoriously dangerous and locals considered the cliff-face impassable. Secured only by ropes, the Sergeant had himself lowered onto a narrow ledge some one hundred feet from the cliff-top and to within fifteen feet of the water. From this position he succeeded in recovering the woman's body. Despite the danger of falling stones Sergeant Collins repeated the exercise in order to recover the body of one of the children.

The presentation of his Scott Bronze Medal by Justice Minister Patrick Cooney on 16 July 1976 at the Templemore Training Centre was no new experience for Sergeant Collins. He was the second member in the history of the Garda Síochána to receive a Scott Medal twice. Michael C. Collins had been awarded the Scott Gold Medal in respect of a rescue-from-drowning incident at Mulranny, County Mayo, in 1967 (see p. 76 above).[88]

Michael J. Reynolds, Garda 17673G

Michael Reynolds, born on 9 February 1945 at Kilconnell, Ballinasloe, County Galway, had worked as a builder's labourer before joining the Guards on 4 March 1970.

On the afternoon of 11 September 1975 the Gardaí began to receive warnings of an armed robbery in progress at the Killester branch of the Bank of Ireland on Dublin's Howth Road. As the police response got under way the raiders made their escape, having taken more than £7,000 from the bank. As they sped away they narrowly avoided a collision with a car driven by off-duty Garda Michael Reynolds who was accompanied by his wife and two-year-old daughter. Believing the car to have been stolen, Reynolds went in pursuit, the chase eventually reaching speeds of sixty miles per hour through a maze of Dublin suburbs. The four raiders abandoned the car at St Anne's Park, Raheny, and attempted to continue their flight on foot still hotly pursued by Garda Reynolds who had driven into the Park almost immediately behind them. Reynolds, who was unarmed, seized and dragged to the ground the nearest of the robbers who, burdened with their loot, were now beginning to tire. On seeing their comrade in Reynolds's hands one of the robbers called in vain for the Garda to release the man, and, when he did not do so, the robber shot Reynolds in the head. Waiting in the car a short distance away Mrs Reynolds heard the sound but thought uncertainly that it might have come from the car stereo. The incident had hardly reached its tragic conclusion before patrol cars began arriving at the scene. Garda Reynolds died in hospital less than two hours later. Convicted initially of capital murder and sentenced to death, two of the raiders, following a retrial, drew life sentences.

At Templemore Training Centre on 16 July 1976 Garda Reynolds's widow, Vera, accepted her husband's Scott Gold Medal from the hands of Justice Minister Patrick Cooney.[89]

Thomas Joseph Callanan, Garda Sergeant 10863D

Thomas J. Callanan was born at Kilsheelan, Clonmel, County Tipperary on 7 November 1931 and left farming for a career with the Gardaí on 27 May 1954.

In the late afternoon of 6 January 1977 he entered the Bank of Ireland at Whitehall, Dublin, unarmed, in plain clothes and on private business only to find an armed robbery in progress. One of the raiders placed the barrel of a sawn-off shotgun against his stomach and ordered him to the floor. Except for the bank staff and one other customer, all lying prone, nobody but Callanan and the raiders were present. Despite the unenviable odds, Callanan instantly struck the gun aside and knocked the raider to the ground. He was then attacked by one of the other men who called to his accomplices to flee while striking Callanan a heavy blow on the shoulder with a krooklock. As one of the fleeing raiders, bag of money in hand, vaulted the counter Callanan seized him and grabbed the bag, throwing it back over the counter. A brief inconclusive struggle followed, during which Callanan managed to pull off the man's mask and found that the robber's features were known to him. All four raiders, put to flight by one intrepid unarmed Guard, were arrested near the bank quite soon afterwards. When examined, the shotgun which had been pressed against Callanan's stomach was found to be loaded with two live cartridges.

A brother to Sergeant Philip Callanan who became a Scott Gold Medallist a year later (see pp 99–100 below), Thomas J. Callanan received his own Scott Gold Medal from Gerard Collins, Minister for Justice, on 24 November 1977 at the Templemore Training Centre. He continued thereafter to serve in the Dublin Metropolitan Division, retiring on 11 June 1984 after 30 years and 16 days. He died on 14 November 1997.[90]

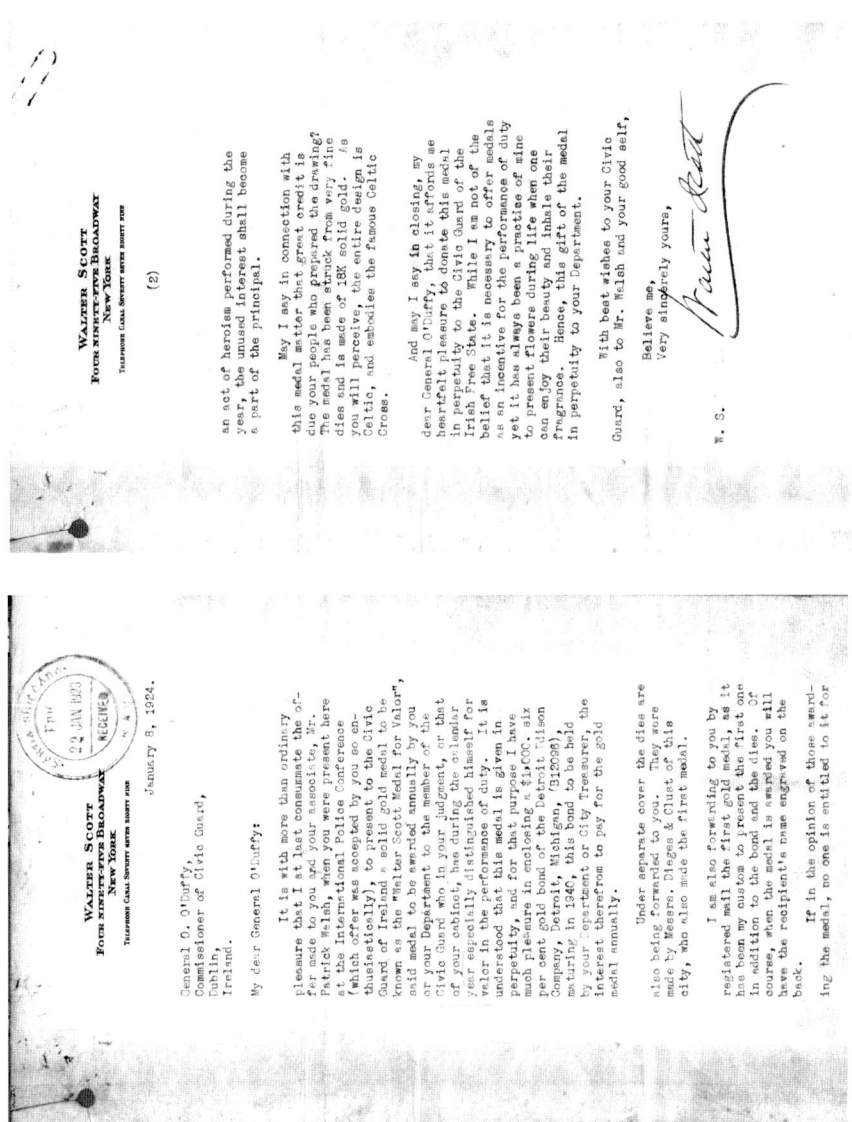

1 The letter of 9 January 1924 from Colonel Walter Scott to Garda Commissioner Eoin O'Duffy confirming the arrangements for the award of the Scott Medal.

2 The design of the Scott Medal is based on a Celtic Cross incorporating elements of the Garda Crest.   3 Garda James Mulroy, first recipient of the Scott Medal.
4 Colonel Walter Scott congratulates Garda Mulroy as Kevin O'Higgins, Minister for Home Affairs, and Commissioner Eoin O'Duffy look on.

5 Gerard Collins, Minister for Justice, and Commissioner Patrick McLaughlin receive from James Mulroy the first Scott Medal for exhibit in the Garda Museum, 15 June 1978. 6 Scott Medallists Garda M.J. Ellis (Silver), Sergeant J. Keely (Gold), Garda J. O'Brien (Silver), and Garda David Hannon (Silver), after presentation, 1928.

 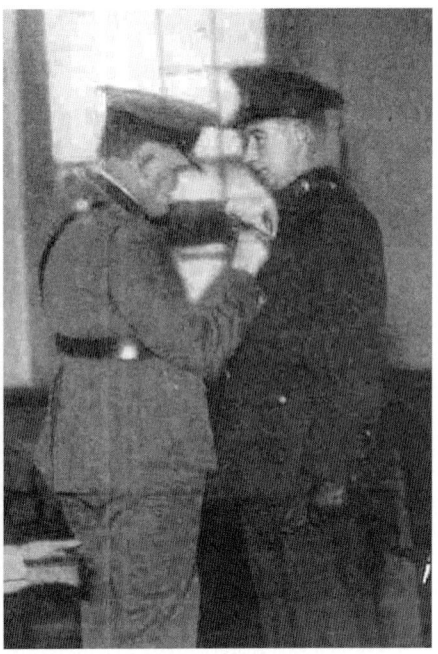

7 Sergeant Laurence Fennelly, Scott Gold Medallist of 1933, rescued children from a burning building in Clonmel, County Tipperary.   8 Garda Patrick Malone, who rescued a man from probable murder by three assailants in Cork City in September 1935, is presented with his Scott Silver Medal by Commissioner Eamon Broy. 9 Detective Sergeant J. Collins, Sergeant J. Driscoll and Garda B. Forde, Scott Bronze Medallists of 1942. Detective Sergeant Collins became the first Garda to win a second Scott Medal; in this photo he is wearing both.

10 Sergeants Michael Flynn and P.J. Tighe after receiving their Scott Gold Medals in 1948. They were the last recipients of Scott Medals for more than a decade. **11** Oscar Traynor, Minister for Justice, and Commissioner Daniel Costigan chat with the first recipients of the 'revived' Scott Medal award, April 1960. The recipients of the bronze medals were Gardaí Patrick Ryan, John Moynihan, Thomas Slattery and Vincent Nolan. **12** Brian Lenihan, Minister for Justice, after the presentation ceremony in 1965. *Left to right*: Sergeant William McCarthy (Gold), Detective Sergeant James Galvin (Silver), Minister, Garda William Blackwell (Silver), and Sergeant John Hennessy (Silver).

13 Scott Medallists of 1976: *left to right – back*: Detective Garda Thomas Connolly (Gold), Detective Garda T. Hickey (Silver), Detective Sergeant P. Morgan (Gold), Detective Garda M. Bugler (Bronze), Sergeant Michael C. Collins (Bronze), Garda John K. Connell (Gold), Garda P.J. Burke (Silver). *Front*: Chief Superintendent E. Kennedy, Assistant Commissioner D. Devitt, Mrs Vera Reynolds (who had received the Scott Gold Medal posthumously on behalf of her husband Garda Michael Reynolds), Patrick Cooney (Minister for Justice), Commissioner E. Garvey.

14 Detective Len Aherne receives his Scott Silver Medal from Gerard Collins, Minister for Justice, in 1978. He had previously been the recipient of a Scott Silver Medal in 1975.   15 Garda Patrick Reynolds, Scott Gold Medallist, was shot dead on duty in February 1982.

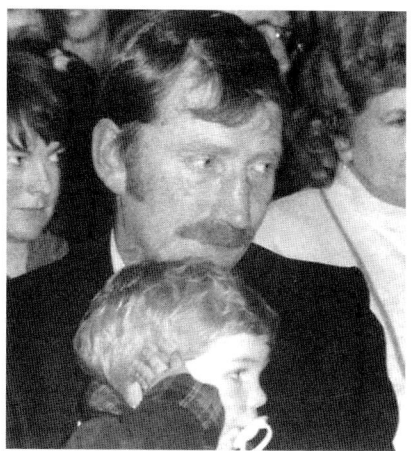

16 Ban Gharda Breda Hand, whose husband Garda Frank Hand was killed on duty in 1984, attended the presentation ceremony with their daughter, Fiona, to receive the Scott Gold Medal on his behalf.   17 Garda Martin V. O'Connor, with family, at the ceremony in 1988 during which he was presented with his Scott Gold Medal. 18 Maire Geoghegan-Quinn, Minister for Justice, pins the Scott Bronze Medal on Sergeant Felix Lunny in 1993.

19 Detective Garda Ben O'Sullivan, severely injured in the incident in June 1996 in which Detective Garda Gerry McCabe was killed, received the Scott Gold Medal for the second time – he had received the gold award previously in 1993.   20 Garda Peter O'Connor and daughter Alicia share a cap after he was was presented with his Scott Gold Medal in 1997.   21 Garda Yvonne Burke (Silver) who in 1998 became the first female officer to receive a Scott Medal.

Anthony B. Sexton, Garda Sergeant 10813H
Born at Breffni Park in Cavan on 7 November 1932, Anthony Brendan Sexton had been a carpenter before joining the force on 27 May 1954.

In the early hours of 27 May 1976 he arrived at the scene of a fire in a two-storey dwelling house at Quin village, County Clare, to be told that two young boys were trapped in an upstairs bedroom. Forcing his way in by the front door, Sergeant Sexton climbed the stairs through a dense pall of smoke and intense heat. On reaching the bedroom he found the floor dangerously weakened by the flames, obliging him to crawl along it towards the boys. Both lads were by now senseless and badly burned, but the Sergeant carried them back through the inferno and to safety. After hospital treatment the boys made a full recovery.

Sergeant Sexton received his Scott Silver Medal from the Minister for Justice, Gerard Collins, on 24 November 1977 at the Templemore Training Centre. He continued thereafter to serve in the Clare Division, retiring on 31 July 1984 after 30 years and 66 days. Sergeant Sexton passed away on 19 January 1996.[91]

Michael G. Neill, Garda Sergeant 14965K
Michael Gabriel Neill was born on 8 January 1940 at Eyeries, Bantry, County Cork, and had driven a van before becoming a Guard on 21 February 1962.

Early on the morning of 18 June 1976 a fire broke out at a three-storey lodging house at Dominick Street, Tralee, County Kerry. At the time Sergeant Neill arrived at the scene witnesses could see through a window that some of the five elderly men who occupied the house were on the third floor and were plainly distraught. Rushing into the blazing building, the Sergeant headed for the stairs. On the flight leading to the second floor a man sat clinging convulsively to the banister rail. As the flames crept closer Sergeant Neill was forced to break the banister in order to release the man's grip; he then dragged the shocked, dazed man back down the stairs to safety. This done, the Sergeant re-entered the house in the hope of rescuing the other men still trapped on the upper floor but by now the heat and flames had grown too intense and he was forced reluctantly to retreat. Then the local fire brigade had arrived and managed to get three of the men to safety through a window. The remaining man died in the fire.

Sergeant Neill received his Scott Silver Medal on 24 November 1977 from Justice Minister Gerard Collins at Templemore Training Centre. Later on Sergeant Neill served in Dublin where he rose to Inspector in 1980 and to Superintendent in 1989. He retired on 7 January 2000 having served 37 years and 321 days.[92]

Dennis Daly, Detective Garda 14851B

Born at Birdhill, County Tipperary, on 27 August 1941, Dennis Daly had worked as a driver before his appointment to the Gardaí on 4 October 1961.

He arrived at the scene of an alleged shooting incident at Church Street, Dundalk, on 10 August 1975 to find a large crowd gathered there. A man who had been shot in the head, he was told, was being cared for at a nearby house, and another man leaving the scene on foot was pointed out to him as the gunman. Detective Daly, who was unarmed, followed the man into a crowded public house and approached him from behind. As the Detective touched him the man pulled a revolver from the waistband of his trousers and spun round. Despite being obstructed by another man, Daly managed to disarm and arrest the gunman. The .38 revolver, as was later discovered, still had five bullets left in its six chambers; one of them, chillingly, had a misfire impression on it.

Detective Daly was presented with his Scott Silver Medal by Justice Minister Gerard Collins on 24 November 1977 at the Templemore Training Centre. He continued thereafter to serve in the Louth/Meath Division until his retirement, after a career of 21 years and 207 days, on 28 April 1983.[93]

James G. Cuffe, Garda 10987H

James Gerrard Cuffe, born on 5 December 1932 at Belmullet, County Mayo, had been a shop assistant before joining the Guards on 3 November 1954.

On the morning of 23 November 1976 he was lodging funds for the Garda Benevolent Society at a bank on Upper Ormond Quay, Dublin, when raiders entered and began to rob the premises. As one of the raiders, carrying a bag of money, was about to leave the bank Garda Cuffe, who was unarmed, jumped on him in an effort to recover the cash. In the course of the struggle the bag burst open, forcing the robbers to depart without at least part of their loot.

Gerard Collins, Minister for Justice, presented Garda Cuffe with his Scott Bronze Medal on 24 November 1977 at Templemore Training Centre. Jim Cuffe continued to serve at Garda Headquarters until his retirement, after 35 years and 89 days in the Force, on 30 January 1990. Sadly he died just a few years later on 12 February 1995.[94]

John Paschal Anders, Detective Sergeant 14810E
James McNamee, Detective Garda 14132A

John P. Anders, born at 16 Walshe's Avenue, Cork, on 23 May 1939, had worked as a lorry driver/salesman before joining the Guards on 23 August 1961. James McNamee from Moyne, County Longford, was born on 14

September 1937 and had been a storeman until he joined up on 10 December 1959.

On the evening of 17 December 1976 the two men were on patrol unarmed and in an unmarked Garda car. Some distance ahead of them was a security van which had just collected a large sum of money from a supermarket at Dublin's Cornelscourt Shopping Centre. As it moved through the car park the van's progress was blocked suddenly by a car bearing false registration plates. Three armed men scurried around the front and side of the van and one of them shouted that unless the security men got out he would start shooting. The security men gamely stayed in the van and the gunmen fired some dozen shots at the windscreen. The two detectives now arrived on the scene. Sergeant Anders drove the Garda car at the gunmen who jumped clear and ran for their own vehicle. Anders rammed the rear of their car. In response the assailants opened fire, hitting the detectives' car several times. The two Guards continued to pursue them as they fled the car park and along the Bray Road, into Cabinteely Village and along Rochestown Avenue. Radio communications had at this point broken down between the detectives' car and Radio Control at Dublin Castle but the members continued on without assistance or radio contact. As they sped along the raiders continued to fire on the pursuing detectives, hitting the car several times. When the chase had reached the Beeches Hotel at Kill Avenue a number of shots penetrated the windscreen of the patrol car. Two bullets struck Sergeant Anders in the head as he drove the car at 60 mph. He nevertheless managed to bring the car to a safe halt, whereupon Garda McNamee flagged down a passing motorist who drove the two Guards to a hospital in Dun Laoghaire. Sergeant Anders, severely wounded, was later moved to the Richmond Hospital. In the course of a follow-up operation the raiders were apprehended and later given lengthy prison sentences.

Detective Sergeant Anders received the Scott Gold Medal and Detective Garda McNamee the Scott Bronze Medal from Justice Minister Gerry Collins at an awards ceremony in Templemore in November 1978. Paschal Anders continued to serve in Dublin and was promoted Inspector in 1984. He retired from the Force on 30 September 1994 after 33 years and 39 days. James McNamee also continued on in Dublin, retiring a fortnight earlier on 13 September 1994 having served 34 years and 278 days.[95]

Philip Francis Callanan, Garda Sergeant 13601M
Philip Francis Callanan, born at Kilsheelan, Clonmel, County Tipperary, on 9 January 1936, left farming for a career in the Guards on 21 August 1958.

He was serving at Tullow in the Carlow/Kildare Division on 16 January 1978 when, in uniform and unarmed, he challenged four armed robbers outside the town's Bank of Ireland. He seized one of the raiders but was shot in the thighs, sustaining severe injuries. Sergeant Callanan (a brother to Sergeant Thomas Callanan who was a Scott Gold Medallist in 1977 – see p. 96 above) received his Scott Gold Medal from Justice Minister Gerry Collins in November 1978 at a ceremony in Templemore. He continued to serve thereafter in the Carlow/Kildare Division, retiring on 31 August 1988 after 30 years and 11 days.[96]

William Grier, Garda Sergeant 13533L
Born at The Glen, Ramelton, County Donegal, on 20 January 1936, William Grier worked in farming before joining the Guards on 10 July 1958.

On the morning of 8 June 1976 Sergeant Grier, stationed at Dundalk, received a report from the Royal Ulster Constabulary that two armed men who had been involved in a murder attempt at Newry were heading towards Dundalk. The Army-assisted Border Patrol were then on a meal break, so Grier and a colleague set off to establish a checkpoint on the main Newry–Dundalk road. As they arrived they noticed a car approaching them which matched that described in the RUC alert. The car carrying two men stopped for the Guards and the driver was asked to step out. He was dressed in clothes so tight-fitting that it seemed improbable that he could be armed, so he was not searched, attention being focused instead on the locked car boot. Sergeant Grier recognized the passenger and asked him to get out. As he tried to search the man Sergeant Grier noticed the butt of a revolver protruding from his inside pocket. Grier seized the man who then called loudly on his accomplice to shoot the two Guards. Clearly the other man was armed also. After a frenzied struggle Grier managed to wrestle his opponent to the ground, pinning him face down. As he tried to disarm his captive two shots rang out. Grier looked up to see the driver standing less than a dozen feet away pointing a handgun at his head. Remembering that a moving target is harder to hit, Sergeant Grier ran bent double in a zig-zag fashion for the relative safety of the patrol car. Both gunmen fired on him as he ran, eventually hitting him in the knee and forcing him to the ground. As he continued to scramble towards the patrol car another bullet narrowly missed his head. He reached the car and managed to radio for assistance. His two assailants made good their escape in the direction of Dundalk, though both were later captured and sentenced to several years in prison.

Sergeant Grier was presented with his Scott Gold Medal by Justice

Minister Gerard Collins at Templemore in November 1978. He continued to serve the people of the Louth/Meath Division, being promoted Inspector in 1989. Inspector Grier retired after 34 years and 204 days on 29 January 1993.[97]

Patrick J.L. Ahern, Detective Sergeant 14814L
Born at Donard, County Wicklow, on 15 April 1940, Patrick Joseph Leonard Ahern had been a student radio operator before joining the Force on 23 April 1961.

Late on the morning of Saturday, 26 November 1976, an attempted robbery of a cash-and-carry store by armed men at Dublin's Richmond Road did not go according to plan. The robbers had taken several customers hostage when Detective Ahern, gun drawn, entered the store and called upon the raiders to drop their weapons. A large revolver and a sawn-off shotgun were pointed at the detective by the men who then threatened to kill him if he did not withdraw. Ahern did not withdraw, and told the men that they were surrounded, causing them to retreat in some alarm further into the store. The detective then moved forward, seized one of the assailants and, after a vicious tussle succeeded in disarming him. Having arrested him, Ahern proceeded to search the man, uncovering a further loaded gun.

Detective Sergeant Ahern received his Scott Silver Medal from Gerard Collins, Minister for Justice at a passing-out parade at Templemore in November 1978. It was his second such award; Detective Ahern had won his first Scott Silver Medal in 1974 (see p. 91 above). Attached at the time of the incident to the Special Detective Unit at Dublin Castle, Detective Ahern continued to serve in Dublin, achieving promotion to Inspector in 1986 and to Superintendent in 1993. He retired after a career of 38 years and 236 days on 14 April 2000.[98]

Seamus Brendan Keys, Garda Sergeant 10926F
Seamus Brendan Keys was born on 9 June 1929 at Cootehill, County Cavan, and had worked as an insurance agent before joining the Gardaí on 2 November 1954.

Sergeant Keys was off duty and out of uniform early in the afternoon of 3 March 1976 when two armed robbers stole a large sum of money from the Bank of Ireland, Navan, having first held the bank manager captive in his office. Keys, accompanied by other Gardaí, entered the bank. The raiders then smashed their way out through a window in the manager's office. The Sergeant darted from the building in time to see one of the gunman, briefcase in hand, heading across the street towards a nearby car park. His accomplice emerged from the window only to be confronted by Sergeant Keys who had armed himself with a piece of wood, the only object to hand, and who was moving forward to make his arrest. As Keys was almost upon him the raider pulled out a revolver and levelled it at him. Keys closed in and as the man sprang back to evade the sergeant's grasp he opened fire, striking the wall above Keys's head. He then made for the getaway car driven by his accomplice shooting as he went. Both raiders initially made good their escape, but were eventually apprehended and charged not only with the robbery but with attempting to murder Sergeant Keys.

Keyes received his Scott Bronze Medal in November 1978 from Justice Minister Gerard Collins at Templemore. He continued to serve in the Louth/Meath Division, being promoted Inspector in 1979. Seamus Keys retired after 31 years and 219 days on 8 June 1986. He died on 15 September 1994.[99]

Daniel McCann, Garda Sergeant 12613D

Born at Swinford, County Mayo, on 6 September 1934, Daniel McCann had been a farmer before opting for a career in the Guards on 10 May 1955.

The man in the car stopped by Sergeant McCann that Sunday night of 24 October 1976 at Castlebellingham, County Louth, was known to the Gardaí and much wanted by them. As McCann tried to arrest him the man produced a gun and pointed it at him. Unarmed himself, McCann seized the gun's barrel and a tug of war began. In the midst of the struggle the sergeant heard the alarming sound of the gun's hammer clicking, but mercifully the weapon failed to actually fire. Other Gardaí came to his assistance and the man was disarmed. The gun, despite its failure to discharge, turned out to be in working order and to have seven rounds in its magazine.

Sergeant McCann was presented with his Scott Bronze Medal by the Minister for Justice, Gerard Collins, at a passing-out parade at Templemore in November 1978. Thereafter he continued to serve in the Louth/Meath Division, and was promoted Inspector in 1983. He retired after a career of 39 years and 119 days on 5 September 1994.[100]

James Brendan Fleming, Garda 17935C

James Brendan Fleming was born on 22 June 1949 at Ballyadams, County Laois, and had been a labourer before joining the force on 21 July 1971.

He and a colleague, both unarmed, were on a mobile border patrol near Monaghan town on the morning of 9 September 1977. They stopped a car carrying two men, one of whom Fleming recognized as an infamous gunman.

Both men were arrested, but on route to Monaghan Station one of the men drew a concealed pistol and pressed it into Garda Fleming's neck. Fleming, though driving the patrol car, turned and lashed out at the man, knocking his gun-hand downwards. He then managed to bring the car to a safe halt and got out. Unfortunately the gunman had by now recovered and held the two Guards at gunpoint while his accomplice fled across nearby fields. An army convoy then appeared on the scene and the gunman surrendered. Garda Fleming took him back into custody. The pistol, when examined, was found to contain five live rounds, one of them in the breech, and its safety catch was 'off'.

Garda James Fleming received his Scott Bronze Medal from Justice Minister Gerard Collins at Templemore in November 1978. Today he still serves the people of the Monaghan area.[101]

John Oliver Hogan, Detective Sergeant 14430D
Michael Patrick Connell, Detective Garda 10964K
Morgan Francis Lahiff, Detective Garda 14647A
John Oliver Hogan, a native of Carrigatoher, County Tipperary, was born on 19 July 1937; he left his previous occupation as a clerk to join the Gardaí on 7 September 1960. Michael Patrick O'Connell, born at Ballina, County Mayo, on 16 February 1930, had been a labourer before joining the Force on 2 November 1954. Morgan Francis Lahiff from Ennis, County Clare, born 30 July 1938, had worked as a salesman until he began a career with the Gardaí on 19 April 1961.

The three detectives arrived at a dairy on Cork's Kinsale Road on the morning of 4 September 1978 in pursuit of routine enquiries when they found that they had interrupted a robbery. As they emerged from their car four raiders, armed and masked, ran from the dairy's main office and opened fire on the detectives, shattering the car's rear window. Hogan, Connell and Lahiff, who were also armed, immediately drew their guns and returned fire on the raiders who withdrew in a hurry behind their getaway car. The exchange of shots continued until Detective Hogan retrived an Uzi subma-chine gun from the detectives' car and levelled it at the robbers, calling on them to surrender. The robbers, outclassed as well as out-gunned, gave up the struggle and were taken into custody. Their fully-loaded weapons, when later examined, included two self-loading pistols, a revolver and a sawn-off shotgun. The detectives recovered cash and cheques amounting to almost £10,500.

Scott Gold Medals were presented to all three men by Justice Minister of

State David Andrews at Templemore in June 1979. The three detectives continued to serve thereafter in the Cork East Riding Division, Hogan being promoted Inspector in 1981. John Hogan retired on 14 July 1994 after 33 years and 311 days. Michael O'Connell and Morgan Lahiff retired on 15 February 1987 and 7 January 1993, having served 32 years 106 days and 31 years 264 days respectively.[102]

Thomas Joseph Tormey, Garda 14986A

Born on 5 September 1941 at Ballinasloe, County Galway, Thomas Tormey left farming for a career in the Guards on 7 March 1962.

At mid-day on 30 May 1978 Garda Tormey, together with Garda Thomas Lavin, arrived at Lord Edward Street in Ballymote, County Sligo, where a house was on fire. The sole elderly occupant was in bed in the upstairs part of the house where the fire was blazing with particular intensity. Garda Lavin and a civilian made an initial attempt to rescue the trapped woman but they were driven back by the intense heat and smoke. A similar attempt by Garda Tormey was also in vain. Tormey tried again, this time crawling up the stairs on his hands and knees. Reaching the bedroom he saw the woman lying on the floor and clearly still alive. He managed to drag her into the corridor but once there was momentarily confused by the choking smoke and almost-unbearable heat. A voice from the stairs enabled him to regain his sense of direction and he carried the woman down to safety. Sadly, she died later that evening.

Thomas Tormey received his Scott Silver Medal at Templemore in June 1979 from the Justice Minister of State David Andrews. He continued to serve the people of the Sligo/Leitrim Division until his retirement on 6 March 1992, after a career of exactly 30 years.[103]

Michael Scanlon, Detective Sergeant 16492E
James Oliver McCarthy, Detective Garda 16928E

Michael Scanlon, born at Tralee, County Kerry, on 9 October 1945, had been a shop assistant before joining the Gardaí on 2 March 1966. James Oliver McCarthy from Miltown, County Kerry, born 28 April 1946, worked as a labourer before joining up on 26 April 1967.

On the morning of 22 February 1979 the two detectives were on armed patrol in the vicinity of the Ford Car Factory in Cork City which, a few minutes earlier, had had its payroll snatched by an armed gang. This had been the latest in a series of armed raids carried out across the region by a unit of the Provisional IRA in which local people had been terrorized and unarmed Gardaí threatened with death. Responding to a call for assistance from their colleagues, Scanlon and McCarthy picked up the trail of the escaping raiders' car and pursued the two robbers at high speed through the Cork suburbs. Shots were exchanged in the course of which the raiders' car was damaged and forced to crash. After an armed stand-off the raiders finally surrendered. The two detectives arrested and disarmed the gunmen and recovered the factory's £40,000 payroll intact, together with a virtual arsenal of weapons. The arrest of the two raiders effectively split the IRA unit; its other two members were later arrested in Limerick. The unit's two-year reign of terror in the Cork, North Kerry and West Limerick region was thus brought to an end.

Michael Scanlon and James McCarthy received their Scott Gold Medals from Justice Minister Gerard Collins at Templemore in June 1980. Detective Scanlon served thereafter in Dublin, Clonmel and Cyprus before returning to Cork. He retired on 8 October 2002 after 36 years and 221 days. Detective McCarthy continued in the Cork Division, retiring on 27 April 2003 after 36 years and 2 days.[104]

Michael P. Greville, Detective Sergeant 15879H
James Fagan, Garda 16483F
Peter P. Canavan, Garda 17441F
Michael Kennedy, Detective Sergeant 10191E
John K. Mullins, Detective Garda 18277L
A Dubliner, born in Rathfarnham on 8 May 1940, Michael Greville had been a clerk before joining the Gardaí on 9 September 1964. James Fagan from Kilcogy Lower, County Longford, born on 16 September 1944, left farming for the Gardaí on 19 January 1966. Peter Canavan, born on 25 January 1949 at Kilkerrin, County Galway, likewise left farming for a career in the Guards on 12 March 1969. Michael Kennedy, born at Newbridge, County Kildare on 10 April 1931, worked as a telephonist before joining up on 18 November 1952. John Kevin Mullins, born 3 June 1953 at Drimoleague, County Cork, was a labourer before joining the force on 8 March 1972.

Responding to a report of an armed raid on a Rathmines post office on the morning of 10 August 1979, Garda Fagan and Garda Mullins, unarmed and on mobile patrol, ran straight into the three armed robbers as they emerged from the building. One raider fired point blank at the Gardaí but missed. The men then fled in their getaway car, one of them shattering a passing motorist's tyre with a shotgun blast as they drove away. The two Gardaí gave immediate pursuit through the busy streets in their patrol car, zig-zagging to avoid being hit by shots fired from the raiders' car. As the chase went on Garda Canavan reported the incident to Garda Communications Centre at Dublin Castle.

Eventually, due to the heavy Friday morning traffic, Fagan and Canavan lost sight of their quarry. The report of the robbery was picked up by Detective Sergeant Greville who was driving in the Palmerstown area. He then spotted the robbers' car and took up the chase. The raiders fired at him also, but Greville, who was armed, returned fire blowing out the rear window of the raiders' car. After a further exchange of shots the gunmen abandoned their car in a driveway. Detectives Kennedy and Mullins now arrived to assist Greville. After yet another exchange of fire the raiders, now faced with a level playing field, surrendered. The entire proceeds of the robbery, some £20,000, were recovered.

Detective Greville was awarded the Scott Gold Medal, Garda Fagan and Garda Canavan the Silver, and Detectives Kennedy and Mullins the Bronze. All were presented at Templemore in June 1980 by the Minister for Justice, Gerard Collins. Michael Greville retired on 17 September 1994 after 30 years and 9 days; James Fagan (promoted Sergeant in 1980) on 15 September 2001 having served 35 years and 240 days; Michael Kennedy on 4 August 1988 after 35 years and 144 days. Peter Canavan retired on 2 December 2004, followed by John Mullins on 3 June 2006. With the exception of John Mullins (promoted Sergeant in 1986) who moved to West Cork, all the members involved in the incident continued to serve thereafter in Dublin.[105]

Kevin Lynch, Garda 20698K

Born in Croom, County Limerick, on 5 April 1958, Kevin Lynch had been a student before entering the Gardaí on 3 August 1977.

On the evening of 30 March 1979 he was detailed with two colleagues to be part of a mobile patrol that would monitor the roads and border crossings around Scotstown, County Monaghan. In the townland of Lanacht, on the border, they stopped and questioned a young man known to them as a dedicated member of the Provisional IRA. The man claimed to be on his way home, so the Guards drove him there while they continued to question him. Some ninety minutes later they again spotted him making his way through a field near the border. When Garda Lynch, accompanied by Garda John Barron, tried to follow discreetly, the man caught sight of them and took to his heels. Lynch and Barron had scarcely returned to the patrol car when they saw another known member of the Provisional IRA driving along a nearby road in a transit van. The Gardaí stopped and searched the van, finding several sets of military fatigues concealed under a pile of building material. The driver was arrested on suspicion of membership of the PIRA and taken to Monaghan Garda Station, where a further search of the clothing from the van unearthed a live bullet. The activity in the area was thought sufficiently alarming and suspicious to warrant a further mobile patrol, this time involving a car with two armed detectives as well as a uniformed patrol car from Monaghan Station. Garda Lynch remained with the Scotstown car which then also returned to the area. After searching vacant and occupied houses in the district where the young PIRA member had first been seen, Garda Lynch and Garda Barron set up a checkpoint on a narrow road. As darkness fell two cars approached, stopped some thirty yards short of the checkpoint and made frenzied efforts to turn back. Garda Lynch shouted for assistance and, with Garda Barron, got into the Scotstown patrol car as it drew level with them. The patrol car sped in pursuit of the fleeing motorists, but, rounding a bend came across a number of men running along the road. One of the men then opened fire on the Scotstown car with a rifle, shattering the windscreen and peppering the car with bullets. Both Garda Barron and Garda Lynch were hit. The Monaghan patrol car had by now arrived behind the Scotstown car on the narrow track, making escape difficult. During an apparent lull in the shooting Garda Lynch got out of the car and ran for the cover of a drain. As he lay there he heard Garda Barron, seriously wounded in the shoulder and back and trapped in the car's footwell, shout for help. Though wounded himself, Garda Lynch returned to the car and, under renewed fire, dragged Garda Barron, who was the larger and heavier of the two, from the car and through a ditch into an adjacent field. Both Gardaí were quickly taken to hospital where Lynch was found to have been shot in the left side of the back. Both Guards made a good recovery.

Garda Lynch was presented with his Scott Silver Medal at Templemore in June 1980 by Justice Minister Gerard Collins. He was promoted Sergeant in 1990 and Inspector in 1998, eventually coming to serve as a Detective Superintendent at Garda Headquarters.[106]

Thomas Joseph Commons, Garda 18035A

Thomas Joseph Commons was born in County Mayo on 4 January 1950 and was a junior clerk before joining the Gardaí on 17 November 1971.

While on motorcycle patrol in Dublin on the evening of 22 July 1978 he stopped and questioned two men whom he suspected of having viciously assaulted and robbed a petrol attendant at gunpoint. Without obvious warning the men attacked Garda Commons. One of them attempted to shoot him in the face at point-blank range, but the gun misfired. The two miscreants fled, and there followed a chase during which Garda Commons caught them, lost them, and eventually after a violent struggle, succeeded in pinning the gunman to the ground. Other Gardaí arrived on the scene and the other man was later arrested. Under examination it was discovered that the gun was in working order and that Garda Common's life had been saved only due to the fact that it had been loaded with the wrong type of bullet.

Garda Commons received his Scott Bronze Medal from Justice Minister Gerard Collins in June 1980 at a passing-out parade at Templemore. He has since risen through the ranks of the force, becoming Sergeant in 1980, Inspector in 1994, and Superintendent in 1998. He is still serving.[107]

Patrick Sweeney, Garda 15311G

Born on 29 June 1942 at Ballylar, Letterkenny, County Donegal, Patrick Sweeney had been training to be a nurse before opting instead for a career in the Gardaí on 25 September 1963.

Early on the afternoon of 4 April 1979 he was standing, unarmed, off duty and in plain clothes at the counter of a bank in Dublin's Talbot Street. Hearing a disturbance behind him he looked around to see a man holding a gun to the head of the bank porter. Unless the staff threw him the money, he threatened, the porter would die. Money was thrown towards the gunman from behind the counter. As the robber's attention became fixed on the cash Garda Sweeney tried to slip around behind him. The man, however, spotted him and threatened to shoot him if he moved any further. As soon as the raider had scooped up the money and left the building Garda Sweeney set off in pursuit. He sighted the robber, gun still in hand, get on a bicycle. Surging forward, Sweeney knocked the man to the ground and, after considerable resistance, managed to subdue and disarm him. The gun proved to be an imitation.

Garda Sweeney received his Scott Bronze Medal from Justice Minister Sean Doherty at a passing-out parade at Templemore in September 1982. He retired on 28 June 1999, having served 35 years and 277 days.[108]

Patrick J. Stokes, Garda 21128A
David Joseph Dowd, Garda 17942D

Patrick Stokes was born at Milford, Tullylease, County Cork, on 11 March 1956. Before joining the Gardaí on 15 February 1978 he had been a farmer. David Dowd, born at Drogheda, County Louth, on 16 April 1950, had worked in a factory before becoming a Garda on 21 July 1971.

Both men were based at Naas and were on mobile patrol in the early hours of 25 August 1979 when they were instructed to investigate an anonymous report of suspicious activities connected with vehicles parked in a lay-by at Palmerstown, Kill, County Kildare. In pitch darkness and in the midst of a driving rainstorm boxes were apparently being transferred from a van to a lorry. There were several men standing between the two vehicles and another beside the door of the lorry. While Garda Dowd approached the men who were moving the goods Garda Stokes went to speak to the lone figure beside the lorry. From somewhere a handgun came flying through the air and was caught by the man facing Garda Stokes, who immediately seized him. As they grappled the gun fell to the ground and Garda Stokes managed to kick it under the lorry, shouting a warning as he did so to his colleague that the men were armed. The man tore himself loose from Garda Stokes, ran to a nearby car and, accompanied by another man, drove off at speed for Dublin. Garda Dowd had arrested one of the group of men who had been positioned between the van and the truck, and together with their prisoner, the two Guards set off in pursuit of the speeding car. As the chase developed momentum Stokes and Dowd alerted their Station at Naas as well as Dublin Control. After almost seven miles had been covered the fleeing men turned onto a narrow by-road but crashed as they attempted to negotiate a junction. The pursuit then continued on foot. As Garda Stokes caught up with one of them, the man, half-way over a gate, shouted that he was armed and would shoot. Stokes felled him with his baton. Garda Dowd then stood guard over the stunned criminal and the search for the man's accomplice ended when Garda Stokes came upon him lying in a ditch. By now other patrol cars were arriving on the scene, and the two men were taken away. Subsequent examination of the vehicles in the lay-by revealed the presence of nearly two dozen metal containers filled with cannabis resin the value of which, on the street, was above a million pounds. The lorry was carrying boxes of bananas and these were intended to be used as camouflage for the drug consignment. The handgun was found to be in full working order and loaded with eight rounds, one of them in the breech.

Garda Stokes received his Silver and Garda Dowd his Scott Bronze Medal from Justice Minister Sean Doherty at a passing-out parade at Templemore on 16 September 1982. Garda Stokes later transferred to Mallow and was promoted Sergeant in 1994; he is still serving. Garda Dowd remained in the Carlow/Kildare Division until his retirement, after 35 years and 150 days, on 17 December 2006.[109]

Daniel Bartholomew Prenty, Garda Sergeant 14004L
Thomas Duffy, Garda 21401K
Born at Claremorris, County Mayo, on 2 August 1935, Daniel Prenty left farming for a career in the Guards on 2 October 1959. Thomas Duffy, born

on 15 December 1956 in County Westmeath, had been a quality controller before joining the force on 26 July 1978.

On the late afternoon of 9 May 1980 a report was received at Dundalk Station that a robbery was in progress at a local jeweller's. Sergeant Prenty and Garda Duffy, in the company of Garda Thomas Mulligan, drove to the scene and began to set up checkpoints in response to further reports regarding the robbers' whereabouts. They then spotted two youths strolling casually, one of them carrying a blue bag. Further information was then received from other Gardaí in the vicinity that the robbers' getaway car was parked close by. Prenty, Duffy and Mulligan immediately drove in pursuit of the youths, catching up with them within seconds. When challenged one of the men drew a revolver and fired two shots at Sergeant Prenty and Garda Duffy who were no more than four feet from him. The man then menaced Garda Mulligan, who was still at the wheel of the patrol car, with the gun. Garda Mulligan ran the patrol car against a pillar, blocking the gunman's path. The two raiders then took to their heels, hotly pursued by Prenty and Duffy. Soon the youths dropped their bag, but the one with the gun turned and fired further shots at the two Guards, forcing at least one of them to dive for cover. The men then fled into a nearby house; this was promptly surrounded by other Gardaí acting on Sergeant Prenty's directions, and the robbers were arrested. Garda Duffy and Sergeant Prenty were unarmed, as was Garda Mulligan. The abandoned bag was found to contain the proceeds of the robbery, jewellery valued at almost £16,000 and over £230 in cash.

Sergeant Prenty received the Scott Gold Medal and Garda Duffy the Scott Silver Medal from the Minister for Justice at Templemore during the early summer of 1981. Dan Prenty continued thereafter to serve in the Louth/Meath Division, being promoted Inspector in 1983. He retired on 28 July 1995 after 35 years and 300 days. Tom Duffy (promoted Sergeant in 1993 and Inspector in 2007), after brief postings to Ballyhaunis and Dromad, returned to Dundalk where he continues to serve the community as a member of the Detective Bureau.[110]

John F. Morley, Detective Garda 15543H
Henry G. Byrne, Garda 18300H
James P.D. O'Kelly, Garda 16611H
Michael J. O'Malley, Sergeant 14508D
John Morley, born at Kiltimagh, County Mayo, on 6 October 1942, had worked in farming and as a clerk before joining the Gardaí on 31 March 1964. Henry Byrne was born on 24 March 1951 at Knock, Claremorris, County

Mayo, and had been a shop assistant until opting for a career in the Gardaí on 8 March 1972. James O'Kelly, born 1 July 1946, came also from Kiltimagh, County Mayo, and had worked as a storeman before joining the force on 15 June 1966. Michael O'Malley from Louisburgh, County Mayo, was born on 8 February 1939 and had left farming for the Guards on 14 December 1960.

On the afternoon of 7 July 1980 the Bank of Ireland at Ballaghaderreen, County Roscommon, was robbed of some £41,000 by two armed and masked men. A number of shots were fired and even the arrival of Gardaí at the scene while the robbery was in progress was unable to prevent the robbers' escape. The raiders (three of them in all) burned their immediate getaway car and transferred to another a short distance from the town before driving towards Castlerea. News of the robbery had been flashed to Castlerea Station and immediately Garda O'Kelly, Garda Byrne, Sergeant O'Malley, and Detective Garda Morley (armed with an Uzi submachine gun) sped off in a patrol car to intercept the fleeing robbers. Some five miles from Ballaghaderreen, at Shannon's Cross, the robbers collided with the patrol car. The thieves then reversed a couple of yards to free their vehicle. One of them emerged and blasted the windscreen of the patrol car with a shotgun, barely missing Garda O'Kelly who dived beneath the steering wheel. The other two raiders then opened fire on the patrol car also, mortally wounding Garda Byrne who was hit in the head. They then attempted to reverse away from the scene but an open door snagged on a telegraph pole forcing them to abandon the car and take to the fields. One of them took refuge in bushes at the roadside as Garda Morley emerged from the stricken patrol car. Morley fired a warning shot over the bushes, and then he and Garda O'Kelly went in pursuit of the other two. Sergeant O'Malley remained with the patrol car radio performing the vital duty of seeking assistance and keeping the station informed of developments. The raiders ran back to the roadway and took cover at a small bridge. There Morley confronted them, but before he could fire more than a single shot a passing cyclist came between him and the gunmen. The gunmen, unconcerned for the safety of the cyclist, used the moment to fire at the detective, hitting him and severing the principal artery in his left leg, from which wound he eventually bled to death. All three raiders were arrested within a short time.

Detective Garda Morley and Garda Byrne were posthumously awarded the Scott Gold Medal. Sergeant Michael O'Malley and Garda James O'Kelly received Scott Silver Medals. These were presented by the Minister for Justice, Sean Doherty, at Templemore on 16 September 1982. Both O'Malley and O'Kelly continued to serve in the Roscommon/Galway Division,

Sergeant O'Malley retiring after 35 years and 56 days on 7 February 1996, and Garda O'Kelly on 30 June 2003 having served 37 years and 16 days.[111]

Seamus Quaid, Detective Garda 13497L
Donal D. Lyttleton, Detective Garda 14401M

Seamus Quaid came from Ballinakill, Kilmeedy, County Limerick; born on 16 November 1937, he left farming for a career with the Gardaí on 22 May 1958. Donal Lyttleton, born at Rathnapish, County Carlow, on 7 August 1940, had been a clerk before joining the Guards on 7 September 1960.

On 13 October 1980, a day which had seen two armed bank raids take place at Callen, County Kilkenny, Detectives Quaid and Lyttleton were checking up on local suspects in the Wexford area where both men were stationed. It was late that evening when they stopped a van at Ballyconnick Quarry near Cleristown. The van was being driven by Peter Rogers, a Belfast man and a known member of the Provisional IRA who had escaped from the internment ship, the *Maidstone*. He had been living in the Ballyconnick area where he had married a local girl. His van was normally in use for vegetable deliveries, but earlier that day it was said to have been seen in Callan. When Quaid and Lyttleton stopped it that night it was filled with explosive materials. As the detectives searched the van Rogers suddenly drew a gun and ordered them out onto the roadway. Both detectives were armed, but Lyttleton had left his gun in the patrol car. Rogers ordered them into the nearby quarry, responded with kicks when Lyttleton tried to reason with him, but then demanded that the two Gardaí should let him go. At one point he fired a shot over their heads. Detective Quaid took advantage of Rogers' evident agitation to quietly draw his own weapon, but the gunman spotted the movement and a brief but lethal gun battle took place. Quaid, aiming low to disable and bring down his quarry, shot Roger four times in the left leg. Rogers managed to shoot Quaid in the lower abdomen. The fatal bullet, however, was the one which cut through the main artery in the detective's leg, causing him to bleed to death within a matter of minutes. As Quaid lay dying, Rogers fired further shots at Lyttleton who, unable to reach the car in any safety, had set off across country to seek help. The wounded Rogers attempted to escape in the van but found that a bullet had punctured one of its tyres. He then stole a car from a nearby farm, but within a few hours his injuries and the hopelessness of his position led him to give himself up.

Seamus Quaid was awarded posthumously the Scott Gold Medal, and Donal Lyttleton the Scott Silver Medal. Both medals were presented by Justice Minister Sean Doherty during a passing-out parade at Templemore on 16 September 1982. Detective Lyttleton continued to serve in the Wexford Division until he retired, after a career spanning 35 years and 135 days, on 19 January 1996.[112]

William Daly, Detective Garda 13794L
Richard Curran, Detective Garda 9925B
Martin Donnellan, Detective Sergeant 17179D
Martin J. Doyle, Detective Garda 20091C
Kieran Brennan, Detective Garda 16476C
John (Sean) Keeley, Detective Garda 19161B

William Daly, Richard Curran and Kieran Brennan had all worked in farming before joining the Guards. William Daly, born on 6 November 1937 at Kylegrove, Portlaoise, joined on 19 February 1959. Richard Curran, from Johnstown, County Kilkenny, was born on 31 August 1925 and attested on 16 May 1947. Kieran Brennan came from Wolfhill, County Laois, where he was born on 8 March 1946; he joined up on 19 January 1966. Martin Donnellan, born at Ballymoe, County Galway, on 7 June 1948, had been a cabinet maker before joining the force on 20 March 1968. Martin Doyle from Dublin's Upper Leeson Street was born on 1 October 1951, and had been a customs clerk before opting for a career with the Guards on 2 April 1975. Sean Keeley, born in Galway on 19 July 1953, had worked as a hospital attendant before joining the Guards on 28 March 1973.

On the afternoon of 30 December 1980 four heavily-armed men smashed their way through a plate glass window into a bank at Dublin's Stillorgan Shopping Centre, threatened the staff and made off towards a waiting van with £102,000. Detective Garda Keeley, armed but off duty, who was in the shopping centre, went to the scene in time to see the robbers piling into the van where a fifth man waited at the wheel. As he ran towards it to get its registration number the raiders inside the van broke the rear window and levelled their guns at him. Keeley drew his sidearm and fired a single round but was then forced to take cover behind a nearby car as the raiders responded with a burst of rifle fire. The van then left the scene at high speed. All Gardaí in south Dublin, whether in stations or on mobile patrol, had by now been alerted. One such mobile patrol, manned by Detective Gardaí Daly (who was armed) and Curran, headed for Foxrock Village where they believed they could intercept the van. They were no sooner on the robbers' tail, however, when they were fired upon and forced to keep at a safe distance during a chase that ended dramatically at Carrickmines Cross. The raiders, realizing that their aged van was never going to outdistance the powerful Garda patrol car, stopped out of sight of the pursuing detectives and set up a hastily-prepared ambush. Daly and Curran caught up with the van before they spotted the danger. Their car was savagely raked with bullets and both men severely injured. The robbers then continued in their flight. Within a short time they abandoned their van, which by now had become a liability, and hijacked a passing Fiat 132. A few miles further on, however, in the Dublin Mountains, they managed to crash this car. They then hijacked a passing Datsun, but as they piled into it they were discovered by Detective Garda Martin Doyle who approached from the direction in which the robbers were fleeing. Doyle, armed and on duty (but driving his own car), was immediately confronted by the raiders' firearms. He reversed away to a safe distance where he came upon Detective Sergeant Donnellan and Detective Garda Brennan, both of whom were unarmed. Realizing that the raiders could scarcely head back towards Dublin, the three detectives used their cars to block the narrow road. The robbers in their stolen Datsun appeared within seconds and stopped a few yards from the improvised roadblock. The three detectives took cover, Doyle pointing his pistol while Donnellan and Brennan pointed cupped hands to give the impression that they also were armed. Panic now seized the raiders. In a frenzied attempt to reverse out of the situation they slid into a drain and overturned. They then tried to escape on foot as the intrepid detectives closed in, Doyle firing first a warning shot over the raiders' heads and firing again when it seemed that fire might be returned. One raider was wounded and two others then gave up the struggle. The remaining two made good their escape.

Detectives Daly and Curran recovered from their injuries in time to receive their Scott Gold Medals from the Minister for Justice, Sean Doherty, at Templemore on 16 September 1982. On the same occasion Scott Silver Medals were presented to Detectives Donnellan, Doyle and Brennan, together with the Scott Bronze Medal to Detective Keeley. William Daly continued to serve in Dublin until his retirement, after 30 years and 258 days in the force, on 3 November 1989. Richard Curran preceded him into retirement on 4 July 1985, having served 38 years and 50 days. Kieran Brennan retired on 7 March 2003 after a career lasting 37 years and 48 days. Martin Donnellan, promoted Sergeant in 1981, is still serving, having since risen to the rank of Assistant Commissioner. Martin Doyle and Sean Keeley likewise are still serving the community.[113]

John Oliver Doyle, Detective Garda 17846B
Born in Wexford on 14 July 1951, John Doyle left farming for a career in the Garda Síochána on 14 April 1971.

On the evening of Saturday, 17 February 1979, Detective Garda Doyle was on duty in the Smithfield area of Dublin in plain clothes and in an unmarked patrol car together with a colleague. As they were checking a car, parked suspiciously outside a business premises on a weekend, they were confronted by a number of armed men who emerged suddenly from the building, having just carried out a robbery therein. The men ordered the two Guards out of the car. On emerging, Detective Doyle immediately tacked one of the raiders, ignoring the gun which was pointing straight at him. The gunman fired, hitting Doyle in the right leg. Doyle, undaunted, continued to struggle with the man until a sawn-off shotgun, fired by another of the assailants, blasted him in the stomach. Detective Doyle recovered from his injuries, though some thirty-five pieces of lead still remain lodged in his stomach, hip and side.

He was presented with the Scott Gold Medal at Templemore on 4 June 1981. Promoted Sergeant in 1990, he continues to serve the people of Dublin.[114]

Seamus Murphy, Detective Garda 15887K
Martin Gleeson, Detective Garda 16452F
John P. Fortune, Detective Garda 19469G
Seamus Murphy, born in Dublin on 25 July 1944, had been a clerk before joining the Guards on 9 September 1964. John P. Fortune, also a Dubliner, was born on 28 April 1950 and had worked as a salesman before joining up on 2 January 1974. Born in Mallow, County Cork, on 8 October 1942, Martin Gleeson had been a farm steward before joining the force on 30 December 1965.

On 27 August 1980 all three men, duly armed, mounted surveillance on a house in Dublin's Crumlin district in which, it was believed, a dangerous criminal, armed and perhaps possessed of explosives, was living. They watched as their quarry approached the house before emerging from cover and confronting him. The man produced a pistol and levelled it at the three detectives, warning them to keep their distance. The Guards immediately leaped over the four-foot railing which stood between them and the gunman and closed with him, disarming him only after a fierce struggle. The gun was later found to have been loaded and ready to fire.

Detectives Murphy, Gleeson and Fortune were presented with their Scott Bronze Medals by Justice Minister Sean Doherty at Templemore on 16 September 1982. John Fortune (himself the son of a Scott Medallist – see p. 86 above) is still serving. Seamus Murphy, promoted sergeant in 1990, retired on 24 February 1997 after 32 years and 169 days. Martin Gleeson followed him into retirement on 7 October 1999, having served 33 years and 282 days.[115]

Noel Conroy, Detective Sergeant 15295A
John Muldoon, Detective Garda 15977H
Timothy Mulvey, Detective Garda 18114E
Patrick Conway, Garda 17752M
John Costello, Garda 20482L

Noel Conroy, born on 21 November 1942 in County Mayo, worked as a machine operator before joining the Gardaí on 25 September 1963. John Muldoon from Rhode, County Offaly, was born on 31 January 1945 and had been a boilerman before joining the force on 24 November 1964. Timothy Mulvey, a Dubliner born on 31 January 1951, left the post office for a career with the Guards on 5 January 1972. Patrick Conway from Mayo, born on 24 February 1951, worked as a labourer before joining up on 2 September 1970. John Costello, born in County Clare on 23 October 1957, was a student before joining the Guards on 29 June 1977.

On 12 September 1978 Detectives Muldoon and Mulvey, on receiving word of an armed robbery in the area, set off in the Finglas detective patrol car. They were followed soon after by a 'uniform' (or 'marked') patrol car responding to a call for assistance from colleagues. Gardaí Conway and Costello, manning this car, were accompanied by Detective Sergeant Conroy. On route to the incident the 'uniform' car came upon the raiders' speeding getaway car and began to pursue it in the direction of the city centre. The robber in the car's front passenger seat leaned from the window and fired a number of shots from a sawn-off shotgun at the pursuing Gardaí, forcing them to maintain a safe distance from their quarry. The raiders turned from the Old Finglas Road into Tolka Estate where a fresh car was parked awaiting them. As the pursuing Guards entered the estate they were again fired upon by the raiders and forced to withdraw. Their alternative car having been seen by the Guards, the robbers abandoned their plan to change to it and returned to their original getaway vehicle. They took off towards Griffith Avenue, now pursued not only by the car carrying Conway, Costello and Conroy but also by the detective car manned by Muldoon and Mulvey, all now repeatedly under fire from the robbers' car. The chase went on until the raiders finally abandoned their car close to the city centre and continued to fire on the Gardaí who now resumed the pursuit on foot. Within a short time three raiders were apprehended and the stolen money recovered.

All five Gardaí were presented with their Scott Silver Medals at

Templemore on 4 June 1981. Noel Conroy, who had been promoted Inspector in the interval between the incident and the medal presentation, thereafter rose steadily through the ranks of the Gardaí, becoming Superintendent in 1986, Chief Superintendent in 1991, Assistant Commissioner in 1994, Deputy Commissioner in 1996, and finally Commissioner in 2003. He retired in 2007 after 44 years service. John Muldoon continued to serve in the Dublin area until his retirement on 24 November 2001 after 37 years and 1 day. Timothy Mulvey likewise remained in Dublin, rising to Sergeant in 1989 and Inspector in 1993. He retired on 4 January 2002 having spent 30 years in the force. Patrick Conway and John Costello are still serving.[116]

Robert E. Conroy, Garda 20439M

Born in Dublin on 15 October 1958, Robert Conroy had been a student before opting for a career with the Guards on 26 June 1977.

Garda Conroy was one of a party of Gardaí who responded to a report of an aggravated burglary at a dairy in Swords, County Dublin, on 15 February 1980. On arriving at the scene the Guards looked in at the lighted windows and saw two masked raiders, one of them armed. Unarmed except for their batons, Garda Conroy and Garda Michael Johnston rushed into the building. Garda Johnston closed with one of the raiders. Standing over a bound and gagged victim the other raider levelled his sawn-off shotgun at Garda Conroy's chest from a distance of four feet. Garda Conroy immediately rushed at the gunman, grappling with him and eventually knocking the weapon from his hand and kicking it aside. He then subdued and arrested the gunman. A detective had by now come to Garda Johnston's aid and the other raider was soon in custody also. Examined later, the gun was found to be fully operable and loaded.

Garda Conroy received his Scott Silver Medal at Templemore on 4 June 1981. Robert Conroy was promoted Sergeant in 1986 and now serves in County Leitrim.[117]

John M. Roche, Garda 20773L

John Roche, born in Fermoy, County Cork, on 29 April 1955, had worked as a laboratory assistant before joining the Guards on 7 September 1977.

He had been stationed for two years at New Ross on the morning of 10 April 1980 when he stood chatting to a friend outside the Allied Irish Bank. Three armed and masked men suddenly emerged from a car. Startled perhaps at the unexpected appearance of a Garda immediately outside the bank they intended to rob, they forced him at gunpoint inside the bank and made him lie on the floor. While on the floor he managed to activate his radio and alert his colleagues both at the station and in the patrol car. A slight noise from the radio betrayed him and one of the raiders began kicking Roche viciously in the ribs. As the gunmen began to seize cash from various areas of the bank a patrol car arrived in response to Roche's message. Its two Garda occupants were confronted in the street outside by an armed man who ordered them from the car and then shot out their tyres. The gunman attracted so much attention that by the time his comrades emerged, laden with bags of money, some one hundred people had gathered. As the robbers left the building Garda Roche scrambled after them but was unable to prevent their escape.

Garda Roche received his Scott Bronze Medal at Templemore on 4 June 1981. He is still serving.[118]

William J. Keane, Garda 19967B

Born at Newmarket, County Cork, on 14 January 1955, William Keane had been a clerk before joining the Guards on 8 January 1975.

In the early hours of 18 April 1980 Garda Keane was on duty with the fishery protection staff at Fenit, County Kerry, when they heard a woman screaming 'fire' and calling for help. At a nearby house they came upon the woman perched on the roof of a glass porch which was burning fiercely. She told Garda Keane that her husband and six children were still asleep inside. An immediate attempt by Keane to enter the house failed in the face of smoke and searing heat. His attention arrested by the sound of a child crying in an upstairs room, Garda Keane then climbed a ladder to a bedroom window and smashed it with his baton; as he did so a piece of glass caught one of his eyes. He climbed into the room through a barrier of choking smoke and made his way towards the crying three-year-old girl and lifted her to safety. As he made his way down the ladder he sustained a further injury, this time to his right leg. Notwithstanding his injuries and the ever-intense heat and smoke Garda Keane made further attempts to get inside the house, but all to no avail. The trapped father and remaining five children perished.

William Keane was presented with his Scott Bronze Medal at Templemore on 4 June 1981. Since then he has risen steadily through the ranks, being promoted Sergeant in 1984, Inspector in 1992, Superintendent in 1999, and Chief Superintendent in 2004. He now serves at Henry Street, Limerick.[119]

John McCoy, Detective Garda 10716F

John McCoy, born on 7 April 1934 at Crossmaglen, County Armagh, left farming for a career in the Guards on 25 May 1954.

He and two colleagues, Detective Sergeant Moroney and Detective Garda Hugh Brennan, all armed, were on mobile patrol in Monaghan town on the afternoon of 31 December 1981. They confronted a man armed with a rifle who ordered them from the car and threatened to shoot them. As they tried to persuade him to part with the gun the man fired at Detective McCoy's feet and, immediately re-loading, pressed the weapon against Detective Moroney's stomach. He then withdrew into the hallway of a public house. The Guards, notwithstanding the gunman's threats, followed cautiously. As McCoy confronted him the man demanded that the detective surrender his sidearm, a demand that was instantly rejected. A noise from inside the bar distracted the gunman and McCoy seized the opportunity to grab the barrel of the rifle. A struggle began and, with help from Detective Brennan, the gun was wrenched from the man's grasp and he was arrested. The rifle was found to be in full working order and loaded with nine rounds; the man had a further 77 rounds in his possession.

John McCoy received his Scott Silver Medal on 7 June 1984. Thereafter he continued to serve in the Cavan/Monaghan Division until his retirement on 6 April 1994 after 39 years and 317 days.[120]

Terence Hynes, Detective Garda 16508E
Thomas Molloy, Detective Garda 19017K
Born at Athlone, County Westmeath, on 10 February 1944, Terence worked as a weaver before joining the Gardaí on 2 March 1966. Thomas Molloy, born on 14 July 1953 at Claremorris, County Mayo, had been a barman before joining up on 7 February 1973.

The two men were on mobile patrol in a Dundalk housing estate on 29 November 1981 when they attempted to speak with the driver of a car. However, the car sped off. The two detectives followed and got close enough to see the man lift a submachine gun from the back seat and place it next to him. Detective Molloy had his service weapon but Hynes was unarmed. They pursued the car at high speed for several miles until the man lost control and crashed. He was unhurt, and, gun in hand, ran off down a side road hotly pursued by the two detectives, now also on foot. They had almost caught up with him when the man spun round and pointed the gun at them. As the detectives called on him to drop the weapon he fumbled ineffectually with it in an apparent attempt to open fire, simultaneously retreating behind a tree. Seizing the moment the two Gardaí parted and rushed the man from opposite directions, quickly overpowering and disarming him. The submachine gun was found to contain eighteen rounds and, notwithstanding the gunman's clumsiness, was in working order. A search of the crashed car revealed a hand grenade and a loaded pistol.

Detectives Hynes and Molloy received their Scott Silver Medals on 29 September 1983. Both men continued to serve in the Louth/Meath Division, Terence Hynes until his retirement on 9 February 2001 after 34 years and 345 days. Thomas Molloy is still serving.[121]

John Donohoe, Detective Garda 18944H
Aidan Boyle, Detective Garda 20760H
Born in Cavan on 21 January 1952, John Donohoe had worked as a butcher before joining the Guards on 10 January 1973. Aidan Boyle was born in Carlow on 8 March 1958 and was training to be a shop manager before he joined the force on 7 September 1977.

On the afternoon of 26 May 1981 Donohoe and Boyle were part of two mobile units of the Special Task Force which responded to a report of two men loitering in the vicinity of a post office in Dublin's North Strand. Also in the units were Detective Gardaí Michael J. Conboy and Anthony G.V. Flynn. All were armed. When Conboy and Flynn emerged from their car to question the two men they were confronted with handguns. Donohoe, in the same car, had had just enough time to draw his gun, but as he emerged the gunmen rushed at him, clubbing him savagely over the head with their weapons and tried to wrench his gun from him. Conboy and Flynn were ordered to keep still or their colleague would die. As the struggle between Donohoe and his assailants grew more frenzied two shots rang out and the men ran off. Donohoe, shot in the groin and bleeding profusely from a severed artery, staggered from the car towards his colleagues who rendered him immediate assistance. Garda Boyle, who had alighted from the car before the violence began was making enquiries in a local shop nearby. His attention attracted by the shooting, he rushed out in time to see a man with a handgun running along the street. Drawing his own gun Boyle took off after the man, calling on him to halt. The man responded by firing two shots at the detective, who immediately returned fire. The chase continued as the gunman made vain attempts to hijack several passing cars. Realizing that Boyle was closing the distance between them the man turned and took careful aim at him. Boyle, however, fired first, hitting the gunman in the neck, after which he moved forward and arrested him. Both the gunman and Detective Donohoe recovered from their injuries, though the Garda had lost one third of his body's blood supply in the incident and doctors were unable to safely remove the bullet.

Both detectives were presented with their Scott Silver Medals by Justice Minister Michael Noonan at Templemore on 24 October 1985. John Donohoe is still serving. Aidan Boyle, also still serving, was promoted Sergeant in 1989 and Inspector in 2002.[122]

Francis J. Corrigan, Detective Sergeant 13338H
Thomas A. McDonald, Detective Garda 13688C
Michael J. Sullivan, Detective Garda 14522L

Francis Corrigan from Clones, County Monaghan, was born on 1 December 1936, and had been a rates clerk before joining the Guards on 24 January 1958. Thomas McDonald, born on 9 August 1935 at Bantry, County Cork, was also a clerk until he joined the force on 13 November 1958. Michael Sullivan, born on 8 March 1937 at Cappamore, Kenmare, County Kerry, left farming for a career with the Gardaí on 14 December 1960.

All three detectives were armed and on mobile patrol near the sub-post office on Cork City's Togher Road on the morning of 6 October 1981. They saw three armed and masked men run from the post office and into a waiting car. Detective McDonald used the patrol car to block their escape. The robbers from within the car opened fire on the detectives. Leaving the relative safety of the patrol car Detective Sergeant Corrigan fired a warning shot in the air and then a second, puncturing one of the raiders' tyres. The armed driver heard Corrigan call on him to surrender. As he did so, Detectives Sullivan and McDonald, who had also emerged from the patrol car, ran with guns drawn to the passenger side of the raiders' car, McDonald firing a shot into another of the car's wheels. Realizing that escape was now impossible, the driver's two accomplices sheepishly obeyed the detectives' orders and put down their weapons. The three were then arrested and searched. The raiders' firearms were all found to be loaded and in working order, their lethal potential clearly visible in the bullet-shattered windscreen of the patrol car and that of another nearby vehicle.

The three detectives received their Scott Bronze Medals from Justice Minister Sean Doherty at Templemore on 16 September 1982. All three continued to serve in the Cork East Riding Division until they retired. Francis Corrigan's last day in the force was 30 November 1993; he had served for 35 years and 311 days. Michael Sullivan followed him on 7 March 1994 after 33 years and 84 days. Thomas McDonald stayed on for a further year, leaving on 3 August 1995 after a career spanning 36 years and 264 days.[123]

Daniel Marion Kenna, Detective Garda 20505B
Kevin Joseph Fields, Garda 20635M

Born in Laois on 14 February 1954, Daniel Kenna had been a management trainee before joining the Gardaí on 6 July 1977. Kevin Fields was born in Dublin on 17 September 1956 and had worked as a security guard before joining the force on 20 July 1977.

Both members were unarmed, in plain clothes, and on mobile patrol in an unmarked car on the afternoon of 20 October 1981. As they drove past a small grocery shop on Dublin's North Strand they saw two youths run from the shop with the owner in pursuit. One of the youths pulled a sawn-off shotgun from under his jacket and pointed it at the shop-owner who then gave up the chase. Both Gardaí recognized the armed youth as a local criminal who lived nearby. Detective Kenna got out and took up the chase on foot while Garda Fields drove round the block to cut off the youths' escape route. Detective Kenna had got within three feet of the culprits when the armed one turned and pointed the gun at him, forcing him to take cover at the roadside. The detective continued his pursuit at a safer distance, but the two youths soon disappeared. He then retrieved an iron bar and a knitted hat which he had seen one of the youths throw under a parked car. The chase was now taken up by Garda Fields who had arrived and parked at a point ahead of them. On being challenged the armed youth menaced the Guard with the shotgun, again from a distance of no more than three feet. Garda Fields reached inside his jacket as if to draw a pistol. The youth took fright and ran off still pursued by Fields. In his flight he discarded gloves, a balaclava, his jacket, and eventually the gun itself before vaulting a set of railings and vanishing into a nearby maze of flats. He was arrested later that afternoon. The shotgun, later examined, was found to be loaded, in working order, and with the safety catch in the 'off' position.

Detective Kenna and Garda Fields were presented with their their Scott Bronze Medals at Templemore on 29 September 1983. Both Guards are still serving the community.[124]

Ronald D. Mangan, Garda 10937C
Terence F. Allen, Garda 21848M

Ronald Mangan, born in Roscommon on 1 June 1949, had been a bus conductor before joining the force on 28 March 1973. Terence Allen was born in Lambeth on 16 September 1960 and had worked as a machine operator before becoming a Guard on 31 December 1979.

The two men were on mobile patrol, in uniform and unarmed, in Dublin's

Upper Dorset Street on the night of 16 May 1981. At a junction they were faced with a group of men gathered in the middle of the road and evidently being menaced by a man standing a short distance away holding a gun. As the patrol car stopped at the scene the gunman fired a single shot and then ran to the side of the car. Garda Allen opened the door and the man leaned into the car pointing the gun at the two officers. Quickly noting the awkwardness of the man's posture, Garda Allen seized his shoulder and forced him down on his knee, at the same time dragging him into the car where Garda Mangan was able to wrench the gun from his grasp. The gun, when examined, was found to contain two further live rounds.

Garda Mangan and Garda Allen received their Scott Bronze Medals from Justice Minister Sean Doherty at Templemore on 16 September 1982. Terence Allen was promoted Sergeant in 1990, and both men are still serving.[125]

Patrick Gerard Reynolds, Garda 21281D
Leo Kenny, Garda 15282L
Patrick Reynolds, from Barroe, Boyle, County Roscommon, was born on 16 December 1958; he left farming for a career with the Gardaí on 21 June 1978. Leo Kenny, a Dubliner born on 11 December 1940, had been a clerk before joining the force on 26 July 1963.

Gardaí Reynolds and Kenny, together with three colleagues (Sergeant Patrick O'Brien, Gardaí Larry McMahon and Tom Quinn) arrived at a semi-derelict block of flats in Dublin's Tallaght area in the early hours of 20 February 1982. All were in uniform and unarmed and they were responding to an anonymous phone tip-off that three suspicious-looking men were carrying bags into a flat at Avonbeg Gardens. While Reynolds and O'Brien checked out the rear of the block, Kenny and the others made their way to the flat named by the anonymous caller as number 33 on the first floor. On entering the flat the Guards found a gang of six heavily armed men and women engaged in counting what later proved to be the proceeds of a bank robbery which had taken place in Askeaton, County Limerick a couple of days previously. Garda Kenny had a lucky escape when a gun pointed at him misfired. Likewise Garda Quinn, whose baton stopped a bullet which might otherwise have killed him. Despite their superior firepower the gang began to panic. One man seemed about to jump from a rear window when the sight of Garda Reynolds and Sergeant O'Brien frightened him back inside the flat. The sergeant remained at the rear to cut off any similar escape attempt while Garda Reynolds ran towards the sounds of confrontation emanating from the flat itself. The Guards inside the flat had by now begun to withdraw from the unequal, close-order struggle, and one of the gunmen was on the first-floor landing when Garda Reynolds reached the top of the steps. Despite the fact that the young Garda was actually turning away from him the man fired at him twice, one bullet wounding Reynolds fatally in the back. The man was finally arrested in 1997.

Garda Reynolds, less than four years in the force at the time of his death, was posthumously awarded the Scott Gold Medal. Leo Kenny, who so narrowly avoided death during the incident, received the Scott Bronze Medal on 29 September 1983; he retired on 10 December 1997, having served the community for 34 years and 138 days, and died on 5 April 1998.[126]

Michael Flanagan, Garda Sergeant 14365M

Born at Boyle, County Roscommon, on 19 July 1937, Michael Flanagan left farming for a career in the Gardaí on 13 July 1960.

Not only was Sergeant Flanagan off duty, in plain clothes and unarmed in the Cabra Allied Irish Bank on 6 April 1982, but he was in the company of his four-year-old son. As father and son stood in a queue an armed man entered and approached the counter. He seized a woman who was standing in the queue, held a gun to her head shouting threats that he would kill her, and threw a plastic bag to the cashier. Sergeant Flanagan surged forward, grabbing the gunman and, after a frenzied struggle, succeed in wresting the gun from his grasp. As the weapon fell it was kicked out of reach by the bank manager. Other bank staff then came to Sergeant Flanagan's assistance and the man was duly arrested. The gun turned out to be an imitation firearm.

Michael Flanagan was presented with his Scott Bronze Medal at Templemore on 29 September 1983. He continued thereafter to serve in the Dublin area until his retirement on 18 July 1994 after a career of 34 years and 6 days.[127]

Kevin McGeough, Garda 15329L
Patrick Whitney, Garda 17852G

Kevin McGeough, born in Trim, County Meath, on 10 May 1940, had been a shop assistant before joining the Guards on 25 September 1963. Patrick Whitney from Dungarvan, County Waterford, was born on 23 July 1951, and had worked as a storeman before opting for a career in the Guards on 14 April 1971.

On the morning of 10 April 1982 a house occupied by an aging widow in Dublin's Clonsilla district caught fire. Garda Whitney, who was off duty, went to the scene along with a civilian. He managed to enter the house through a side window but was soon driven back out by dense smoke. He and the civilian then broke in by the front door. Garda Whitney crawled into the sitting-room and called the woman's name but got no reply. A faint sound reached him from across the room and, through a wall of flames and smoke he caught an horrific glimpse of the woman, seated in a blazing armchair, her clothes on fire and a facing lighted gas heater. Garda McGeough, also off duty, had now arrived on the scene and had joined Garda Whitney in the sitting-room on his hands and knees. McGeogh crawled towards the woman and made a vain attempt to turn off the gas heater, burning his right hand as he did so. He then pressed forward and lifted the woman from the chair, carried her out of the house and onto the front lawn where he rolled her on the grass until the flames were extinguished. Both Gardaí were barely clear of the house when the gas cylinder in the sitting-room exploded. Sadly, the woman was too badly burned for any recovery to be expected and she died on route to hospital.

Garda Whitney was presented with his Scott Bronze Medal on 7 June 1984. Tragically, Kevin McGeough was not present to receive the Scott Silver Medal awarded to him; he had been killed in a road accident on 4 January 1984, having served the community for over twenty years. Patrick Whitney retired on 2 October 2000 after a career lasting 29 years and 172 days.[128]

Patrick G. English, Garda 20949L
Michael A. Murphy, Garda 21032C
A native of Tipperary Town, Patrick English was born 20 October 1957 and left farm labouring for a career in the Guards on 11 January 1978. Michael Murphy from Wexford, born on 5 February 1957, had worked in a factory before he joined the force – also on 11 January 1978.

On 20 April 1982 two men, one of them armed with a sawn-off shotgun, held up the Ulster Bank at Kilcock, County Kildare, making off in a stolen car with more than £1,800 in cash. They had not gone far when their car was spotted and pursued by Garda English and Garda Murphy, both unarmed. On two occasions during the chase the robbers halted to brandish their weapon at the Guards and warn them off. English and Murphy, however, stayed as close to their quarry as they dared. But on reaching Maynooth they found that the raiders had abandoned their car and taken off on foot across the fields. The two Guards followed likewise on foot and caught up with the raiders in a field. As they closed until a distance of only half-a-dozen yards remained between them and the robbers, the man with the gun turned and pointed it straight at them. Garda Murphy called on the man to be sensible and to drop the gun. After a moment's hesitation the raider capitulated, breaking the gun and ejecting two live cartridges onto the ground. The raiders were then arrested.

Gardaí English and Murphy were presented with their Scott Bronze Medals on 29 September 1983. Garda Murphy was promoted Sergeant in 1989, and both men are still serving.[129]

John T. Farrelly, Garda 20386F
James Ryan, Garda 22083C

John Farrelly was born at Ballybay, County Monaghan, on 15 January 1956, and had been a bar manager before joining the Guards on 1 September 1976. James Ryan, born on 9 June 1960 at Soloheadbeg, County Tipperary, had worked in a creamery before joining the force on 25 June 1980.

The two were on mobile patrol duty at Howth, County Dublin, on the afternoon of 22 November 1982 when word reached them that a young man had fallen down a nearby cliff. On arriving at the scene at Balscadden Road they saw the youth hanging over a 120-foot drop by his foot which had caught in a tree branch some 80 feet from the top of the cliff. The boy was unconscious. Farrelly and Ryan, realizing that the branch might give way at any moment, immediately scrambled down the treacherous cliff face clinging as they went to such jutting stones and vegetation as they could grasp. They reached the boy and pulled him onto a ledge to relative safety. A return journey to the cliff-top with the senseless youth was clearly impracticable, but eventually help arrived and both rescuers and rescued were hauled to safety.

Gardaí Farrelly and Ryan were presented with their Scott Bronze Medals at Templemore by Justice Minister Michael Noonan on 7 June 1984. Both men are still serving, John Farrelly having risen through the ranks to Chief Superintendent.[130]

Michael G. O'Brien, Garda 19741F

Born in Monaghan on 3 July 1955, Michael O'Brien had worked in insurance before opting for a career in the Gardaí on 14 August 1974.

Shortly before midnight on 16 July 1983 he and a colleague, Garda Laurence Witherow, both unarmed, were on mobile patrol in Dundalk. At Marches Upper they stopped a container truck which, they noticed, had no rear lights. The driver and passenger got out and, without warning the passenger fired a shot from a handgun at the astonished Gardaí standing eight feet away, who immediately took cover. The gunman, accompanied by the truck driver, fled into the dark recesses of a nearby housing estate hotly pursued by O'Brien and Witherow. Under a street light the gunman turned and fired another shot at the two Guards, forcing them again to dive for cover. At this Garda Witherow headed back to the patrol car to radio for assistance. Garda O'Brien meanwhile continued to follow the men, eventually catching up with the driver and arresting him. The gunman temporarily made good his escape but was later taken into custody.

Garda O'Brien received his Scott Silver Medal from Justice Minister Michael Noonan at Templemore on 24 October 1985. He was promoted Sergeant in 1984 and Inspector in 1994, and still serves the community to this day.[131]

Joseph Delaney, Detective Garda 16416L

Born at Borris-in-Ossory, County Laois, on 22 November 1943, Joseph Delaney had been a clerk before joining the Guards on 29 December 1965.

In the aftermath of a robbery early on the evening of 15 November 1983 in which £40 had been taken at gunpoint from a motorist in Dundalk, Detective Delaney, accompanied by Sergeant Thomas Brady, went to a house in the town to identify the suspect. As they approach the house they were fired on from within. Coming round the side of the house Delaney attempted to persuade the gunman to give up, but the man responded only with threats. More Gardaí appeared on the scene and the man fired again. Despite the obvious danger Detective Delaney went to the front door and again tried to reason with the gunman. This time he was more successful. The gunman asked for a local priest and, on his arrival, both he and Delaney were allowed into the house, still, however, at gunpoint. The three sat at a table and talked. After further persuasion from Detective Delaney the man at last laid down the .22 rifle. However, a sudden noise at the rear of the house caused him to become alarmed and agitated and he again reached for the gun. Seizing the moment Delaney knocked the weapon aside, grabbing it as he did so. A struggle followed at the end of which Delaney succeeded in subduing the man and taking him into custody. The rifle, under subsequent examination, was found to be loaded and ready to fire.

Detective Garda Delaney received his Scott Bronze Medal from Michael Noonan, Minister for Justice, at Templemore on 24 October 1985. He was promoted Sergeant the following year, but, sadly, died still in service on 27 April 1988, after more than 22 years in the Guards. He was 44 years old.[132]

Edward J. Connor, Garda 12780K

Born near Strokestown on 8 April 1933, Edward Connor left farming for a career with the Gardaí on 12 May 1955.

On 24 June 1983 Garda Connor, Garda Michael O'Driscoll and Sergeant W. Grier were on mobile patrol in Dundalk when they were alerted to an armed robbery in progress at the nearby Windmill Bar. As the two masked raiders emerged from the premises they were confronted by the three Guards who had just pulled up opposite the front door. One of the men made flustered attempts to cock a firearm as the two backed away from the Guards, issuing threats and warnings as they did so. The Gardaí, undeterred by the threats or by the gun which was continally pointed at them, pursued the men at walking pace along several streets. Eventually the raiders took to their heels, dropping their loot as the ran. One of them was later arrested nearby.

Edward Connor was presented with his Scott Bronze Medal at Templemore on 24 October 1985 by Justice Minister Michael Noonan. He retired, after 37 years and 310 days, on 17 March 1993, and died almost exactly eleven years later on 10 March 2004.[133]

Anthony Tighe, Garda 18101C
Declan W. O'Brien, Garda Sergeant 19889G
Patrick T. Kavanagh, Garda 20892B

Anthony Tighe, born in County Mayo on 1 February 1951, had worked as a fitter-turner before opting for a career with the Guards on 5 January 1972. Declan O'Brien from Athlone, County Westmeath, born on 3 March 1953, changed the uniform of military policeman for that of a Garda on 27 November 1974. Patrick Kavanagh, born on 16 February 1958 in County Kildare, left his labouring job to become a Garda on 28 December 1977.

During the early hours of 22 March 1984 a man living in Dublin's Crumlin district was taken from his house by armed men, bundled into a stolen van and driven away. At 7.10 a.m. the van was spotted by a Tallaght mobile patrol manned by Tighe, O'Brien and Kavanagh who were aware of the incident. Having informed Radio Control the Gardaí shadowed the van as it headed down the South Circular Road, and were joined within minutes by two other patrol cars from Ballyfermot and Kilmainham. When the van turned into Phoenix Park an attempt was made by the Kilmainham car to overtake it. The van driver tried to ram the patrol car and a man in the front passenger seat pointed a handgun at the Guards, forcing them to pull swiftly ahead of the van and maintain a safe distance. Garda Tighe, driving the Tallaght patrol car, continued some 15 yards behind the van, followed by the Ballyfemot car. The side door of the van suddenly opened and a masked man leaned out and fired at the Tallaght car. The bullet ricocheted off the base of the windscreen in front of Garda Tighe, whose only reaction was to drive the car in a zig–zag pattern as more bullets were fired from the van. At one point a shotgun blast fired through the van's rear window hit the lower part of the patrol car. Garda Tighe, unruffled, doggedly stayed behind the van. Before long the kidnappers gave way to panic. The van swerved into a side road and stopped, disgorging four men who fled down an embankment, and some of whom continued to shoot at the pursuing Gardaí who were unarmed. Gardaí from the patrol cars then went to the assistance of the kidnapped man who had been abandoned in the van. Armed reinforcements arrived almost immediately and the four cornered kidnappers, after further exchanges of shots, surrendered.

Garda Tighe received his Scott Silver Medal, and Sergeant O'Brien and Garda Kavanagh their Scott Bronze Medals from Justice Minister Michael Noonan at Templemore on 24 October 1985. Declan O'Brien was promoted Inspector in 1993 and Superintendent in 2002. Patrick Kavanagh rose to Sergeant in 1986, to Inspector in 1995, and to Superintendent in 2002. Kavanagh and O'Brien are still serving, but Anthony Tighe retired on 2 December 2006, having served for 34 years and 332 days.[134]

John B. Mullarkey, Garda Sergeant 18367K
John A. Scanlon, Garda 16333C
Born in County Roscommon on 21 June 1949, John Mullarkey left farming for a career in the Guards on 17 May 1972. John Scanlon, born near Boyle, County Roscommon, on 11 September 1945, had been a miner before joining the force on 22 September 1965.

Both men, attached to Roosky Station, County Leitrim, were manning a road checkpoint on the main Sligo–Dublin road on the night of 4 November 1983. Shortly before midnight they stopped a Dublin-bound Ford Granada car carrying three men. The men initially seemed co-operative but not all of them gave the same account of where they had come from. The car had a false tax disc and the driver's documentation was of doubtful authenticity. On Sergeant Mullarkey's instructions the men pushed the car to the side of the road and began to line up behind it. Suddenly two of the men rushed towards Mullarkey and Scanlon as if to attack them. The man who had been the front-seat passenger and was then standing close to Garda Scanlon drew a firearm and shot the Guard in the stomach at point-blank range. As he fell to the ground the gunman fired again, this time hitting him in the left hip. Scanlon scrambled desperately to his feet and tried to get out of reach as the gunman continued to fire at him and bullets whistled past his ear. He managed to hobble behind a nearby house. Meanwhile the two other men were scuffling with Sergeant Mullarkey who had seized the driver's arm. Moments after the shots rang out and Scanlon had limped to safety, the gunman moved across to menace Mullarkey. At the urging of the car's driver the gunman shot Sergeant Mullarkey in the left buttock and then in the right leg. The men sped off, leaving the two wounded Guards to seek what assistance they could. The next day Mullarkey and Scanlon were able to pick out the car driver from a set of Garda photographs, and some five months later Mullarkey was able to identify both the driver and the gunman at the Special Criminal Court.

John Mullarkey and John (Aidan) Scanlon recovered from their injuries and were presented with their Scott Bronze Medals at Templemore by the Minister for Justice, Michael Noonan, on 24 October 1985. Sergeant Mullarkey, having served 34 years and 35 days, retired on 20 June 2006. Garda Scanlon retired after a career of 36 years and 223 days on 2 May 2002.[135]

John J. O'Sullivan, Garda 20481A
Nicholas Marnell, Garda 23282C

Born in Killarney, County Kerry, on 25 February 1957, John O'Sullivan had worked as a labourer before joining the Guards on 29 June 1977. Nicholas Marnell from Cuffes Grange, Kilkenny, born in 1961, had been a storeman before joining up on 30 December 1982.

The Royal Oak public house in Dublin's Parkgate Street was open for business on 20 June 1985 when, soon after 6 p.m. two men, one armed with a sawn-off shotgun, came in, ordered the customers against the back wall and demanded that the manager open the safe. A warning shot was fired when two customers tried to seize one of the men. This caused the unarmed robber to lose his nerve and flee, pursued by the pub manager and a customer. The remaining robber then decamped with two bags of coins and a bundle of banknotes. Gardaí O'Sullivan and Marnell were off duty, out of uniform and out for a run in the Phoenix Park. As they emerged into Parkgate Street they saw the commotion and took off after the armed raider. Soon realizing that he was being followed, the gunman pointed his weapon at Garda Marnell and pulled the trigger. Luckily, the gun misfired. This occurred again a few minutes later when the man attempted to shoot Garda O'Sullivan. Seizing the moment, Garda O'Sullivan then closed with the man and arrested him. The gun, when examined at the scene by Garda Marnell, was found still to contain one live cartridge.

Garda O'Sullivan was presented with his Scott Gold Medal, and Garda Marnell his Scott Bronze Medal, by Justice Minister of State Nuala Fennell on 4 December 1986. John O'Sullivan was promoted Sergeant in 1989 and later rose to Inspector. Both men are still serving.[136]

Patrick J.A. Morrissey, Garda Sergeant 14545K

Born at Belturbet, County Cavan, on 7 March 1936, Patrick Morrissey worked in the building trade before joining the Gardaí on 14 December 1960.

On the morning of 27 June 1985 Gardaí Peter Long and Paul Flynn were on mobile patrol at Ardee, County Louth. As they approached the town's Labour Exchange they came upon a robbery in progress. Two armed men had ambushed the manager and had just taken a bag from his car containing over £25,000 in cash. When they saw the patrol car they fled in the manager's car, firing wildly at the two Guards as they went. Pausing only to pick up Sergeant Morrissey, who was in Ardee to attend court that morning and had heard about the robbery, Long and Flynn renewed the pursuit. None of the three uniformed Guards was armed. Cutting across the raiders' escape route, Long, Flynn and Morrissey attempted to block the road at Tallanstown. But the raiders had by now abandoned their original getaway car for a fast motorbike they had concealed at nearby Pepperstown before the robbery, and they managed to elude the roadblock. The three Gardaí got back into their patrol car and again took up the chase. The motorized pursuit ended abruptly near Rathbrist Cross where the raiders collided with an approaching car, injuring the driver and her young daughter. Long and Flynn stayed with the injured mother and child while Sergeant Morrissey ran after the robbers, both of whom also had been hurt in the collision. The final phase of the chase ended in the grounds of Rathbrist House where Sergeant Morrissey succeeded in outflanking the gunmen. When he demanded that they give themselves up one of them shot him in the stomach. As he tried to regain his feet the gunman then stood over him and shot him in the face at a range of a few inches. The Sergeant died within minutes. A short time later the two raiders were cornered in a barley field and arrested. They are both still in prison.

Sergeant Morrissey was survived by a widow and four children. He was awarded posthumously the Scott Gold Medal on 4 December 1986.[137]

Francis B.M. Hand, Detective Garda 20594L

Frank Hand was born in Athlone, County Westmeath, on 29 August 1957. He had worked as a labourer before joining the force on 20 July 1977.

On the morning of 10 August 1984 Detective Gardaí Frank Hand and Michael Dowd were in an unmarked car acting as armed escort to a post office mail van. Both Gardaí had handguns and Detective Dowd held an Uzi sub-machine gun on his lap. The van, carrying £202,000, was on its way from Dublin's GPO to make cash deliveries in the North West Dublin and South East Meath areas. As the two Guards pulled up behind the van at Drumree

Post Office, some 25 miles from Dublin, the little convoy was attacked by two armed and masked men. One of the men fired a handgun through the rear of the car while the other, from the passenger side, sprayed the windscreen with a machine gun. Detective Dowd's head was grazed by a fragmenting bullet and he slumped sideways; the Uzi slid towards the floor. He was then dragged from the car and forced to lie flat. Meanwhile Detective Hand had emerged from the driver's side, gun in hand, and fired two shots, one of them hitting the post office wall. The raider with the machine gun fired a further burst, one bullet hitting Detective Hand in the chest, fatally wounding him. Up to eight men may have been involved in the robbery at Drumree. The three most closely concerned with the shooting of Detective Hand were convicted in March 1985 and imprisoned.

On 4 December 1986 Frank Hand's wife of five weeks, Ban Gharda Breda Hand, together with the daughter he was never to know, received on his behalf the Scott Gold Medal from Justice Minister of State Nuala Fennell.[138]

Kieran J. Egan, Detective Sergeant 15976L
Phillip P. Kelly, Detective Sergeant 17792L
Dermot A. Jennings, Detective Sergeant 19163K
Brendan M.G. Loughnane, Detective Garda 19139F
John G. Lee, Detective Garda 20574E
Michael M. Shanahan, Detective Garda 19855B
Christopher G. Power, Garda Sergeant 20940F
Michael J. Prendergast, Detective Garda 20367L

Kieran Egan, from Ballinasloe, County Galway, was born on 31 August 1945; he joined the Guards on 24 November 1964. Phillip Kelly, born in 1950 at Clonmany, Lifford, County Donegal, left farming for a career in the Gardaí on 13 January 1971. Dermot Jennings, born at Ballindoon, Boyle, County Roscommon on 30 August 1954, joined the force on 28 March 1973. Brendan Loughnane, a Galwayman born on 6 September 1954, had been a student before opting for a career with the Gardaí on 28 March 1973. Dubliner John Lee, born 30 December 1957, had worked as a psychiatric nurse before joining the Guards on 20 July 1977. Michael Shanahan, born in Dublin in 1954, had been a quality inspector before becoming a Garda on 25 September 1974. Christopher Power, also a Dubliner, was born on 9 April 1958, and had clerked at the post office before joining the force on 11 January 1978. Michael Prendergast, from Claremorris, County Mayo, born on 25 April 1954, worked as a laboratory assistant before attesting for the Guards on 1 September 1976.

Soon after dawn on 17 March 1984 the eight Gardaí listed above surrounded a house near Newmarket-on-Fergus, County Clare, the hideout for a group of armed and wanted criminals. Sergeants Egan and Kelly, together with Gardaí Loughnane, Prendergast and Shanahan, stormed into the building. Sergeant Jennings, standing behind an unmarked Garda car stationed nearby, then demanded through a loud-hailer that the gunmen surrender. Only one surrendered. As he did so his accomplices opened fire on the Gardaí outside from an upstairs window. The unmarked car from behind which Sergeant Jennings, moments before, had addressed the gunmen, was raked with machine-gun bullets. One of the men then stepped onto a flat roof and began firing a submachine gun. The Gardaí stood firm, returned fire and forced the gunmen to retreat. Sergeant Power was wounded during the exchange. From positions inside the house Sergeant Egan and his colleagues continued the gun battle. At one point Sergeant Egan, despite the danger, stepped from cover and demanded that the gunmen surrender. The men, realizing that there was no prospect of dislodging the determined Guards, ceased firing and threw down their guns. So unnerved were they that a priest had to be summoned to act as mediator before they would agree to be taken into custody. Large sums of money and a substantial quantity of guns and ammunition were discovered at the house.

Detective Sergeant Egan received his Scott Silver Medal and the other members of the team their Scott Bronze Medals from Justice Minister Nuala Fennell on 4 December 1986. Kieran Egan rose through the ranks to Inspector (1989), Superintendent (1991), Chief Superintendent (1995), and to Assistant Commissioner in 1997. Phillip Kelly was promoted Inspector (1991), Superintendent (1995), and Chief Superintendent in 2001. Dermot Jennings became an Inspector (1989), Superintendent (1994), Chief Superintendent (1997), and Assistant Commissioner in 2001. Brendan Loughnane, Michael Shanahan, Christopher Power and Michael Prendergast were promoted Sergeant in 1986, John Lee in 2000. All those involved in the incident are still serving, except Sergeant Loughnane who retired on 12 January 2007 after 33 years and 291 days, and Sergeant Power who preceded him into retirement less than a fortnight earlier, on 1 January 2007, having served 30 years and 294 days.[139]

John J. Smith, Garda Sergeant 15078B
Brendan O'Connor, Garda 18759C
Born at Rathmoyle, Castlerea, County Roscommon, on 9 April 1942, John Smith had worked in the building trade before becoming a Garda on 4

October 1962. Brendan O'Connor from Sligo, born on 17 May 1947, had been a bus conductor before joining the Guards on 15 November 1972.

Sergeant Smith and Garda O'Connor, together with Garda Thomas Rourke, were unarmed and on mobile patrol in Bray town centre on the morning of 20 April 1984. As they were making routine checks on business premises in Quinsboro Road they saw two men armed with handguns inside a jewellery shop. Garda Rourke stood at the front of the shop while Sergeant Smith and Garda O'Connor ran to a side door which was ajar. One of the gunmen tried to slam the door as they approached, but the combined weight of the two Guards forced the door open and trapped the gunman against the wall behind it. Seizing the moment, Sergeant Smith tore the gun from the raider's hand and pushed him before him into the shop. Unconcerned for his colleague in the line of fire, the other gunman threatened to shoot the encroaching Gardaí. From their momentary vantage point behind their captive Smith and O'Connor sprang forward and grabbed the robber, disarming him and taking him into custody. Later, when Garda O'Connor examined the handgun brandished at them by the second gunman, he found it to be loaded, the safety catch 'off', and the cap of the bullet marked by the firing pin – as if the weapon had been on the very point of discharge.

Sergeant Smith and Garda O'Connor were presented with their Scott Silver Medals by Justice Minister of State Nuala Fennell on 4 December 1986. Both men are now retired, John Smith, after 36 years, on 3 October 1998, and Brendan O'Connor, after 31 years and 144 days, on 6 April 2004.[140]

Brendan Johnson, Garda 17606M

Brendan Johnson from Killarney, County Kerry, was born on 2 May 1950, and resigned his apprenticeship as a mason to join the Gardaí on 12 November 1969.

In the early hours of 2 November 1984 Garda Johnson, together with Gardaí Cotter, White and O'Connor, arrived at Waterford's Jail Street in response to a report of a building on fire. The fire was out of control; the door was ajar and smoke billowed forth revealing the intensity of the inferno within. Through the roaring and crackling Garda Johnson caught the sound of somebody moaning from inside the house, but nobody could be seen from the street. Followed by his three colleagues, Johnson crawled into the hallway keeping as close as possible to the ground. The smoke and heat were now unendurable, but, moving forward, Garda Johnson crawled on his own into the blazing sitting room where he found a man, now quite unconscious, lying on the floor. Seizing him by the legs, Johnson dragged him into the hallway where his colleagues were able to give assistance. The house from which the man was rescued was reduced to ashes within a short time, but the man himself made a good recovery.

Brendan Johnson received his Scott Silver Medal on 4 December 1986 from Justice Minister of State Nuala Fennell. He retired, having served his community for 33 years and 63 days, on 13 January 2003.[141]

Brendan Connolly, Garda Sergeant 16652K
Patrick McGee, Garda 20793F
Born at Ballybay, County Monaghan, on 9 January 1947, Brendan Connolly joined the Guards on 13 July 1966. Patrick McGee, born on 8 April 1956 at Adamstown, County Wexford, had been a clerk before joining the force on 7 September 1977.

A break-in by five armed men at Alphonus Road, Dundalk, on the night of 9 August 1984, was interrupted by the occupants who raised the alarm. The raiders fled in a car as Detective Garda Joe Flanagan, armed, arrived on the scene. Closely pursued by Detective Flanagan, the gunmen eventually lost control and crashed at Hoey's Lane. As Flanagan caught up with them there was an exchange of shots, after which the gunmen ran away, leaving three loaded weapons behind. Following the progress of the incident on their radio, Garda McGee and Sergeant Connolly, unarmed and in a marked patrol car, drove into Muirhevnamore where they hoped to head off the fleeing raiders. Finally, at Dulargy Avenue the two Guards came across a masked and armed man running in their direction. The gunman raised a sawn-off shotgun and fired at the patrol car. Undeterred, McGee and Connolly leaped on him and, after a tussle, disarmed and took him into custody. A search revealed that, along with the shotgun, the man had a loaded revolver.

Sergeant Connolly and Garda McGee received their Scott Silver Medals from Justice Minister of State Nuala Fennell on 4 December 1986. Brendan Connolly, now sadly deceased, retired from the force on 2 June 1997, having served the community for almost 31 years. Patrick McGee was promoted Sergeant (1986), Inspector (1995), Superintendent (2002) and Chief Superintendent in 2005. He is still serving.[142]

David Cherry, Garda 22597E
A Dubliner, born on 2 October 1959, David Cherry had been a clerk before joining the Gardaí on 27 April 1982.

In the early hours of 21 November 1985 Garda Cherry, together with Garda Terence Allen, attended the scene of a fire at a lock-up shop in

Dublin's Middle Gardiner Street. They spotted inside a small front window on the first floor a young woman trapped in her flat above the blazing shop. Unable to find a way through the inferno on the ground floor, Garda Cherry scrambled onto the narrow ledge over the shop front and broke the window. Seizing the woman by the arms he tried desperately but in vain to drag her through the small window. An attempt by a fireman to reach them with a ladder had to be abandoned as the heat from the ground floor spread upwards and the fire threatened to consume the entire building. Firemen turned the hose on Cherry's uniform to dampen it as he continued to try to pull the woman to safety and cries from below urged him to jump and save himself. Eventually the woman's strength gave out and she slumped back into the room, never to be seen alive again.

Garda Cherry was presented with his Scott Bronze Medal by Justice Minister of State Nuala Fennell on 4 December 1986. He was promoted Sergeant in 1999 and is still serving.[143]

Eunan Dolan, Detective Garda 20645H

Born in Dublin in 1957, Eunan Dolan had been an insurance clerk before opting for a career with the Guards on 3 August 1977.

On the evening of 8 November 1985 Detective Gardaí Eunan Dolan and Walter O'Connell were on mobile patrol in Dublin's North Wall when they stopped a taxi which had just turned into Sheriff Street. The three youths who emerged from the car were known offenders. Suddenly one of them, Christopher Griffin, produced a handgun and pointed it at Detective Garda Dolan. Dolan immediately rushed at him, causing the gunman to panic and take to his heels. He then fled towards a nearby block of flats hotly pursued by Detective Dolan, and eventually threw away his weapon. Seeing that the gun had been abandoned in a public street, Detective Dolan stopped chasing Griffin and recovered it – a loaded semi-automatic pistol in working order. A follow-up search of the taxi uncovered £5,800 in cash. The cash was the proceeds of a robbery which had taken place the previous evening when three armed and masked men had held up a supermarket, threatening the life of a manager as they did so. The three youths were later arrested and convicted.

Detective Garda Eunan Dolan received his Scott Bronze Medal from Justice Minister Gerard Collins at Templemore in November 1988. Promoted Sergeant in 1989, Inspector in 2002, and most recently Superintendent, he is still serving.[144]

John B. Collins, Garda 13115F
Thomas J.F. Myers, Garda 23960G
John Collins, born at Kilkee, County Clare, on 9 August 1935, left farming for a career with the Gardaí on 7 November 1956. Thomas Myers from Cork City, born on 29 November 1963, had been a clerical assistant before joining the Gardaí on 28 February 1984.

Early on the afternoon of 15 November 1986 Garda Myers, together with his colleague Garda Kenneth Creegan (both with the Crime Task Force) were on mobile patrol in Dublin's Dorset Street area. In uniform but unarmed, they stopped a motor cycle in Lad Lane. The pillion passenger suddenly pulled a sawn-off shotgun from a plastic bag and levelled it at the two Guards, threatening to kill them if they moved. The two men then abandoned the bike and ran into a maze of nearby flats, where Garda Creegan seized and arrested one of them who proved to be unarmed. The armed man, still hotly pursued by Garda Myers, fled into Granby Lane, at which point he turned and fired at the Garda who was no more than ten yards from him. When the chase began Garda John Collins, off duty, out of uniform and with his wife, was driving in his own car along Dorset Street. He spotted the fleeing gunman, weapon in hand, and drove after him into Granby Lane. The gunman came towards him and ordered him and Mrs Collins from the car, following this with threats and pointing the gun straight at Collins. As Garda and Mrs Collins emerged from the car the gunman, momentarily distracted by a movement from Garda Myers, shifted position. The moment the gun's muzzle moved out of line with his chest Garda Collins leaped at his assailant and grabbed hold of the weapon. Garda Myers joined in and during the fierce struggle that followed the shotgun went off, blowing out the windscreen of a nearby truck. The man was eventually subdued and arrested.

John Collins received his Scott Gold Medal and Thomas Myers his Scott Silver Medal from Justice Minister Gerard Collins in November 1988. By this time John Collins, having served his community for 31 years and 254 days, had left the force on 17 July 1988. Garda Myers was promoted Sergeant in 1993 and Inspector in 2000; he is still serving.[145]

John A. Leonard, Garda 16549B
Patrick D. McNicholas, Garda 22433B
John Leonard, born on 1 July 1942 at Moycullen, County Galway, left labouring for a career with the Gardaí on 20 April 1966. Patrick McNicholas from Swinford, County Mayo, born on 2 June 1962, had been an insurance clerk before joining the force on 31 March 1982.

On the afternoon of 19 February 1987 a number of armed men who had robbed a builders' suppliers at Dublin's Robinhood Road were making their escape in a van. Gardaí Leonard and McNicholas spotted the getaway vehicle and began to give chase. They followed the van until it stopped in the driveway of a private house at Tibradden Grove and there attempted to arrest the raiders. The men resisted violently, one of them kicking Garda Leonard so that he was forced to release his grip. Another levelled a gun at Leonard's head and pulled the trigger, but the gun failed to fire. Unfazed, Garda Leonard seized another of the armed robbers as the latter jumped from the van; this one managed to fire his weapon, shooting Leonard in the upper left forearm. Leonard had to release the man, who then escaped. Meanwhile Garda McNicholas took off after one of the other armed men who had emerged from the van. The gunman turned to confront McNicholas at a distance of five yards and tried to shoot him. The gun initially misfired but on the second attempt the weapon went off, the bullet missing McNicholas' head by inches. Two of the other robbers then fired at McNicholas' feet. Before eventually escaping they fired futher shots at both of the unarmed Gardaí.

Garda Leonard received his Scott Gold Medal and Garda McNicholas his Scott Bronze Medal from Gerard Collins, Minister for Justice, in November 1988. A year later McNicholas would be presented with a Scott Silver Medal (see pp 145–6 below). Promoted Sergeant in 1989, John Leonard retired on 30 June 1999, having served 33 years and 72 days. Patrick McNicholas, promoted Sergeant in 1995, is still serving.[146]

Martin V. O'Connor, Garda 17981G

Born on 20 July 1951 at Cashel, County Tipperary, Martin O'Connor had worked as a clerk before attesting for the Gardaí on 8 September 1971.

On 5 November 1987 Garda O'Connor and Sergeant Henry Spring knocked on the door of a house in Dublin's Camlough Road. They were pursuing enquiries in connection with the notorious kidnapping of the businessman John O'Grady. Once inside the house Garda O'Connor became suspicious of the occupants and went to the patrol car to summon assistance. As he did so one of the men from the house reached into the car and pushed a handgun against his chest. O'Connor, still seated in the car, seized the gunbarrel and tried to turn it away from him. At this point a second assailant approached and attacked him, grabbing at his face and mouth. To gain more freedom of manoeuvre, O'Connor scrambled from the car, but then a third man shot him in the stomach from a distance of two feet. Undefeated, O'Connor drew his own handgun and fired at the assailant. He was then shot again, this time in the shoulder. As he fell backwards one of the men kicked him. Luckily the assistance he had called for on the car radio just before the men launched their attack on him now arrived and Mr O'Grady was freed from his captivity.

Garda O'Connor was presented with his Scott Gold Medal by Justice Minister Gerard Collins in November 1988. He retired from the force on 15 March 1989, having served 17 years and 189 days.[147]

Patrick Moriarty, Garda Inspector 12868F
Patrick J. O'Rourke, Garda Sergeant 15556L
Born at Oola, County Limerick, on 5 August 1934, Patrick Moriarty had been a driver in the Irish army before joining the Guards on 8 November 1955. Patrick O'Rourke from Crusheen, County Clare, born on 20 June 1944, left farming for a career with the Gardaí on 31 March 1964.

On 27 November 1987 Inspector Moriarty, Sergeant O'Rourke and other Gardaí were assisting members of the army who had set up a roadblock near Balief Cross, County Kilkenny. While their colleagues helped to man the roadblock Moriarty and O'Rourke established a routine checkpoint some distance away. Both men were keenly aware of the possibility that they might soon be faced by armed and desperate men. Inspector Moriarty was unarmed. At 1.40 p.m. a car was stopped at the checkpoint and Moriarty spoke to the driver and passenger. The driver, he noticed, closely resembled a man wanted for serious crimes. He ordered the passenger out of the car, but the man responded by pulling out a gun and pointing it at Moriarty. The driver then drove off at high speed towards the roadblock where the car crashed. The men were still not ready to give up and there was a brief but furious exchange of shots. Moriarty and O'Rourke approached and called on the gunmen to surrender, which they eventually did.

Patrick Moriarty, newly promoted to Superintendent, received his Scott Silver Medal, and Sergeant O'Rourke his Scott Bronze Medal from Justice Minister Gerard Collins at Templemore in November 1988. Superintendent Moriarty retired after a career spanning 38 years and 270 days on 4 August 1994. Patrick O'Rourke followed him into retirement, having served 37 years and 81 days, on 19 June 2001.[148]

Joseph Fitzpatrick, Garda 21846D
Joseph Fitzpatrick was born in Dublin on 10 August 1957, and had worked as a clerk before joining the Gardaí on 31 December 1979.

Garda Fitzpatrick, who was unarmed, was one of number of Gardaí who on the morning of 13 April 1987 went in pursuit of three masked men, one of them equipped with a shotgun, who had just robbed a bank on Dublin's Arran Quay. The raiders had fled the scene in a stolen car driven by an accomplice. Closely pursued by the Gardaí, the robbers crashed at Chapizod Bridge. Three of the men were arrested as they jumped from the car. The fourth man, however, ducked back inside the car and grabbed the sawn-off shotgun. Garda Fitzpatrick, who had spotted the man, instantly jumped into the car and, after a violent struggle, succeeded in disarming and arresting his quarry.

Garda Fitzpatrick received his Scott Silver Medal from Gerard Collins, Minister for Justice, in November 1988. Promoted Sergeant in 1996, he is still serving.[149]

Joseph A. Neilan, Garda 11046K

Born at Bruff, County Limerick, on 15 February 1933, Joseph Neilan had worked in a bar before joining the Guards on 3 November 1954.

On 25 June 1987 a party of Gardaí attended an incident at a private house at Newtownmountkennedy, County Wicklow, on foot of a report that shots had been heard. At 3.30 p.m. they watched as a man carrying a shotgun walked with a woman to a van. He fired a shot towards the waiting Gardaí and then drove the van for some distance until a collision with a patrol car ended his flight. Garda Neilan arrived on the scene fully aware that the man was armed. He called to the man and woman in the van but they made no reply. Undeterred either by the weapon within or by the ominous silence, Neilan approached the van, threw open the door and seized the driver in a bear-hug. He now saw that the gun, clearly loaded, was laid between the seats, its muzzle pointing towards the windscreen. At this moment other Guards came to his aid and Neilan was able to move the gun into the rear of the van where it could be safely secured.

Garda Neilan was presented with his Scott Silver Medal by Justice Minister Gerard Collins in November 1988. He continued thereafter to serve in the Wicklow/Wexford Division, but sadly, he died still in service, on 21 June 1991, after a career of 36 years and 231 days.[150]

Thomas G. Mahon, Garda Sergeant 17920E
Stephen J. Flaherty, Garda 23328E
Michael J.M. Brennan, Garda 15135A

Born in 1952 near Hollymount, County Mayo, Thomas Mahon had been a vet's assistant before attesting for the Guards on 16 June 1971. Stephen Flaherty from Tralee, County Kerry, born on 22 January 1959, left factory work for a career with the Gardaí on 26 January 1983. Michael Brennan, a

Dubliner, was born on 11 October 1942, and changed his original career as a prison officer for that of a Garda on 21 November 1962.

All three men were unarmed and on mobile patrol together in Limerick in the early hours of 14 October 1986 when a radio message directed them to go to John Carew Park; a man there, it was reported, was acting suspiciously. When they arrived at the scene they found that the man was in possession of a shotgun. As Mahon and Flaherty approached him he walked away. They called on him to stop only to see him turn and point the gun straight at Sergeant Mahon, who was no more than ten feet away. The man vowed that he would shoot them unless they kept their distance. Repeating his threats he began to back away from the Guards and then turned and ran onto a nearby grassy area. Again the two Guards moved closer and again he threatened to kill them. Meanwhile Garda Brennan, having radioed for assistance, drove the patrol car onto the green to cut off the gunman's retreat. The shotgun swung once, then twice, in the direction of the car, as the man tried to cover both the car and the two Gardaí. The threats continued. Now, in response to Garda Brennan's alert, two more Guards – Garda Cornelius Daly and Garda Anthony Maher – joined the scene. Garda Daly drew his revolver and demanded that the man surrender, which he eventually did. The shotgun was found not only to have a live cartridge in its breech, but to be cocked also.

Scott Bronze Medals were presented at Templemore to Sergeant Mahon and to Gardaí Flaherty and Brennan by Gerard Collins, Minister for Justice, in November 1988.

The eldest of the three, Michael Brennan, retired on 10 October 1999, having served his community for 36 years and 324 days. Stephen Flaherty was promoted Sergeant in 1998. Sergeant Mahon rose to Inspector in 1996 and to Superintendent in 2002. Both he and Sergeant Flaherty are still serving.[151]

Christopher O. Mangan, Garda 22825G
Michael T. Minogue, Garda 23832E
Christopher Mangan, born on 31 March 1962 at Dunshaughlin, County Meath, had been a farm worker before joining the Guards on 21 July 1982. Michael Minogue from Limerick, born on New Year's Day 1963, also left farming for a career with the Guards, attesting on 4 January 1984.

Both members were unarmed and on mobile patrol on Christmas Eve 1986 in Dublin's Drimnagh district when they came upon an attempted robbery at a shopping centre. A black English-registered car sat parked outside a drapery shop. As the patrol car passed the driver tried to hide his face and an armed, masked youth was seen to run from the car into the shop. Garda Mangan instantly drove the patrol car in front of the parked car and he and Garda Minogue jumped out. Mangan ran to the driver's door while Minogue ran behind the car in pursuit of the gunman who had entered the shop. The driver of the getaway car suddenly reversed, trapping Garda Minogue between the rear of the car and the vehicle behind. Inside the shop two armed raiders, on catching sight of the Gardaí around their car, decided to abandon the robbery and ran from the premises. The two menaced the Guards with handguns and threats as they scrambled into the car. By now, however, Garda Minogue had managed to free himself and the two Gardaí rushed at the raiders, grabbing the nearest one. A fierce struggle began. Mangan and Minogue eventually succeeded in disarming and pinning down one raider, but the other man and the driver managed to drive off. The handgun taken from the captured raider turned out to be a replica, but one which even at close quarters was virtually indistinguishable from a real firearm.

Gardaí Mangan and Minogue received their Scott Bronze Medals from Justice Minister Gerard Collins at Templemore in November 1988. Both are still serving, Garda Mangan having been promoted Sergeant in 1992 and Inspector in 2000. Christopher Mangan was awarded a further Scott Medal in 1996 (see pp 175–6 below).[151]

Noel Crotty, Garda 20434L

Born at Cahir, County Tipperary, in 1957, Noel Crotty had been a welder's mate before opting for a career with the Gardaí on 22 June 1977.

Garda Crotty was on duty at the bus depot in Dublin's Ringsend on the morning of 5 March 1987 when the depot was robbed. Four masked men, two of them with handguns, had just carried out the raid when Garda Crotty approached a car parked outside, at the wheel of which sat the gang's getaway driver. The man took fright and sped off. Crotty turned and saw two armed men standing inside the depot's front entrance. Fortunately armed, Garda Crotty drew his weapon and demanded that the raiders surrender. Then the getaway car re-appeared and made several attempts to run over him. The two armed raiders, pointing their guns at Crotty, began to move towards the car. Crotty fired three shots at them, forcing one of them to drop his weapon. The circling car eventually collected all except one of the robbers. Garda Crotty then ran into the depot where he seized and arrested the fourth raider as the man attempted to escape through a window.

Noel Crotty was presented with his Scott Bronze Medal by Gerard Collins, Minister for Justice, in November 1988. He was promoted Sergeant in 2000 and is still serving the community.[153]

Michael J. Biggins, Garda 21637B

Born in Cong, County Mayo, on 18 March 1956, Michael Biggins left farming for a career in the Guards on 28 March 1979.

Early in the evening of 28 March 1987 Garda Biggins and two colleagues attended an incident at a private house in Swords, County Dublin. He took up a position outside, but when his colleagues entered they were confronted with a man wielding a shotgun. After fruitless attempts to reason with the man the two members withdrew, followed outside by the man who then pointed the gun at Garda Biggins, standing some ten feet away. As the gunman readjusted his stance in an attempt to keep all three Gardaí in his sights he momentarily turned his back on Biggins. Biggins sprang at him and, with the help of his two colleagues, managed to disarm him.

Michael Biggins received his Scott Bronze Medal at Templemore in November 1988 from Justice Minister Gerard Collins. He was promoted Sergeant in 1997 and is still serving.[154]

Martin Caine, Garda 21206G

Martin Caine was born at Kilmeena, County Mayo, on 7 November 1956. He had worked in farming before joining the Guards on 10 May 1978.

Garda Caine had just come off duty on the evening of 6 December 1986 and went to pick up his sister-in-law at a clothing shop in the Drimnagh area of Dublin. He was told by other members of the shop staff that he had just missed her. He stayed and chatted with them for a few minutes when suddenly three armed masked men burst through the door shouting their intention to rob the premises. Amid a scene of panic and confusion Garda Caine, who was in plain clothes, assessed the situation as the robbers, clearly unfamiliar with the shop, terrified staff and customers and made inept attempts to open the cash register. When they demanded to be told the where-abouts of the office and the manager Caine pointed them towards the office and told them that the manager was not present. Clearly taking Caine to be the manager one raider pressed a shotgun against his temple and demanded the keys of the safe. He was then frog-marched into the office where, despite his protestations that he was a customer, the raiders pushed him behind a table and made it clear that they would shoot him if he did not open the safe. Caine, realizing that the crucial moment had arrived, suddenly grabbed the table and rammed the raiders with it, trapping them momentarily against the door. As he dropped the table one of the raiders lost his balance. Caine seized him round the neck and smashed his fist into him, letting go only when the other raider in the room aimed a blow at his head with a pistol. The two raiders then fled in panic towards the main door, preceded by their accomplice who had remained in the outer shop. Garda Caine ran after them into the car park and was merely a dozen feet from them when the raider with the shotgun turned and shot him in the right leg. The raiders continued their flight and Garda Caine, undeterred, continued to pursue them until his injuries forced him to give up. Later in hospital a number of shotgun pellets were removed from his leg.

Martin Caine received his Scott Silver Medal from Justice Minister Ray Burke at a ceremony in Templemore on 4 December 1989. He recovered from his injuries and is still serving the community.[155]

Stephen Coughlan, Garda 22444H
Paul Greene, Garda 24109A

Dubliner Stephen Coughlan, born on 25 May 1962, had been a barman before entering the Garda Síochána on 31 March 1982. Also from Dublin, Paul Greene, born on 9 December 1963, had worked in a bakery before joining the force on 12 December 1984.

The two Gardaí were returning from a court appearance at Kilmainham in Garda Coughlan's private car on the afternoon of 18 January 1988. They were unarmed and were dressed partly in Garda uniform but with civilian jackets. As they drove by the Bank of Ireland in Great James Street they saw three men donning masks before entering the building. One, they noticed, had a handgun and another a hammer. On following the men into the hallway they immediately saw that one of them was at the counter holding staff and customers at gunpoint inside the main chamber. Garda Coughlan slipped his baton between the handles of the two swinging doors in order to impede the robbers' escape. He was spotted in this by one of the men who tried to force open the door, but the weight of both Guards on the other side held it fast. Seeing the commotion, one of the other raiders ran to the door gun in hand. Failing likewise to dislodge the two Guards, he levelled the gun at Garda Coughlin's head and threatened to shoot if the door was not opened. He then pulled the trigger, but the gun failed to fire. The third raider then approached the door and, using the hammer he had carried into the bank, smashed the glass panelling, showering the two Gardaí with shards and splinters. This enabled the three robbers to gain a better purchase and, despite their best efforts to keep the door closed, Coughlin and Greene soon began to get the worst of the struggle. The door at length gave way and, as the raiders pushed past him, Garda Coughlan seized the man with the gun and dragged him to the floor, causing him to drop both the weapon and a bundle of banknotes.

Meanwhile Garda Greene grabbed the second raider and both men likewise fell wrestling on the hall floor. At this point the third raider savagely attacked Garda Greene with the hammer, raining blows on his head and neck until he was momentarily stunned. The unarmed raider and the man who had wielded the hammer then escaped, but left their armed accomplice in the hands of Coughlan and Greene who then arrested him. Their captive's gun was later found to be an imitation firearm.

Justice Minister Ray Burke presented Gardaí Coughlan and Greene with their Scott Silver Medals at Templemore on 4 December 1989. Both men are still serving.[156]

Patrick D. McNicholas, Garda 22433B
Patrick Flynn, Garda 21161C
Gerard Carney, Garda 23646B
Patrick McNicholas, born at Swinford, County Mayo, on 2 June 1962, had been an insurance clerk before joining the Guards on 31 March 1982. Patrick Flynn, from Carrick-on-Shannon, County Leitrim, was born on 21 November 1956, and had worked as a storeman before attesting for the Guards on 10 May 1978. Gerard Carney, a Dubliner born on 7 October 1960, had been a stores manager before opting for a career with the Gardaí on 21 September 1983.

On the morning of 25 February 1988 Garda Flynn and Garda Carney, both unarmed, were on mobile patrol when in Walkinstown Road they saw a man wearing a wig leap into a blue Mazda car which then took off at speed. As they followed the car into Walkinstown Parade the man leaned from the passenger window and fired a handgun at the patrol car. The pursuit continued, and the gunman then produced a weapon with a longer barrel and again fired at the two Guards. Each time he fired he chose a moment when the patrol car was negotiating a corner – in other words when the Guards within were most exposed. Prudently the two Gardaí dropped back a little though still keeping the Mazda in sight. At a cul-de-sac in the Robinhood Industrial Estate two men were seen to abandon the Mazda. One of them fled into the car park of a nearby restaurant while the other stood on a low embankment and turned to confront Gardaí Flynn and Carney. The patrol car had stopped some twenty yards behind the Mazda, and as they emerged Carney and Flynn had to dodge a shot fired from he embankment. The man then ran into the car park still followed by Carney and Flynn. Again they were forced to dive for cover as the man turned and pointed a gun at them. At this point Garda McNicholas, driving a Garda van with a colleague, spotted a man with a handgun running frantically along the Naas Dual Carriageway. It was one of the men from the Mazda. Throwing the patrol van into a U-turn, McNicholas drove in pursuit. As he came within ten yards of his quarry the gunman turned and levelled the gun at the approaching car. McNicholas drove on regardless and managed with considerable skill to strike the man a glancing blow with the van and knock the gun from his grasp. He then took the man into custody.

At a ceremony at the Garda College, Templemore, on 4 December 1989, Justice Minister Ray Burke presented Scott Silver Medals to Garda McNicholas and Garda Flynn, and a Scott Bronze Medal to Garda Carney. It was Garda McNicholas' second Scott Medal; the previous year he had received a Scott Bronze Medal in respect of an incident in February 1987 (see pp 137–8 above). Garda McNicholas was promoted Sergeant in 1995, Garda Flynn in 1994. All three men are still serving.[157]

Dominick Hutchin, Detective Garda 18182L

Born in Dublin on 19 April 1949, Dominick Hutchin had worked as a shop assistant before joining the Gardaí on 23 February 1972.

Detective Hutchin was on duty at the Men's Labour Exchange on Dublin's North Cumberland Street on the morning of 1 September 1987 when the Exchange was raided by two men armed with a sawn-off shotgun, a revolver and a sledgehammer. As it was usual for an armed detective to be on duty in the premises during pay-out periods, Hutchin was on the 'staff' side of the counter. On hearing the glass shatter in one of the pay-out hatches he went to the 'public' area where he saw a masked raider brandishing the sawn-off shotgun. Hutchin drew his handgun, identified himself as a Garda, and ordered the man to drop his weapon. He was now standing between the raider and the 'exit' door. The raider pointed the shotgun at Hutchin who again ordered him to drop it. The second raider then emerged from the broken hatch window, bag of loot in one hand and revolver in the other. The first raider quickly exchanged his shotgun for his accomplice's revolver and advanced on Hutchin firing two bullets which embedded themselves in wood-work close to the Garda. The raider who was now in possession of the shotgun then fired at Hutchin, wounding him in the face and body. The detective continued to stand his ground and focussed his attention on the man with the revolver, sensing him as the greater danger. As the raiders closed on him from two different angles in their determination to reach the exit, Hutchin fired six shots at the man holding the revolver. The wounded raider fell into a sitting position a short distance from Hutchin, but with the revolver frozen in his hand and still pointed at the detective. Hutchin then withdrew through a door in a nearby partition to reload his gun and radio for help. When he re-emerged into the 'public' area both raiders had fled, leaving behind the shotgun and a pool of blood. It was later learned that they had escaped the scene in a stolen car and then changed to a pre-arranged getaway car driven by a third man. The raider wounded by Detective Hutchin had been hit by five bullets. Had he been brought to a hospital soon after the incident his life could have been saved. As it turned out, his callous friends flung him from the getaway car in the course of the escape, and he died. Detective Hutchin was taken to hospital where he was found to be badly injured, more than thirty pellets having been embedded in various parts of his body. He was to remain on sick leave for five months.

Dominick Hutchin was awarded the Scott Silver Medal in 1989. He retired on 18 April 2006, having served the community for 34 years and 55 days.[158]

Daniel Albert Kelly, Garda 18355E
David L. Condren, Garda 23071E

Daniel A. Kelly, born in Cork on 15 February 1953, had been a shop assistant before opting for a career with the Gardaí on 12 April 1972. David L. Condren, a Dubliner born on 15 June 1962, had worked in telephone installation before joining the force on 6 October 1982.

On the morning of 6 May 1988 Gardaí Condren and Kelly were on duty as armed escorts to the mail delivery vehicle as it made its rounds to post offices in the area around Killaloe, County Clare. Garda Condren, who was personally unarmed and driving the marked patrol car, was in part-uniform and Garda Kelly (who carried an Uzi sub-machine gun) was in plain clothes. When they arrived at Feakle Post Office they were greeted with the alarming news that Caher Post Office had been robbed. Condren and Kelly immediately headed towards Caher at high speed with siren blaring. Less than two miles from Feakle they met a white van the driver of which was wearing a balaclava. The two Guards turned the patrol car and began to follow the van, radioing for assistance as they went. After a mile or so the raiders decided to make a stand. Rounding a bend Condren and Kelly were confronted with the sight of two masked men one of whom was pointing a revolver at them. As they drew nearer Garda Kelly seized the initiative and fired a burst from his Uzi – not at the van but in the air as a warning. The speed of the patrol car carried them past the van and, glancing in his mirror, Garda Condren could see the man with the revolver firing at them. Bullets began to strike the patrol car. Kelly got out, Uzi in hand, and identified himself as a Garda. Condren took cover as best he could on the front seats, and by adjusting the mirror was able to watch as Kelly and the raiders exchanged fire. In now transpired that both raiders were armed, one with a rifle. Eventually Kelly's shots hit the van driver and the revolver was seen to fall from his grasp as he slumped forward. Due to the position in which the patrol car had stopped, however, the two Guards were at a disadvantage. Kelly therefore got back into the car and, still under fire, he and Condren drove on a short distance until they had the additional cover afforded by a lorry parked between them and the van. The rifleman, however, also took advantage of the lorry: Climbing in at the passenger side he drove off towards Caher. The two Gardaí then summoned an ambulance and a priest for the wounded raider, whom they made as comfortable as possible until he was removed to hospital. The gunman, soon identified as a member of the Provisional IRA, died later that day.

Daniel Albert Kelly received his Scott Silver Medal and David Condren his Scott Bronze Medal from Ray Burke, Minister for Justice, at Templemore on 4 December 1989. David Condren is still serving, but Daniel Kelly retired on 6 June 2007 after a career of 35 years and 56 days.[159]

Patrick Campbell, Detective Garda 18011D
Born in Newbliss, County Monaghan on 1 December 1946, Patrick Campbell had been a fireman before joining the Garda Síochána on 8 September 1971.

Under the watchful eyes of Garda Campbell (armed) and his colleague, Garda William Craven (unarmed), the Securicor van stopped to make a routine cash delivery at the Atlantic Homecare Store in Dublin's Stillorgan Industrial Park. It was the afternoon of 26 March 1988. Moments after the two Guards had watched the security man enter the store they spotted two men wearing obviously false beards follow him in. Gardaí Campbell and Craven followed likewise and, on seeing one of the men reach into his jacket pocket they realized that he was probably armed. They both jumped on the man who struggled violently. Campbell and Craven managed to pull his hand from his pocket and, on searching him, found in the pocket a fully-loaded handgun. However, while they struggled to secure their captive, the man's bearded colleague had placed a gun to the head of the security guard. On request a member of the store security staff helped Garda Craven to hold the prisoner. Garda Campbell then drew his handgun and, identifying himself as a Garda, ordered the gunman to drop his weapon. The gunman instantly sought cover behind some shopping trollies and made his way along a row of them. At the entrance to the store's carpet section he emerged and pointed his gun at Garda Campbell. Reacting swiftly, Campbell fired a shot in the gunman's direction forcing him to flee further into the store, still pursued by the detective. As he took cover and tried to assess the situation amid the crowds of panic-stricken shoppers milling about the store, Garda Campbell turned to check on Garda Craven who was still holding the captured raider. He saw that a third raider was entering the store, gun gripped in both hands, and was pointing it at Craven and the store security man who was helping him. The security man ran for cover, leaving Craven still holding the prisoner. Focussing on the third gunman, Campbell identified himself as a Garda and ordered him to drop his weapon. When the man continued to point his gun at Craven, Campbell fired a single shot at him, shattering a glass door that stood in the line of fire. The third gunman immediately dropped his weapon and fled, escaping in a stolen car driven by a fourth raider. When Campbell turned his attention back to the second armed raider he found that the man had escaped through an exit at the rear of the store. The two Guards were then assisted by a Garda Chief Superintendent who had been shopping in the store with his wife. Before long, two more colleagues arrived from Blackrock Station. The raider captured during the incident received a lengthy jail sentence.

Patrick Campbell received his Scott Bronze Medal from Justice Minister Ray Burke during a ceremony at Templemore on 4 December 1989. Thereafter he continued to serve the community (collecting a further Scott Bronze Medal in 1995 – see pp 170–2 below) until his retirement on 30 November 2003, after a career of 32 years and 84 days.[160]

Patrick G. Kelly, Detective Garda 22528B

Paddy Kelly was born in Limerick on 19 October 1957 and left his former occupation as a prison officer for a career with the Garda Síochána on 13 April 1982.

Detective Garda Kelly was off duty, unarmed, and on his way into the Bank of Ireland at Mobhi Place in Dublin's Glasnevin district on the afternoon of 15 August 1988 when he found himself in the middle of an attempted robbery. Two motorcycles had just drawn up outside the bank and their two pillion passengers got off and approached the entrance, one of them pulling out a sawn-off shotgun. One motorcyclist then sped off, soon followed by the other when Kelly ran towards him and attempted to knock him from the bike. One of the motorcyclists then returned, driving his machine along the footpath. Kelly lunged at him but the man evaded him and drove off. Kelly then turned to confront the two pillion passengers who had now emerged from the bank. The pair took to their heels, hotly pursued by Detective Kelly. The raider with the shotgun made one attempt to menace Kelly with it, but the detective took evasive action and the chase continued over a high wall and across the River Tolka. At this point the raiders took refuge in the undergrowth. A number of Gardaí now came to Kelly's assistance and the detective was able to point out the robbers' location. The raiders were arrested, the bank's takings recovered, and the loaded shotgun seized and made safe.

Paddy Kelly received his Scott Bronze Medal at Templemore on 4 December 1989 from Justice Minister Ray Burke. He is still serving.[161]

John D. Leahy, Garda 24349H
Gerard L. Walsh, Garda 23898H

John Leahy, born on 2 June 1963 at Kilmallock, County Limerick, left unemployment behind and joined the Gardaí on 6 November 1985. Gerard Walsh, a Dubliner born on 17 September 1964, had been a bus conductor before joining the force on 4 January 1984.

The two men were on mobile patrol at Dublin's Capel Street Bridge in the early hours of 18 November 1988 when they noticed a man waving frantically at them from an upper window at the corner of Upper Abbey Street and Capel Street. When they went to investigate the man told them that smoke was seeping from underneath the door of the top-floor flat (on the fourth floor) and that a man was trapped inside. On approaching the door of the flat the two Guards saw for themselves that the smoke had now begun to pour thickly through the surrounds. From within groaning sounds could be heard. Leahy and Walsh forced open the door and were immediately engulfed in dense, choking black smoke, forcing them to retreat momentarily down a few steps of the stairs. They then rushed forward into the flat but could see nothing and were unable to breathe. With the aid of a couple of wet towels wrapped round their heads they tried again, this time on hands and knees, feeling their way forward. The man, however, had now ceased to groan, making their task more difficult. Suddenly a burst of flame lit up the room and they spotted the man lying motionless some six feet away. Despite fears for their own safety they moved forward, grabbed the man and dragged him from the inferno into the corridor and down the stairs. Garda Leahy rendered first aid to the man, who was still unconscious, as they waited for the ambulance. Only then did the two Guards learn that another man was likewise trapped in his flat on the second floor; by now the entire building was ablaze. Three other Gardaí had by now arrived at the scene. Accompanied by Garda Walsh the three climbed the stairs and forced their way into the second-floor flat. Not only were they obstructed by choking smoke but the heat from the fire in the floors overhead was virtually unbearable. Nevertheless the four Guards located the man, still in bed, and dragged him to safety. Both men rescued that night made a good recovery.

Gardaí Leahy and Walsh were presented with their Scott Bronze Medals at Templemore on 4 December 1989 by Justice Minister Ray Burke. Gerard Walsh was promoted Sergeant in 1993, and both men are still serving.[162]

William P. McCaffrey, Detective Garda 14285K
James T. Mulloy, Detective Garda 17086M
Born in Ballina, County Mayo, on 7 January 1937, William McCaffrey had worked in a factory before joining the Guards on 20 April 1960. James Mulloy, also a Mayoman, born at Achill on 25 November 1945, left the building trade for a career with the Guards on 15 November 1967.

Both detectives, armed and in plain clothes, were on escort duty on the evening of 15 October 1988, and they waited outside the greyhound track at Garryowen, Limerick, where they were due to accompany a man carrying tote money to a night safe. As they prepared to get under way Detective Mulloy walked towards their client's car while Detective McCaffrey reversed the patrol car into position. Suddenly there was a commotion and two shots rang out. Four masked and armed men, two of them carrying a box between them, ran across the road and got into a parked car. Detective McCaffrey swung the patrol car around, directing its headlights on the gunmen's car. Meanwhile Detective Mulloy drew his firearm, and after identifying himself as a Garda ordered the raiders to drop their weapons and surrender. As Detective McCaffrey jumped from the patrol car Mulloy fired twice at the front of the raiders' car, some fourteen feet from him. McCaffrey then moved to within ten feet of the car and pointed his gun at the occupants repeatedly calling on them to get out of the vehicle. Some fifteen seconds elapsed before the doors opened and the raiders got out of the car. The detectives took all four men into custody. A search of the car revealed two handguns, a sawn-off shotgun, and a powerful assault rifle, all loaded.

Detective Gardaí McCaffrey and Mulloy were presented with their Scott Bronze Medals at Templemore on 4 December 1989 by the Minister for Justice, Ray Burke. Both men continued thereafter to serve in Limerick. James Mulloy retired on 24 November 2002 after 35 years and 10 days. William McCaffrey, after a career lasting 33 years and 262 days, retired on 6 January 1994; sadly he died on 3 September 2001.[163]

Thomas Declan Murray, Garda 24675H

Thomas Declan Murray, born in Carrickmacross, County Monaghan on 26 May 1962, had worked as a fork-lift driver before attesting for the Gardaí on 10 December 1986.

Garda Murray was on patrol at Glendalough Road in Dublin's Glasnevin district when, soon after midnight on 8 November 1988, a man ran up to him and reported that his home was on fire. The man also told Murray that one of the occupants was trapped inside the building which was divided into flats, and that all efforts to free him had so far failed. With one of the occupants to act as guide Murray began to make his way upstairs, but was initially driven back by dense smoke. Wrapping a wet shirt round his face the Garda tried again, crawling up the stairs with one of the house's occupants bringing up the rear. The occupant waited at the top of the stairs while Murray moved forward into the flat where the man was said to be trapped. No flames were visible, but the smoke rendered his torch useless; the heat, though, was intense. Eventually, feeling his way about, he found an unconscious man lying on his back in the centre of the room. Garda Murray seized him and dragged him from the room, and, assisted by one of the other occupants, managed to get the man downstairs. The man later made a full recovery.

On 4 December 1989 Justice Minister Ray Burke presented Garda Murray with his Scott Bronze Medal during a ceremony at Templemore. Today, having collected a further Scott Bronze Medal in 1995 (see p. 170 below), he still serves the community.[164]

Gerard J. Barry, Garda 23341B
Paul T. Duffy, Garda 24014A

Born at Midleton, County Cork on 5 June 1961, Gerard Barry had been a student before joining the Gardaí on 26 January 1983. Paul Duffy from Ballyshannon, County Donegal, was born on 11 July 1962 and had worked as a barman before attesting for the Guards on 30 May 1984.

Both men were on mobile patrol in the Crumlin district of Dublin in the early hours of 21 February 1988 when word reached them that a house was on fire at Rutland Avenue. They were met at the scene by a distraught woman who told them that her husband was trapped in an upstairs room of the two-story terraced house. The two Guards tried to reach the first floor but on their first attempt were driven back by smoke and choking fumes. They tried again this time reaching the top of the stairs, but having searched one room and found nobody they were again compelled to retreat downstairs. With the added protection of wet towels around their faces they made a third attempt.

Again they reached the landing and again they opened a bedroom door, braving as best they could the rush of escaping smoke and flames. Garda Duffy entered and felt his way about until at last he came across a man lying senseless face down on a bed. Working in a confined space made infinitely worse by the surrounding inferno, Duffy and Barry managed to manoeuvre the man out of the room and down the narrow staircase to the front garden. The man later made a full recovery, as did Garda Duffy and Garda Barry both of whom had to be treated for smoke inhalation.

Gardaí Duffy and Barry were presented with their Scott Bronze Medals at a ceremony at the Garda College, Templemore, on 23 November 1990 by Justice Minister Ray Burke. Gerard Barry was promoted Sergeant in 1998. Both men are still serving.[165]

Gerard J. O'Grady, Garda 21747F
Michael J. Jordan, Garda 22394H
Brian P. Brunton, Garda 24349C
Gerard O'Grady, born at Castlebar, County Mayo, on 17 January 1956, left the building industry for a career with the Gardaí on 5 December 1979. Michael Jordan, also from Castlebar and born on 26 January 1962, had been a fireman before attesting for the Guards on 10 March 1982. Brian Brunton, a Dubliner born on 13 September 1964, spent some time as a trainee manager before joining the force on 6 November 1985.

On the morning of 15 September 1988 Garda O'Grady, on beat patrol on Dublin's Navan Road, called into the Employment Exchange. Garda Alan Murphy and the building's caretaker, Jack Lawlor, were already there. O'Grady then walked to the junction of Navan Road and Old Cabra Road to await the arrival of the Securicor van due that morning at the Exchange. Having stood there long enough to take the particulars of a a passing van, he then returned in time to see the Securicor vehicle drive into the Exchange, and took up a position nearby. As Jack Lawlor unlocked the gates O'Grady spoke briefly to Garda Brunton and Garda Jordan who had just pulled up in a patrol car. Suddenly Lawlor came running towards the car yelling 'raid, raid'. Inside the building Garda Murphy was being held at gunpoint, his radio taken from him, and some £107,000 stolen. At Lawlor's cry O'Grady turned in time to see two masked men run out of the Exchange door and round the back of the building. He immediately alerted Cabra Station by walkie-talkie that a robbery was in progress and dashed after the raiders whom, he suspected, were making for the Dunard Estate behind the Exchange. He now saw five men running towards the Estate, two armed with rifles and two with sawn-off shotguns. Also in pursuit of the men as they fled the Exchange was Garda Murphy. The robber closest to O'Grady, some sixty yards ahead, pointed his shotgun at the Guard causing him to detour behind some bushes. When O'Grady emerged a moment later the man fired at him, pellets from the shot barely missing the unarmed Guard. Undeterred, he continued to pursue the men who vanished through an opening in the perimeter wall of the Dunard Estate. When Garda O'Grady climbed onto the wall he was again shot at. The raiders then got into a waiting green car and sped off towards Blackhorse Avenue. Accepting the offer of a civilian car, O'Grady took off after the getaway vehicle but lost sight of it in the Phoenix Park. Meanwhile the Cabra patrol car, manned by Garda Jordan and Garda Brunton, and the Blanchardstown patrol car, had joined the pursuit. The raiders fired repeatedly at the pursuing Gardaí as they drove madly through the city. Brunton and Jordan nevertheless persevered until the men abandoned their car at Claddagh Road in Ballyfermot. Here, surrounded by armed detectives, the men were arrested as they made a hurried attempt to bury their loot and equipment in a back garden.

Gardaí O'Grady, Jordan and Brunton received their Scott Bronze Medals from Justice Minister Ray Burke at a Garda College ceremony on 23 November 1990. Gerard O'Grady was promoted Sergeant in 1989, Brian Brunton in 1997, and Michael Jordan in 1998. All three men are still serving.[166]

John Aiden Donnelly, Garda 20051D

John A. Donnelly, born in Ballinasloe, County Galway, on 15 February 1952, had been a bus conductor before joining the Garda Síochána on 8 January 1975.

Garda Donnelly was off duty and accompanied by his two-year-old daughter on the evening of 26 January 1989. He arrived at the supermarket in his own car just as three armed raiders were leaving the store. Garda Donnelly moved his car so as to block the raiders' getaway vehicle. The gunmen then fired a shot at his car window and tried to hijack the car. Garda Donnelly steadfastly refused to give them his car keys, forcing the raiders to flee from the scene on foot. One of them was eventually arrested and received a prison sentence for the robbery.

Garda Donnelly received his Scott Bronze Medal at Templemore from Ray Burke, Minister for Justice, on 23 November 1990. He was promoted Sergeant a month later and is still serving.[167]

John P. Moore, Garda 24592E

Born in Kanturk, County Cork, on 10 May 1961, John Moore had been a prison officer before opting for a career with the Gardaí on 10 December 1986.

On the morning of 8 January 1990 Garda Moore and a colleague, both in uniform and unarmed, were on mobile patrol when they received a radio report that a personal attack alarm had been activated at the Allied Irish Bank in Dublin's Ranelagh district. When they arrived at the bank they were met by the porter who said that the premises had been robbed and indicated that the raiders were escaping by a rear exit. Garda Moore ran to the back of the building and was in time to see two men emerge from the laneway behind the bank. Startled by the sight of Moore the robbers turned back into the laneway. Losing sight of them initially Garda Moore, after a quick look round a small adjacent house, ran along the laneway towards the carpark at the rear of the Crosbie Tavern. On reaching the carpark he saw three men making their way into Ranelagh Park and then on across a flooded pathway towards Chelmsford Avenue. Realizing that Moore was almost on top of them the raider nearest to him drew a pistol and shot Moore in the arm. Moore continued to pursue them. Near Chelmsford Avenue one of the other raiders turned and shot him in the right leg. Now in considerable pain, Moore continued the chase collapsing, recovering, but inevitably collapsing again. Eventually, assisted by local people, he radioed his Station at Donnybrook and requested an ambulance. The patrol car got to him first and took him to hospital. His leg wound mercifully proved to be superficial but a .25 inch calibre bullet had to be removed from his forearm, and he was unable to return to duty for eight months.

Garda Moore was presented with his Scott Gold Medal by Justice Minister Ray Burke in November 1991. He was promoted Sergeant in 1996 and is still serving.[168]

Thomas K. Mansfield, Garda 23549M
Gerard H. Quinn, Garda 24634D

Thomas Mansfield, born in Dublin on 14 December 1957, had served in the Irish Defence Forces Air Corps before joining the Gardaí on 7 September 1983. Gerard Quinn, also a Dubliner, born on 27 February 1964, left a managerial post for a career with the Guards on 10 December 1986.

Both men were on mobile patrol in Dublin's Rathmines district on the morning of 8 April 1988 when they noticed smoke rising thickly from the roof of an apartment block at Frankfort Avenue. Making his way through flames and dense smoke, Garda Quinn entered the rear of the building and let Garda Mansfield in at the front door. While they managed to alert the tenants upstairs, conditions in the building forced the two Guards to resort to the use of wet towels to allow them to take more direct action. Their heads swathed in the sopping towels they moved along the ground floor on hands and knees, but before long they were forced back out into the garden for air. From the garden they spotted at an upstairs window a man clearly trapped in his apartment. They made a desperate but futile attempt to reach the man by re-entering the building. They then seized a ladder and managed to get the trapped man onto the window ledge. Now their difficulties multiplied as it became clear that the man was disabled, having had a leg amputated. Smoke had begun to engulf the window ledge by the time the fire brigade arrived minutes later, but the man was brought to safety.

Gardaí Mansfield and Quinn were presented with their Scott Bronze Medals by Ray Burke, Minister for Justice, in November 1991. Thomas Mansfield was promoted Sergeant in 1994 and Gerard Quinn in 1996. Both men are still serving.[169]

Francis P. Dunleavy, Garda 21099D
Peter J. O'Boyle, Garda 22653L

Born at Edgeworthstown, County Longford, on 10 March 1958, Francis Dunleavy had been a storeman until joining the Guards on 15 February 1978. Peter O'Boyle from Ballyhaunis, County Mayo, born on 20 July 1960, left his third-level studies to become a member of An Garda Síochána on 1 July 1982.

Early on the afternoon of 29 April 1990 the two men, together with Student Garda Christopher Morrison, all unarmed, were on mobile patrol when they were alerted to go to a cash and carry premises at Dublin's Robinhood Industrial Estate; a personal attack alarm had been activated. When Garda Dunleavy and Student Garda Morrison entered the building to check out the alarm they were confronted by a youth brandishing a sawn-off shotgun. The gun was raised until Dunleavy was looking down its barrels. Dunleavy grabbed the weapon by its stock and jerked it up towards the roof. He then grappled with the raider and was on the point of wrenching the gun away from him when a second raider appeared and the Guard found himself at close quarters with another shotgun – this one pressed against his cheek. The second raider shouted that he would kill him, and Dunleavy had little choice but to release his grip on his original assailant. He and Student Garda Morrison were then forced to lie on the floor. From inside the patrol car Garda O'Boyle could see what was taking place through the glass door of the building, and was in the process of radioing for help when he felt a shotgun being pressed into the back of his neck. O'Boyle seized the gun and tried to force it downward away from his head but the awkward angle allowed the raider to pull the gun out of his grasp. Soon Garda O'Boyle joined his two colleagues and the warehouse staff on the floor of the premises. While O'Boyle was engaged in the struggle at the patrol car, however, Garda Dunleavy seized the opportunity to summon help via his walkie-talkie, throwing the radio under some boxes thereafter in case his captors had over-heard him. As the raiders climbed into their getaway car the three Gardaí scrambled to their feet, but as they approached the door they were again faced with a shotgun and the robbers made good their escape.

Gardaí Dunleavy and Boyle received their Scott Bronze Medals from Justice Minister Ray Burke at Templemore in November 1991. Francis Dunleavy was promoted Sergeant in 1993 and Inspector in 2003. Peter O'Boyle was promoted Sergeant in 1994 and Inspector in 2005. Both men were to be awarded Scott Medals again in later years (see pp 168 and 175–6 below). They are still serving.[170]

John M.G. Galvin, Garda 23990K
Kieran P. Carroll, Garda 22457L
John Galvin was born on 23 February 1963 at Rathea, Listowel, County Kerry, and had worked in a factory until attesting for the Gardaí on 30 May 1984. Kieran Carroll from Ballinlough, County Roscommon, born on 6 May 1963, had been a student before joining the force on 31 March 1982.

Early on the morning of 30 April 1991 Gardaí Galvin and Carroll were on mobile patrol near Dublin's Blackrock College when they smelled burning and heard the sounds of a fire in progress. They drove into the College grounds and learned from a group of elderly people that a building blazing a short distance from them was the staff quarters and that two people were still inside. They managed to get in through a window but the heat and smoke were already unbearable. The two Guards pressed on regardless as ceilings burned overhead and pieces of flaming timber showered on them. As they forced open an inside door a gust of smoke and heat knocked Garda Galvin off his feet, singeing his hair and skin. They located an elderly man still in his bed and carried him to safety through a corridor that was burning from one end to the other. To the obvious horror of the onlookers the two Guards then returned to try to find the other missing man. But by now all movement inside the building was impossible, and with the collapse of the roof Galvin and Carroll were forced to get back out again on their hands and knees. They believed that they had come to within a dozen feet of the man's probable location, but it was there that the inferno was at its hottest. The two Gardaí were themselves taken to hospital suffering from smoke inhalation.

Scott Bronze Medals were duly presented to Garda Galvin and Garda Carroll by the Minister for Justice, Ray Burke, at Templemore in November 1991. John Galvin was promoted Sergeant three weeks later and Inspector in 2004. Kieran Carroll was promoted Sergeant in 2000. Both men are still serving the community.[171]

Geoffrey V. Power, Garda 16755L

Born on 22 January 1947 at Bundoran, County Donegal, Geoffrey Power joined the force on 29 December 1966.

He was on his way back to Mill Street Station in Galway in heavy rain early on the morning of 10 April 1991 when a young man approached him to report that his friend had fallen into the river. Sending the boy on to the Station to raise the alarm, Garda Power himself hastened to the scene of the incident. The lad's friend had fallen from a footbridge at a point where the River Corrib is about 75 yards wide. Such was the severity of the weather, however, that not only the bridge but its handrail – some four feet high – were both under water. No street lights were nearby to alliviate the poor visibility. But Garda Power's keen eyes picked out the figure of the youth in the centre of the river, pinned against a staunchion. The Guard climbed down keeping as close as he could to the river bank, and lowered himself the remaining ten feet into the near-freezing water. Gripping the handrail to prevent himself being swept away, Power moved along the rail hand-over-hand, his feet unable to grip on anything, until he reached an eight-foot-high security gate on the bridge. This gate was topped with barbed wire but Garda Power clambered over it regardless and pressed on until he reached the staunchion where the boy hung barely breathing. Power held the youth's head above the raging waters until the fire brigade arrived. The lad later made a full recovery.

Garda Power, who had spent 45 minutes that night in the cold angry Corrib, received his Scott Silver Medal and, uniquely, a kiss from the Minister for Justice Maire Geoghegan-Quinn, at the Garda College, Templemore, in the spring of 1993. He continued thereafter to serve in Galway until his retirement, after a career lasting 30 years and 276 days, on 30 September 1997.[172]

Felix Lunney, Detective Garda Sergeant 14690M

Born on 21 April 1940 at Castleshane, County Monaghan, Felix Lunney embarked on his career in the Garda Síochána on 19 April 1961.

On the afternoon of 19 August 1989 Sergeant Lunney, together with two colleagues from the Detective Unit at Donnybrook Station, were on patrol in plain clothes. His two colleagues were armed but Lunney himself had no firearm. They were in Pembroke Park when the sound of a burglar alarm was heard from a private house. Finding a rear window suspiciously open, Sergeant Lunney and one of his colleagues quietly slipped inside. While Lunney checked out the ground floor his colleague went upstairs and came face-to-face with a man wielding a large knife. The detective made an attempt to seize the man but, after a tussle, the assailant pushed his way past him and down the stairs. He ran straight into Sergeant Lunney who, on hearing the rumpus, had come to the bottom of the stairs. The man shouted at Lunney, challenging the detective to shoot him and jabbed at him with the knife. As he reached the foot of the stairs the man made a serious attempt to drive the knife into Lunney's chest. Not giving an inch, Lunney seized the assailant's arm forcing the weapon upwards and away from his body. A fierce struggle took place during which the burglar grabbed the knife blade in his hand to prevent Lunney taking it from him, and cut himself badly. The fight ended with the burglar pinned against the bannister and the knife in Lunney's possession.

Justice Minister Maire Geoghegan-Quinn presented Detective Sergeant Lunney with his Scott Bronze Medal at Templemore in March 1993. He continued to serve the people of Donnybrook until he retired on 12 April 1997 after 35 years and 359 days.[173]

Bernard P. Jones, Garda 23843M

Born at Ballina, County Mayo, on 23 January 1964, Bernard Jones had been a student before joining the Gardaí on 4 January 1984.

Garda Jones was observer in the mobile patrol car being driven by one of his colleagues on the evening of 11 February 1990. Near Dublin's Frank Sherwin Bridge the two Guards saw a man running towards Heuston Station apparently fleeing from another who was trying unsuccessfully to conceal a shotgun. The patrol car went in pursuit. As the car drew level with the gunman the Guards noticed that he was now holding the weapon across his chest with both hands. The driver skilfully guided the car until it bumped the man, knocking him off his feet. He didn't, however, stay down and was upright again in a moment gun still in hand. Immediately Garda Jones, who was unarmed, leaped from the car and bore the man to the ground. The gunman still clung to his weapon and struggled desperately, but with the help of the patrol car driver he was subdued and taken into custody.

Garda Jones received his Scott Bronze Medal from Maire Geoghegan-Quinn, Minister for Justice, at the Garda College, Templemore, in March 1993. He was promoted Sergeant in 1997 and is still serving.[174]

Michael R. McKeon, Chief Superintendent 13059A

Michael McKeon was born at Glin, County Limerick, on 1 October 1935, and had been a student before beginning a distinguished career in the Guards on 16 May 1956.

The agitated man with the rifle who arrived at the doctor's surgery at Clane, County Kildare late on the afternoon of 12 July 1990 had a grievance against the doctor and intended to shoot him. After a long moment in which he levelled the gun at the doctor's head the man lowered the barrel and shot the doctor in the right hip. Luckily the injury did not prevent the doctor from running out of the surgery. The gunman followed firing four further shots, but seemed to have a poor aim and the doctor escaped. Now more agitated than ever the man went to a nearby field where he spent the next hour during which several watchful Gardaí tried in vain to cajole him into parting with the weapon. When the situation had still not been resolved by 7 p.m. Chief Superintendent McKeon arrived on the scene. He managed to engage the man in easy conversation for a brief period, but again he became agitated. Threats to kill himself were followed by threats aimed at everybody looking on. He demonstrated to McKeon how he had removed the trigger guard with a view to turning the rifle into a rapid-fire weapon. Two more hours passed and the shadows began to lengthen as the man paced about the field swallowing bullets and repeating his threats of suicide. It was becoming clear to McKeon that the threats of suicide were real and that the man was trying to find the necessary courage. An opportunity to overpower him had to be watched for carefully. It was almost dark when the man sat down on a mound of earth next to a stream, his introspection deepened by McKeon's carefully-modulated voice. McKeon moved ever closer until he was within a dozen feet of the man. Suddenly the moment arrived. Confused by the problem of lighting a cigarette while holding a heavy rifle the man's attention was distracted for the crucial space of time needed for McKeon to spring forward and pin the gun to the ground while another Guard came from behind and overpowered the man himself. When examined, the rifle was found to be loaded and ready to fire.

Chief Superintendent McKeon, less than a year from retirement at the time of the incident, added a Scott Bronze Medal to his achievements. He left the force on 23 May 1991 having served 35 years and 8 days, but returned in March 1993 to Templemore to receive his medal from Justice Minister Maire Geoghegan-Quinn.[175]

Matthew Oliver Lennon, DetectiveGarda 16173L
Born in Clones, County Monaghan, on 2 April 1944, Matthew Lennon joined the Garda Síochána on 21 April 1965.

Very early on the morning of 16 November 1990 the Garda on duty at Navan Station, County Meath, received the alarming report that a young man had fired a rifle shot through his parents' window at St Brigids Villas in the town. The gun, as well as some ammunition taken from the house earlier, belonged to the young man's father. Sergeant Patrick Gannon, Detective Garda Matthew Lennon, Garda Leslie O'Shaughnessy and Garda Hugh Brady, all of Navan Station and all in plain clothes, immediately went to the scene. Gannon, Brady and Lennon were armed; Lennon was also wearing a bullet-proof vest. Gannon and Lennon approached the end-of-terrace house by themselves, leaving their two colleagues on the street within view of the building. They entered an alleyway alongside the house; from here they could see inside the back garden where the young man was holding the rifle in both hands. From one end of the alley they called on him to give them the gun; from the garden area at the other end came the voices of the man's mother and that of another woman likewise pleading with him to relinquish the weapon. The whole scene was lit up by lights from inside the house. The two Guards moved closer but the young man levelled his rifle at them and threatened to shoot if they did not back off. Gannon and Lennon took such cover as they could at the front corner of the shed which formed one 'wall' of the alleyway. After a short lull Lennon crept again along the alleyway at the end of which was the back garden. He identified himself by name and again called on the gunman to give him the rifle. The approach was low-key rather than peremptory or demanding. At no point did Lennon or any of his colleagues attempt to intimidate or frighten the gunman. If he would surrender the gun, the man was assured, 'everything' would be 'alright'. Lennon had now reached the corner of the rear end of the shed about twenty feet from the gunman. Again came the threat to 'kill' if the Guard did not withdraw. When Lennon did not immediately back away the man rushed towards him, gun pointing straight ahead. Lennon moved swiftly back up the alley but after a short interval moved again towards the garden. Meanwhile Sergeant Gannon had gone round the other side of the shed to a spot from which he had a view of the garden over a low wall. After further futile exchanges, and threats from the gunman, Lennon followed the man's father through the alleyway and into the garden. Clearly provoked by this the gunman came towards them, gun presented, and the two men withdrew quickly through the alleyway. This time, however, the gunman made the mistake of following them through the alley. The moment the gunbarrel appeared at the other end Lennon grabbed it and forced it upward. With his right hand he pushed the gunman; the man's father joined in and seized him round the neck. Sergeant Gannon immediately came to help also and a scuffle developed during which the gun went off, as the man still had his finger inside the trigger guard. The man persisted in his refusal to let go of the gun until eventually Lennon had to hit him with his own firearm. The man was then arrested by Sergeant Gannon.

Detective Garda Lennon received his Scott Bronze Medal from Maire Geoghegan-Quinn, Minister for Justice, at the Garda College, Templemore, in March 1993. He retired on 1 April 2001 having served 35 years and 346 days.[176]

Kenneth A. McGreevy, Garda 23512A
Joseph P. Collins, Garda 24538M

Kenneth McGreevy from Athlone, County Westmeath, born on 26 January 1964, had worked as a security guard before attesting for the Gardaí on 20 July 1983. Joseph Collins, born in County Galway on 23 January 1965, had been a prison officer before joining the force on 8 October 1986.

Early on the morning of 18 December 1990 the two men were on mobile patrol when they saw smoke and flames gushing from a first-floor window of a house in Dublin's Upper Gardiner Street. They ran through the open door of the house – which had been converted into flats – and discovered that the seat of the blaze was in one of the flats. But when they tried to get into this flat they were beaten back by fumes and unbearable heat. Immediately they took steps to evacuate the rest of the building, working their way from the first floor to the ground and then to the basement. Soon the eight occupants were safely off the premises. But no soon had this been achieved than one of the occupants dashed back into the house. Pursued by McGreevy and Collins, the man ran upstairs to the second floor and refused to come down. Thick smoke was now filling every corner and crevice of the building and the two Gardaí could breathe only by covering their faces with the sleeves of their tunics. When they reached the second floor they found the man slumped unconscious at the top of the stairs. With great difficulty and with the flames getting ever closer Collins and McGreevy managed to drag the man down two flights of stairs to the ground floor where other Gardaí helped carry him to an ambulance. The man later recovered.

Joseph Collins and Kenneth McCreevy received their Scott Bronze Medals from Justice Minister Maire Geoghegan-Quinn at the Garda College, Templemore, in March 1993. Both Gardaí are still serving.[177]

John McHugh, Garda 19010A

Born at Ballindrait, Lifford, County Donegal, on 13 January 1954, John McHugh joined the Gardaí on 7 February 1973.

On the afternoon of 16 April 1991 two men noticed that a bungalow at Lerrig North, Ardfert, County Kerry, had caught fire. Knowing that two elderly men lived there they attemped to rescue them but were driven back by dense choking smoke. Alerted to the situation Garda McHugh and a colleague hurried to the scene. McHugh entered the kitchen but, like the civilian would-be rescuers, he had to retreat before the pall of black smoke. He tried once again, this time on his hands and knees. Reaching a bedroom he found an elderly man slumped on the floor and dragged him to the door of the room where fire brigade personnel helped to carry the man outside. Sadly the man died at the scene.

On 24 March 1993 Justice Minister Maire Geoghegan-Quinn presented Garda John McHugh with his Scott Bronze Medal. Thereafter he continued to serve the people of Kerry until his retirement on 15 January 2004 after a career of 30 years and 343 days.[178]

Thomas Aidan McDermott, Garda 25164L

Born at Glenaniff, Rossinver, County Leitrim, in 1964, Aidan McDermott joined the Gardaí in May 1990.

Posted to Clontarf Station, Dublin, after training, Garda McDermott was one of two dozen Guards temporarily sent to Ronanstown in December 1991 in response to a steep rise in criminal activity there. He was on his way to the Station on the evening of 12 December when he spotted two men scaling the wall of a house, one of them equipped with a knapsack. At the sound of McDermott's voice the two startled would-be burglars split up and tried to run for it. McDermott seized the one with the knapsack who immediately began to scream for help. From nowhere two men ran forward and attacked the Garda, beating and kicking him with indescribable viciousness. McDermott's captive managed to pull himself free and joined in the assault in an effort to retrieve the knapsack to which the young Garda still clung with grim determination. Eventually the cowardly trio had to flee empty-handed. The knapsack was found to contain, along with gloves and a balaclava, a sawn-off shotgun. Despite considerable bruising Garda McDermott returned to duty the next day.

Aidan McDermott duly received his Scott Bronze Medal from Justice Minister Maire Geoghegan-Quinn at Templemore on 24 March 1993. He is still serving.[179]

John C. O'Neill, Garda 24328M

Born in Dublin on 16 February 1964, John O'Neill joined the Gardaí on 6 November 1985.

Attached to the motor cyclists unit at Tallaght Station, Dublin, Garda O'Neill was patrolling the Springfield area on the evening of 23 August 1990 when members of the public alerted him that an armed raid was in progress at a nearby supermarket. Three masked men were involved, one of them armed with a sawn-off shotgun. On arrival at the scene Garda O'Neill was on time to see three men run from the supermarket and into a black car in which a fourth man was waiting. The car roared off in the direction of Fortunestown with Garda O'Neill in close pursuit. After a high-speed chase the raider at the wheel misjudged a bend in the road after Fortunestown Supermarket and crashed. The four raiders decamped towards Duncairn Gardens with O'Neill, still astride his motorcycle, close behind. As the distance between Garda and robbers narrowed one of them turned and threatened O'Neill with the shotgun; the voices of his accomplices could be heard urging him to shoot O'Neill. At the last moment the gunman lost his nerve and resumed his flight. Shifting his focus to one of the other raiders, Garda O'Neill left his motor-cycle and followed him over walls and through gardens along Duncairn Avenue until he finally caught and arrested him. A search of the area later turned up the shotgun which one of the raiders had presented at Garda O'Neill; it was loaded.

Garda John O'Neill received his Scott Gold Medal from Justice Minister Maire Geoghegan-Quinn at Templemore on 30 March 1994. He left the force in October 1996.[180]

Benjamin O'Sullivan, Detective Garda 15636A

Ben O'Sullivan, born at Mournabbey, Mallow, County Cork, on 7 February 1944, left farming for a career with the Guards on 6 May 1964.

Based in Limerick, Detective O'Sullivan and a colleague, armed and in plain clothes, were in an unmarked patrol car at Punches Cross on the evening of 30 January 1992. On receiving a radio report that a taxi driver was in trouble in Griffith Avenue they drove immediately to the scene. The shaken taxi driver told them that a man had threatened him with a shotgun. The two Guards drove in pursuit of the man, catching up with him within minutes further along Griffith Avenue. As they approached to within ten yards of him the man pointed the gun at the patrol car causing O'Sullivan and his colleague to stop and take such cover as they could inside the car. He then continued to walk along Griffith Avenue, shadowed from a safe distance by the two Gardaí who decided to continue the pursuit separately and on foot. As he walked the man menaced passers-by with the weapon and, emerging onto Childers Road, stood in the middle of the road levelling his gun at cars approaching him. Several drivers stopped and fled in terror. Unnoticed by the gunman, O'Sullivan and his colleague were edging closer to him. O'Sullivan was twenty yards away when he saw that the man's attention was increasingly occupied by the prospect of terrorizing more drivers. At the approach of yet another car the detective rushed at him, knocking the gunman off his feet and pinning him to the ground. O'Sullivan's colleague joined in and the man was disarmed and taken into custody. The shotgun was found to be loaded and with the safety catch in the 'off' position.

Ben O'Sullivan was presented with his Scott Gold Medal by Maire Geoghegan-Quinn, Minister for Justice, at a Garda College ceremony in Templemore on 30 March 1994. He continued to serve thereafter in Limerick's Henry Street Station, and would collect a further Scott Gold Medal before he retired (see pp 184–5 below) on 6 February 2001, having served for 36 years and 277 days.[181]

Vincent M. Markey, Garda 24145H
Gerard McGrath, Garda 23327G

Vincent Markey, born in Dublin on 21 January 1963, had worked as a storeman before attesting for the Gardaí on 12 December 1984. Gerard McGrath, also a Dubliner, was born on 6 September 1962 and had been a clerical assistant before joining the force on 26 January 1983.

The two Gardaí in the Coolock Station patrol car were on their way to the district court on the morning of 23 November 1990 when they caught sight of four youths walking away from Dorset Street Post office towards Dublin's North Circular Road. The youths were somewhat conspicuous in that they were wearing balaclavas and one of them was brandishing a sawn-off shotgun. The Gardaí followed them for a short distance until they were fired on and forced to leave the car to take cover. At this, the youths piled into the patrol car and drove off. Within seconds Garda Markey and Garda McGrath of Fitzgibbon Street Station, in an unmarked patrol car, appeared on the scene in response to a radio alert that Dorset Street Post Office had just been robbed. Both were unarmed and in plain clothes. One of the Guards from the Coolock car waved them in the direction that the raiders had fled but Markey and McGrath, as they sped onwards down the North Circular Road towards Summerhill, still had no idea that the Coolock car was being driven by the robbers. This changed abruptly as Markey and McGrath rounded a bend near Summerhill and saw that the Coolock car had crashed into a number of other cars. As they approached they saw a youth with a sawn-off shotgun hanging from a cord beneath his arm run from the car into Summerhill Parade. Blue beacon flashing, Markey and McGrath pursued the youth until he ran panic-stricken into a cul-de-sac. As the patrol car slowly glided to a halt a short distance from him the youth, hampered by his gloves, prepared to confront Markey and McGrath. Markey stood cautiously behind the open passenger door and ordered the youth to drop the weapon. McGrath gesticulated a similar command from the driver's seat. The trapped, flustered gunman seemed likely to open fire. Markey unzipped his jacket and reached purposefully inside. The bluff worked; the gunman immediately dropped to the ground and was then arrested. With some difficulty the two Guards undid the white flex which bound the gun to the youth's shoulders, and disarmed him. As they tried to make it safe it went off accidentally. Meanwhile back at the crash scene an angry civilian had collared one of the other raiders and held him until Gardaí arrived to arrest him.

Vincent Markey received his Scott Silver Medal and Gerard McGrath his Scott Bronze Medal from Justice Minister Maire Geoghegan-Quinn at Templemore on 30 March 1994. They were both promoted Sergeant, Markey in 1995 and McGrath in 1998, and they continue to serve the community today.[182]

Ivor J.P. Burlingham, Garda 24305A

Born in Dundalk, County Louth, on 5 September 1959, Ivor Burlingham had been a civil servant for several years in the Department of Education before joining the Gardaí on 14 August 1985.

He was on foot patrol in Dublin's Harcourt Street at midday on 10 March 1991 when a passer-by reported a fire in the basement of a four-storey terraced house. The house was, in fact, a disused and derelict building used commonly by homeless people, and the steep steps to its basement were overgrown and blocked by rubbish. When Garda Burlingham had struggled through the on-lookers and the debris and got into the small smoke-filled basement room he saw two men apparently asleep. One of them was surrounded by flames while the other man's clothes were actually ablaze. He tried to awaken them and then dragged one of them to the foot of the basement steps where other Gardaí had arrived and were ready to assist. Garda Burlingham then turned back into the hellish room where he could barely see the outline of the second victim. The Garda covered the man with his greatcoat in an effort to extinguish the flames which were licking at the man's clothes. At this point the fire brigade arrived to assist and an ambulance took the two men to hospital where, sadly, one of them died three days later.

Garda Burlingham, the burns to his head and hands fully healed, was presented with his Scott Silver Medal by Maire Geoghegan-Quinn, Minister for Justice, at Templemore on 30 March 1994. He was promoted Sergeant in 2002 and is still serving.[183]

Conor P. Comiskey, Garda 24782M

A Dubliner born on 12 July 1967, Conor Comiskey had been training to be an accountant before opting for a career in the Gardaí on 1 June 1990.

Garda Comiskey and a colleague were on mobile patrol in Dublin's Marlborough Street in the early hours of 3 February 1993 when they went to O'Connell Bridge in response to a radio message that a man had jumped into the river. A number of Gardaí and civilians were already at the scene when Comiskey arrived. A man was struggling in the water and the current was carrying him across the river towards Burgh Quay. Running to Burgh Quay Comiskey stripped off his jumper, watch and radio and lowered himself from a ladder into the dark, swirling water. The current and the cold, however, defeated his best efforts. By the time he had reached the middle of the river the man, now no more than five yards away, had ceased to struggle and Comiskey was forced to abandon the rescue attempt and do what he could to save himself. His legs and arms became heavier and heavier as he swam back and the weight of his clothes threatened to drag him under. He barely made it back to the ladder where he was helped to safety. Suffering from hypothermia, shock and the beginnings of a stomach infection, Comiskey was rushed to hospital where he was detained for several days.

On 30 March 1994 Justice Minister Maire Geoghegan-Quinn presented Garda Conor Comiskey with his Scott Bronze Medal at a ceremony in Templemore. He still serves the community.[184]

Michael Tyner, Garda 23556M
Fergal Harrington, Garda 25505L
Francis Dunleavy, Garda 21099D
Gary F. Corrigan, Garda 24256L

Michael Tyner, born in Avoca, County Wicklow on 18 February 1963, worked as a shop assistant before joining the Guards on 7 September 1983. Fergal Harrington, a Dubliner born on 17 May 1969, left an assistant managerial post for a career with the Gardaí on 11 February 1993. Francis Dunleavy was born in Edgeworthstown, County Longford on 10 March 1958 and had been a storeman before attesting for the Gardaí on 15 February 1978. Gary Corrigan from Achill, County Mayo, born on 2 January 1964, had worked as a barman before joining the force on 14 August 1985.

Minutes after receiving the radio alert of an armed robbery in Dublin's Tallaght district, Gardaí Tyner and Harrington, on mobile patrol on the morning of 12 April 1993, spotted the raiders' getaway vehicle and went in pursuit. Responding to an updated radio report that Gardaí were following the robbers in the Naas/Long Mile Road area, Garda Dunleavy and Harrington joined in the high-speed chase, keeping other units fully informed as they did so. At one point a gun was pointed at them from the speeding getaway car. The robbers collided with the patrol car carrying Dunleavy and Harrington at Robinhood Road and eventually crashed. The four raiders jumped from their stricken car, menacing the approaching Gardaí with their weapons as they scattered in different directions. Tyner, Harrington, Dunleavy and Corrigan, undaunted, pursued the men until they had caught and arrested all of them.

On 25 May 1995 all four men were presented with their Scott Silver Medals by Justice Minister Nora Owen. Francis Dunleavy, who had been awarded a Scott Bronze Medal in 1991 (see pp 156–7 above), was promoted Sergeant in 1993 and Inspector in 2003. Michael Tyner was promoted Sergeant in 1994. All four are still serving.[185]

John Cooney, Garda 23915A

Born in Macroom, County Cork, on 14 July 1963, John Cooney joined the Gardaí on 28 February 1984.

Early on the morning of 12 July 1993 ran to Cork's North Gate Bridge where a young man was reported to have jumped into the river. Efforts by members of he public to rescue him with lifebuoys had come to nothing and the youth was now in severe difficulties. Hurriedly throwing off some heavier items of clothing, Garda Cooney climbed down into the water and swam towards the youth. He was almost beyond help and had sunk below the surface just before Cooney reached him. The Guard seized hold of him before he could vanish and, with the aid of a lifebuoy thrown by other Gardaí who had arrived on the bridge, the lad was pulled to safety. He later made a full recovery.

Garda John Cooney received his Scott Bronze Medal from Justice Minister Nora Owen on 25 May 1995. Thereafter he continued to serve in Cork City until his discharge on medical grounds on 27 April 2000.[186]

Thomas Barrett, Garda 23584K

Thomas Barrett, born on 6 November 1962 at Athea, County Limerick, left farming for a career with the Gardaí on 7 September 1983.

He was one of a party of Gardaí who in the early hours of 19 June 1993 were engaged in searching a house in Limerick for a gun which had been used at a shooting incident at Ballysimon, County Limerick, some time previously. The woman occupant of the house insisted that she was alone. But Garda Barrett, when searching through one of the bedrooms, went to check an open cupboard door and was suddenly faced with a man armed with a rifle. Barrett grabbed the gun and a fierce struggle ensued during which the Garda was violently hit over the head by the gunman. Hearing the commotion other Gardaí came to Barrett's aid and the man was disarmed and arrested.

Thomas Barrett received his Scott Bronze Medal at Templemore from Nora Owen, Minister for Justice, on 25 May 1995. He was promoted Sergeant in 1995 and is still serving.[187]

Michael McDonagh, Garda 23607A
Michael Ryan, Garda 21113C

Born at Miltown Malbay, County Clare, on 25 January 1964, Michael McDonagh had worked in farming before attesting for the Gardaí on 7 September 1983. Michael Ryan, born on 23 September 1957 at Ennis, County Clare, had been an export clerk before joining the force on 15 February 1978.

On receiving a report that a house at Crawford Street, Kilrush, County Clare, was on fire, Gardaí Ryan and McDonagh ran to the scene to find the front room of the house ablaze and smoke billowing from the window. The fire was also beginning to spread to the upper floor. Screams from the trapped occupants issued from within but the intense heat and smoke frustrated the two Guards' initial attempt to force their way in. Having got the door open Garda Ryan then tried again on his hands and knees, crawling along the hallway searching as he went. His hands met those of a man lying unconscious in the hallway and the two Guards managed to manoeuvre the senseless man out from the narrow confined space and through the choking fumes to safety. He later made a full recovery.

Gardaí Ryan and McDonagh were presented with their Scott Bronze Medals by Justice Minister Nora Owen at the Garda College, Templemore, on 25 May 1995. They are still serving.[188]

Thomas Declan Murray, Garda 24675A
Fionan Lynch, Garda 24924F

Declan Murray was born at Carrickmacross, County Monaghan, on 26 May 1962 and had been a fork-lift operator before joining the Gardaí on 10 December 1986.

Fionan Lynch, a Dubliner born on 10 November 1962, joined the force in 1990.

Gardaí Murray and Lynch were on mobile patrol when they received word of an armed raid in progress in the Cabra area. They sped to the scene to be informed by onlookers that the criminals were still inside the premises. Garda Lynch approached the front door while Garda Murray went round to the back door. As Lynch made his entrance an armed raider was terrorizing an employee who had been made to lie on the floor. The sudden appearance of Garda Lynch, however, alarmed the raider who made unsuccessful efforts to open an exit door. Enraged, the gunman brandished his weapon and threatened everyone present. Garda Murray, momentarily delayed by an obstinate inner door, then burst onto the scene. The raider, now quite panic-stricken, first pointed the gun at Murray and then struck him over the head with it. Murray, unfazed, immediately seized and overpowered him. Garda Lynch rushed forward, pushed the raider to the floor and helped Garda Murray to disarm him.

At a ceremony in Templemore on 25 May 1995 Justice Minister Nora Owen presented Gardaí Lynch and Murray with their Scott Bronze Medals. Garda Murray had previously been awarded a Scott Bronze Medal in respect of an incident in 1988 (see p. 152 above). Both men are still serving.[189]

Patrick Campbell, Detective Garda Sergeant 18011D
John Sharkey, Garda 24851G
Thomas McKenna, Garda 22118L

Patrick Campbell, born at Newbliss, County Monaghan, on 1 December 1946, had been a fireman before joining the Gardaí on 8 September 1971. John Sharkey was born in Ballinasloe, County Galway, on 5 May 1970 and was a student until opting for a career in the Guards in 1989. Thomas McKenna, a Dubliner born 30 July 1960, had also been a student before joining the force on 30 July 1980.

On 15 April 1993 Detective Sergeant Campbell received reliable information via two Garda colleagues that a security van was to be robbed on 17 April by armed men on a motor cycle while making a cash collection at Castle Street, Bray, County Wicklow. Campbell discussed the matter with his superiors and a decision was taken to give cover to the security van and its personnel. On the morning of the intended robbery a party of eleven Gardaí took up positions in undercover vehicles and business premises in and around Castle Street. As the time approached 11.45 a.m. a motorcyclist was observed circling the area, halting eventually beside a bush at the top of Castle Street. Soon after midday a Brinks Allied Security van with a three-man crew drew up outside a video rental store and came to a stop just a few feet from the rear of an observation vehicle manned by Detective Sergeant Campbell and Gardaí Sharkey and McKenna. A security man entered the store and collected a bag containing over £1,000 in cash. As he returned to the van he was approached by a man who was pointing a gun at him with one hand while simultaneously trying to don a mask with the other. Without any provocation the gunman fired a shot at the security man and then demanded the cash. The security man immediately tossed the bag towards his assailant. As the gunman bent to pick it up he was suddenly confronted by Campbell and McKenna who were both armed. Standing directly behind them was Garda Sharkey who was unarmed. The Guards identified themselves and called on the gunman to drop his weapon. The man, however, ignored them and ran off across the carpark towards Castle Street pursued by the three Gardaí who repeatedly called on him to stop and drop his gun. His response was to turn and fire a shot at Campbell and Sharkey, who were closest to him. Garda McKenna returned fire but the gunman still continued to run. As he approached the footpath on Castle Street the motorcyclist seen earlier came at speed along the footpath and slowed down to collect him. At this point Campbell and Sharkey caught the gunman from behind and prevented him from boarding the motorcycle. The motorcyclist fled and the enraged gunman then tore himself free, turned and fired at his captors. The bullet passed between Campbell and Sharkey narrowly missing them and embedded itself in a parked car. Garda Sharkey knocked the gun from the man's grasp and he and Detective Campbell then subdued and handcuffed him. Garda McKenna gave gun cover to his two colleagues and preserved the culprit's gun as well as the bag of cash until the arrival of other Gardaí.

Detective Sergeant Campbell and Gardaí Sharkey and McKenna duly received their Scott Bronze Medals from Nora Owen, Minister for Justice, at Templemore on 25 May 1995. Patrick Campbell, who had previously been awarded a Scott Bronze Medal in 1989 (see pp 148–9 above), retired on 30 November 2003 having served 32 years and 84 days. Garda Sharkey, promoted Sergeant in 2000, and Garda McKenna are still serving.[190]

Anthony Gallagher, Garda 23907M
Declan Sheeran, Garda 25277H

Born at Navan, County Meath on 13 November 1962, Anthony Gallagher had been an apprentice mechanic before joining the Gardaí on 28 February 1984. Declan Sheeran, born at Ballydingan, County Roscommon on 12 September 1967, had worked in the building industry before joining the force in November 1990.

Gardaí Gallagher and Sheeran, both in uniform and unarmed, were manning the Ballyfermot patrol car on the late afternoon of 31 July 1993 when they were directed by radio to escort a delivery of cash from a butcher shop in Dublin's Ballyfermot Road to the night safe at the Bank of Ireland nearby. Arriving there a few minutes later they found the butcher Sean and his brother George already seated in their white van and ready to proceed. At the bank George got out opposite the night safe followed by Garda Sheeran. Suddenly a masked man appeared pointing a pump-action shotgun at Sheeran's head. Sheeran noticed the expression in the gunman's eyes and, acting on instinct, dived to the ground barely missing the buckshot which flew over his head. As he scrambled for the cover of an adjacent car two more shots rang out, one of which burst a front tyre of the patrol car. Sheeran, keeping his head down, got back into the patrol car. The gunman and the butcher's van had vanished. The butcher's startled brother George also got into the patrol car as Garda Control was alerted and back-up summoned. Garda Gallagher, at the wheel, who had also narrowly avoided being hit, had seen the butcher drive off in the white van pursued by a grey car. A number of people who had witnessed the incident indicated to the two Guards the direction taken by the van and the grey car. As they joined the chase on their remaining three good tyres onlookers continued to point them in the right direction. On Le Fanu Road they saw coming towards them a charcoal grey car with four masked occupants. As they drew abreast one of them leaned through the window and fired a shot directly at the patrol car effectively knocking out its engine. As their assailants disappeared in the direction of Kylemore Road Garda Sheeran noted the exact make of the grey car and Garda Gallagher radioed its registration number to Garda Control. With the assistance of a passing motorist Garda Sheeran along with the butcher's brother George drove in the direction from which the raiders had come until, to their relief, they came across the butcher's van with Sean standing alive alongside it. Two shots, it seemed, had been fired at his van, disabling it. A number of armed masked men had then relieved him of some £20,000 in cash and cheques. Garda Gallagher arrived a few minutes later having managed to re-start the stricken patrol car and before long they were joined by other Gardaí.

On 25 May 1995 Justice Minister Nora Owen presented Gardaí Gallagher and Sheerin with their Scott Bronze Medals. Anthony Gallagher, promoted Sergeant in 1996, and Declan Sheeran are still serving.[191]

James C. Grogan, Garda 22094K

Born in Kilrush, County Clare, on 9 April 1959, James Grogan joined the Garda Síochána on 30 July 1980.

Garda Grogan and a colleague were on mobile patrol in Cork City on the morning of 9 July 1993 when they received a radio alert regarding a suspected stolen car being driven in the Model Farm Road area. The two Guards caught up with the stolen car whose occupants then abandoned it and sought the protection of a gang of hostile youths lurking nearby. One of them felled Garda Grogan with a missile, upon which the mob attacked him, continuing to kick and beat him long after he had lost consciousness. For a time he remained in a coma, regaining his senses only after extensive surgery.

His injuries were so extensive that he was considered unable to return to duty and was discharged from the force on medical grounds in August 1994. He was present at Templemore on 15 February 1996 to receive his Scott Gold Medal from Justice Minister Nora Owen.[192]

Brendan J. Walshe, Detective Garda 21573K

A native of Enniscrone, County Sligo, Brendan Walshe was born on 26 May 1953 and had spent six years in the Army Signals Corps before joining the Gardaí on 28 December 1978.

He was on plain-clothes duty with a colleague in Dublin's Ballyfermot area on 20 June 1994 when they were alerted to a robbery-in-progress at Lally Road. The raiders were still there when the two Guards arrived at the scene. Detective Walshe drew his revolver, identified himself as an armed Garda and ordered the culprits to drop their weapons. One of them responded by firing three blasts from a shotgun at the Guards, damaging a nearby van and the Garda patrol car and wounding Detective Walshe in the hand. Walshe returned fire wounding the gunman who then fired a fourth shot and tried to escape. The two Guards leaped on the gunman and overpowered him, recovering not only the shotgun but also the raiders' loot.

Detective Garda Walshe received his Scott Bronze Medal from Justice Minister Nora Owen at the Garda College, Templemore, on 15 February 1996. He is still serving.[193]

John F. Keyes, Garda 20971F

A Dubliner born on 23 July 1956, John Keyes had been a clerk before attesting for the Gardaí on 11 January 1978.

He was on foot patrol on Dublin's Dame Street on the afternoon of 31 July 1994 when he saw an armed man carrying a bag run from a bank and into a car. Garda Keyes ran over, dragged open the driver's door and in the struggle which followed, managed to wrench the gun from the man's grasp. The robber then seized a knife from the passenger seat and tried to stab the Garda, only for Keyes to disarm him yet again. Keyes then successfully detained the man until help arrived.

Garda John F. Keyes received his Scott Bronze Medal from Nora Owen, Minister for Justice, at Templemore on 15 February 1996. He still serves the community today.[194]

Thomas J. Flaherty, Garda 22405G

Originally from Inverin, County Galway, Thomas Flaherty was born on 15 February 1963 and had been a student before joining the Gardaí on 10 March 1982.

Garda Flaherty was on mobile patrol in Galway on 31 March 1994 when he was alerted that a woman had fallen into the docks at New Dock Road. When Flaherty arrived at the scene minutes later it was to see the distressed woman lose her grip on the lifebuoy she had been clutching and sink underwater. Pulling the clothing from his upper body Garda Flaherty dived off the dock – a height of fifteen feet – and plunged into thirty feet of freezing water. He quickly found the woman and raised her head above the surface. With the help of a lifebuoy thrown by his colleagues he swam with his charge a distance of some sixty yards until they reached the dock wall. Although dazed and barely conscious when lifted from the water, the woman later fully recovered from her experience.

At Templemore on 15 February 1996 Justice Minister Nora Owen presented Garda Thomas Flaherty with his Scott Bronze Medal. He is still serving the community.[195]

Denis Madden, Garda 17523D

Denis Madden was born at Ballinasloe, County Galway, on 22 June 1948, and had worked as a nurse before attesting for the Gardaí on 6 August 1969.

Garda Madden was on mobile patrol in Galway early on 21 December 1994, a night of freezing fog and poor visibility, when he received a radio message that a man 'had fallen' into the canal at Lower Dominic Street. When he reached the scene he was in time to see the man scale the railings and throw himself into the water. Other Gardaí at the scene threw him a lifebuoy but the man would not take it. Removing his jacket and shoes, Garda Madden jumped the twenty feet from the canal wall to the water. The man seemed determined to frustrate all efforts to save him and dragged Madden under the surface with him at least once. In an endeavour which of necessity combined rescue and capture, Madden swam to the canal wall against the man's resistance and there managed to secure him with a rope thrown down by colleagues. The rope, however, became entangled causing the man to break loose. Again he was swept away and again Madden renewed the struggle both above and beneath the surface to drag the man back to the wall. At last, some ten minutes later, Madden's colleagues succeeded in pulling their reluctant rescuee clear of the water. For a brief period Madden himself was in danger of being swept away, but help from the fire service was now available and he himself was finally back on dry land. The rescued man made a full recovery.

Garda Denis Madden in due course received his Scott Bronze Medal from Justice Minister Nora Owen at a ceremony in Templemore on 15 February 1996. Exactly four years later to the day, on 15 February 2000, he retired after 30 years and 194 days service.[196]

Christopher O. Mangan, Garda Sergeant 22825G
Peter J. O'Boyle, Garda 22653L

Born on 31 March 1962 at Dunshaughlin, County Meath, Christopher Mangan left farm work to pursue a career with the Gardaí on 21 July 1982. Peter O'Boyle from Ballyhaunis, County Mayo, was born on 29 July 1960 and had been a student before joining the force on 1 July 1982.

Sergeant Mangan and Garda Boyle, both of them unarmed, were in an unmarked patrol car in Dublin's Crumlin district on the afternoon of 28 October 1993 when they saw a car leaving a shopping centre at a dangerously high speed. While in pursuit they were informed by radio that the car in front contained armed and desperate criminals who had just robbed a building society and had terrorized the staff in the process. With Mangan at the wheel the two Gardaí persevered until the raiders abandoned their car at Dolphin's

Barn and ran towards a flat complex. The chase then continued on foot, pausing several times as the robbers menaced the Guards with guns and ordered them away. As two of them disappeared into a flat Mangan and O'Boyle seized, subdued and disarmed the third man. When back-up arrived the two Gardaí pointed out the flat to their colleagues and the other robbers were arrested. All weapons and the entire proceeds of the raid were recovered.

Sergeant Mangan and Garda O'Boyle were presented with their Scott Bronze Medals at the Garda College, Templemore, by Justice Minister Nora Owen on 15 February 1996. Christopher Mangan, who had been awarded a Scott Bronze Medal previously in 1988 (see pp 141–2 above), was promoted Inspector in 2000. Peter O'Boyle, also a recipient of an earlier Scott Bronze Medal in 1991 (see pp 156–7 above), was promoted Sergeant in 1994 and Inspector in 2005. Both men are still serving.[197]

Richard A. McDonnell, Garda Sergeant 20845M

Richard McDonnell from Dunboyne, County Meath, was born on 8 April 1957 and had installed telephones before attesting for the Gardaí on 30 November 1977.

On 6 July 1990, barely a fortnight after his promotion to Sergeant, Richard McDonnell, in plain clothes and driving a patrol car, received word of a bank raid in west Dublin and that Gardaí were pursuing the raiders through the north of the city. McDonnell was armed and attached to the Emergency Response Unit. He spotted the speeding getaway car and made several attempts to block its progress. The robbers fired repeatedly at him, at least two bullets striking the patrol car. Sergeant McDonnell returned fire, controlling the patrol car as best he could while a raider from the passenger seat of the getaway vehicle kept his gun trained on him. The raiders then crashed into a Garda roadblock and a further exchange of shots took place between them and Sergeant McDonnell. Other Gardaí then fired in support of the sergeant and a brief gunbattle ensued in which two of the raiders were fatally wounded.

Sergeant Richard McDonnell was presented with his Scott Bronze Medal on 15 February 1996 at Templemore by Justice Minister Nora Owen. He was later promoted Inspector and is still serving.[198]

John J. Ward, Garda Sergeant 23579B
Marcus G. Hand, Garda 25482G
Peter O'Connor, Garda 24700F

Sean Ward, born in Dublin on 3 October 1960, had been a clerical officer before opting for a career in the Garda Síochána on 7 September 1983.

Marcus Hand, also from Dublin, was born on 7 August 1969 and had worked as a salesman before becoming a Guard in 1991. Peter O'Connor, again a Dubliner, born on 20 November 1961, had worked in store security before joining the force on 12 May 1987.

Early on 5 March 1995 the three colleagues met to conduct a mobile patrol. As they drove along Dublin's Mary Street in the direction of Capel Street they noticed a car parked outside the Allied Irish Bank (at the unusual hour of 6 a.m.). Also there was the extraordinary sight of a man apparently pointing a sawn-off shotgun at someone. A man bringing the previous night's takings from a pub to the bank's night safe was being robbed. Of the three Guards only Garda Hand, in plain clothes, was armed. Sergeant Ward drove straight at the gunman but avoided any attempt to strike him a glancing blow with the car in case it should cause the gun to go off. As he stopped a few feet away Hand and O'Connor leaped from the car. There were three raiders, one of them holding the shotgun and another armed with a handgun. Hand and O'Connor rushed at two of them while Ward emerged from the car to find himself staring down the barrel of the shotgun. The initial scuffle, during which Garda Hand was threatened with the handgun, developed into a rout as the raiders tried to flee. Garda O'Connor tackled one of them but was then shot in the knee. He was so seriously injured that staunching the loss of blood from his wound had to take precedence over any immediate further pursuit of the culprits.

Sergeant Ward together with Gardaí Hand and O'Connor received their Scott Gold Medals at Templemore on 10 April 1996 from the Tánaiste, Dick Spring. Sean Ward was promoted Inspector in 2002 and later Superintendent. He, Marcus Hand and Peter O'Connor are still serving.[199]

Michael Whelan, Garda 24800B
James J. Nolan, Garda 24660C
Born in Dublin on 4 November 1967, Michael Whelan was a factory foreman before becoming a Garda in 1989. James Nolan from Burren, County Clare, was born on 13 February 1964 and had left labouring for a career in the Guards on 10 December 1986.

Gardaí Whelan and Nolan were in uniform and on mobile patrol in an unmarked car in the Maryland area of Dublin on the evening of 27 October 1994 when they spotted a car carrying two young men travelling at a high speed. When the car stopped to collect another passenger the two Guards decided to investigate. They drew alongside and Garda Whelan got out to speak to the driver. He noticed that the youth in the rear seat - who had just been picked up – had a bag from which a gunbarrel was clearly protruding. As Garda Whelan shouted a warning to Garda Nolan the armed youth and the youth in the front passenger seat suddenly jumped from the car and ran. Whelan and Nolan dashed after them. When the distance between them and the armed youth had narrowed appreciably the lad turned and threatened the officers, pointing the rifle at them. Neither Guard so much as broke stride but threw themselves at the youth whom they quickly overpowered and disarmed. The gun proved to be in working order but was not loaded; it had been stolen in the city centre earlier that day.

On 10 April 1997 the Tanaiste, Dick Spring, presented Gardaí Whelan and Nolan with their Scott Bronze Medals at a ceremony in Templemore. James Nolan (who collected a further Scott Bronze Medal in 2002 – see pp 191–2 below) was promoted Sergeant in 1996 and Michael Whelan the following year. Both officers are still serving.[200]

Christopher Bonar, Garda 25034A

Originally from Tipperary, Christopher Bonar was born on 3 June 1970 and had been a student until opting for a career with the Gardaí in 1990.

Soon after midnight on 26 April 1994 Garda Bonar and a number of colleagues responded to a call to assist Gardaí in Dublin's Ballyfermot area. A stolen car had just been abandoned at Glencullen Park, and Garda Bonar was one of those who took up positions from which they could keep under observation all routes in and out of the Park. As expected four youths appeared and the Gardaí moved to seize them. Suddenly the youth being pursued by Garda Bonar pulled out a sawn-off rifle and turned to face him. Bonar did not hesitate but flung himself straight at the youth, knocking the gun to one side. The youth soon got the worst of the struggle and was disarmed and taken into custody. The gun was found to have a live round in the chamber.

Christopher Bonar received his Scott Bronze Medal from the Tanaiste, Dick Spring, at the Garda College, Templemore, on 10 April 1997. He still serves the community.[201]

Henry Marcus De Long, Garda 24867C

Born in Clonakilty, County Cork, on 24 December 1966, Henry De Long had been an office clerk until he joined the Gardaí in 1989.

On 10 August 1995 Garda De Long was in uniform and on patrol when he was alerted that the National Irish Bank on Dublin's O'Connell Street was being robbed. When he approached the bank on foot he saw a man run from the building carrying a bag and a revolver. As he closed in on his quarry the raider turned and pointed the weapon straight at him. Ignoring the threat De Long tackled the man and knocked him to the ground. As he grappled with him he heard what he took to be a shot; it turned out to be an explosive charge hidden in the security bag. After the robber had been arrested it emerged that the gun was not genuine but a convincing replica of the real thing.

Garda De Long was presented with his Scott Bronze Medal at Templemore by Tanaiste Dick Spring on 10 April 1997. He is still serving today.[202]

Michael Noel Canavan, Garda 21578C

Noel Canavan from Tuam, County Galway, was born on Christmas Day 1958 and had been a clerical officer before joining the Guards on 28 December 1978.

He was off duty on the morning of 16 May 1997 when he observed a man whose behaviour seemed suspicious enter the Bank of Ireland at Foxford, County Mayo. Within moments there was a shotgun blast followed by an exodus of frightened customers, their hands still raised over their heads. Garda Canavan paused only to put his head round a pub door and ask the owner to call the Guards. When he turned back the robber was running towards a parked car. Canavan identified himself as a Garda, pursued and caught the man as he was about to get into the car. Canavan noticed that there was a sawn-off shotgun on the seat of the car. The embattled robber threatened to shoot Canavan and reached into his pocket. The Guard seized his wrist and a violent struggle developed during which the raider managed to dive into the car, grab the shotgun and point it at Garda Canavan. Undeterred, Canavan forced the gun upwards until it pointed at the roof of the car and eventually succeeded in disarming the culprit. A local man then came to his aid and the robber was detained until other Guards arrived. Along with the shotgun which had a live round in one of its chambers, the raider had a loaded handgun in his pocket.

Garda Canavan was presented with his Scott Gold Medal by Justice Minister John O'Donoghue at the Garda College, Templemore, on 23 July 1998. He is still serving the community.[203]

Ciaran C. Doyle, Garda 25251D
David M. Mulhall, Garda 22751L
John D. O'Connell, Garda 24134B

Ciaran Doyle, a Dubliner born on 29 January 1968, worked as a lifeguard and receptionist before joining the Garda Síochána in 1990. David Mulhall, also a Dubliner, was born on 31 August 1958 and had worked in a factory before joining the Guards on 5 July 1982. Sean O'Connell from Waterford, born on 15 May 1964, joined the force on 12 December 1984.

A day of pleasure-cruising on 25 October 1997 for Mr Von Below and the Murphy family on the North Mayo coast went badly wrong. Soon after they began to explore a 300-metre long sea-cave which was surrounded by 90-foot-high cliffs they realized that their currach (some 16 feet long) was about to sink. They were at length washed onto a rocky shore near the back of the cave where they sought safety. Later that afternoon their voices were heard by neighbours who, worried by their failure to return, had set out in search of them. The Garda Underwater Unit was summoned and, using an inflatable boat provided by the Killala Coast and Cliff Rescue Service (whose members accompanied them), headed for the mouth of the cave. With Garda O'Connell providing surface cover, Gardaí Mulhall and Doyle donned scuba equipment and entered the water. Currents and water conditions in general were described as horrific and the three Gardaí were buffeted and hurled against rocks and the sides of the cave. Underwater Mulhall and Doyle found that their torches were beginning to fail. A decision was taken that Mulhall and Doyle, together with members of the CCRS would enter the cave on the inflatable boat and try to float in two buoys with a line attached to rescue the Murphys. It became known that Mr Von Below and another member of the rescue services had perished. Garda Doyle volunteered to swim with the end of a 700-foot-long heavy climbing rope tied to a life-ring round his body. It was now dark and conditions were no better. As he went the long rope was reeled out by his colleagues. Inside the cave the other end of the tow-rope was attached to the inflatable boat and the Murphy family, husband, wife and daughter, were helped on board. On radio instructions the inflatable was then pulled through the huge angry waves with Mulhall and Doyle steadying it as it went. The Murphys were then air-lifted to hospital where they made a full recovery.

Garda Doyle received his Scott Gold Medal, and Gardaí Mulhall and O'Connell their Scott Silver Medals from John O'Donoghue, Minister for Justice, at Templemore on 23 July 1998. Ciaran Doyle and David Mulhall are still serving. Sean O'Connell decided to leave the force in September 2002 having served 16 years and 260 days.[204]

William M. Brady, Garda 24976G
Brigid Yvonne Burke, Garda 00566E

Born in Dunboyne, County Meath, on 6 November 1969, William Brady had been a draughtsman before joining the Gardaí in 1989. Yvonne Burke, born in County Clare on 20 April 1970, had been a student before joining the force in 1990.

Gardaí Brady and Burke were on mobile patrol in the Navan Road area of Cabra on 13 November 1993 when a panic alarm was activated at a supermarket on Ashtown Road. They arrived there in time to see two men leave on a motorcycle in suspicious circumstances. Brady and Burke pursued the men who after a short distance fell from the motorcycle. As the patrol car drew near one of the men fired at it with a sawn-off shotgun shattering the windscreen on the passenger side. The two fugitives then re-mounted their bike and the chase began again, along Navan Road towards Blanchardstown. Before very long the men again lost control of their machine and they fell heavily. The pillion passenger lay dazed on the ground and this time Brady and Burke were able to seize the shotgun. While they were doing so, however, the motorbike rider recovered himself sufficiently to re-mount and make another attempt to escape. He had no better luck. Soon, after a collision with a vehicle, he ran off into a field where he was later arrested.

William Brady and Yvonne Burke were presented with their Scott Silver Medals by Justice Minister John O'Donoghue at the Garda College, Templemore, on 23 July 1998. Garda Yvonne Burke was the first-ever woman Garda to be awarded a Scott Medal. Both members still serve the community today.[205]

Peter T. Burke, Garda 26282L

Peter Burke, a Dubliner born on 8 January 1970, had worked in a bank before joining the Garda Síochána in 1995.

On the afternoon of 16 June 1996 a man armed with a handgun robbed a travel agency in Dublin's Tallaght district and assaulted the manager. Garda Burke, who was on beat patrol, saw the man run from the premises. On being told by the staff of what had occurred, he set off in pursuit. As he ran the man drew a handgun and, as Garda Burke's footfalls sounded just behind him, he turned and pointed the weapon at the Garda. After a tense stand-off the man took to his heels again, still hotly pursued by Garda Burke. As he got within range the Guard, who was otherwise unarmed, drew his baton and struck the man on the arm causing him to drop the gun. He then grabbed the robber and, after a struggle, overpowered and arrested him. All the cash stolen from the travel agency was recovered.

On 23 July 1998 Justice Minister John O'Donoghue presented Garda Burke with his Scott Bronze Medal at the Garda College, Templemore. Peter Burke, who been less than a year in the force at the time of the incident, was promoted Sergeant in 2004 and still serves the community today.[206]

Augustine Fox, Garda Sergeant 22441K
Patrick J. Molloy, Garda 22601G
Patrick D. O'Callaghan, Garda 25126G

Augustine Fox, born at Newmarket-on-Fergus, County Clare, on 29 August 1961, had been a marketing manager before joining the Gardaí on 15 June 1983. Patrick Molloy from Renmore, Galway City, was born on 11 March 1961 and had worked as a computer operator before attesting for the Guards on 27 April 1982. Patrick O'Callaghan from Tipperary, born on 13 March 1970, was a security officer until he joined the force in 1990.

In the early hours of 14 July 1996 the three colleagues were patrolling Sarsfield Barracks housing estate in Limerick when they saw that one of the buildings was on fire. Gardaí Molloy and Callaghan forced their way into the two-storey house by the front door and were met by a blast of intense heat and a pall of oily black smoke. Garda O'Callaghan, crawling about on all fours, found two terrified children standing in a corner. He and Garda Molloy grabbed a child each and managed to get them past the blazing hallway and out the front door to safety. Having learned that a child was still trapped in another of the bedrooms, the two Guards together with Sergeant Fox went back in, again on their hands and knees, this time to the room which seemed to be the seat of the fire. They were driven back by the choking smoke and searing heat. Sergeant Fox made a last desperate attempt to reach the upstairs bedroom but was again forced back. Fortunately the fire brigade had now arrived and the third child was found and brought to safety. All three Gardaí needed hospital treatment for smoke inhalation and cuts to their hands and elbows.

Sergeant Fox and Gardaí Molloy and O'Callaghan were presented with their Scott Bronze Medals at Templemore on 23 July 1998 by Justice Minister John O'Donoghue. Patrick O'Callaghan was promoted Sergeant in 2003. All three officers are still serving.[207]

John Noel Jones, Detective Garda 20383A
James Breslin, Detective Garda 22319M

Noel Jones from Moyne, County Longford, was born on Christmas Eve 1955 and had been a hospital attendant before joining the Garda Síochána on 1 September 1976. James Breslin, born on 19 April 1961 at Mountcharles,

County Donegal, had worked as a carpenter before joining the force on 29 April 1981.

Early on the morning of 27 October 1996 Detectives Jones and Breslin were on mobile patrol in the Malin Head area of North Donegal. As they conducted a search of a shed which adjoined a dwelling house they came upon five masked men dressed in waterproof oilskins. Also in the shed was a cache of firearms, ammunition, explosives and similar devices. The two officers, both armed, arrested all five men. They were later convicted and received prison sentences for possession of the materials discovered in the shed.

Noel Jones and James Breslin received their Scott Bronze Medals from Justice Minister John O'Donoghue at the Garda College, Templemore, on 23 July 1998. Both men are still serving.[208]

Patrick J. Murphy, Garda Sergeant 22557F
John J. Synnott, Garda 20734K
Padraic E. O'Malley, Garda 26284F
Born at Carrigtohill, County Cork, on 10 May 1958, Patrick Murphy had worked as an electrician before becoming a member of the Garda Síochána on 27 April 1982. John Synnott from Thomastown, County Kilkenny, was born on 1 August 1956 and had been a mechanical engineer before attesting for the Gardaí on 3 August 1977. Padraic O'Malley, born in Kildare on 18 December 1972, was a student until he joined the force in 1994.

Sergeant Murphy and Garda O'Malley were on mobile patrol in Wexford in the early hours of 14 January 1996 when they spotted smoke rising from the roof of a two-storey terraced house in Upper John Street. They contacted Garda Synnott for assistance and he was at the scene within a few minutes. In the course of alerting the neighbours in adjoining and nearby houses the Guards learned that an elderly lady lived alone in the blazing house. No response being received to their frenzied hammering on the front door, they kicked it in. As they stepped inside the house the intense heat and smoke forced them into a crawling position. After a few minutes Murphy and Synnott began to beat their way upstairs, initially leaving O'Malley to continue the search of the downstairs rooms. Garda Synnott, who reached the top of the stairs on his hands and knees just ahead of Sergeant Murphy, came upon the house's elderly occupant barely conscious, her hands gripping the newel post. The two Guards lifted and carried her downstairs through the growing inferno and out to safety. She was then resuscitated by firemen who had just arrived, and later, despite her advanced years, made a full recovery. The inner rooms of the house were completely gutted by the fire.

Scott Bronze Medals were presented to Sergeant Murphy and Gardaí Synnott and O'Malley on 23 July 1998 by Justice Minister John O'Donoghue at a ceremony in Templemore. All three officers are still serving.[209]

Michael G. McConalogue, Garda Sergeant 21942H
Jude E. Ainsworth, Garda 23685C

Michael McConologue, a Dubliner born on 27 August 1959, had been a clerk before attesting for the Gardaí on 14 May 1980. Jude Ainsworth, born in Mayo on 30 March 1964, worked as a labourer until joining the force on 21 September 1983.

The two colleagues were patrolling in Dublin's Aughrim Street area on 9 December 1996 when they noticed smoke billowing from the roof of a house. A group of people were standing around the doorway from which black smoke was likewise issuing. They told the Guards that someone was trapped in an upstairs flat. The initial attempt by McConologue and Ainsworth to climb the stairs failed in the face of the intense heat and smoke which made breathing all but impossible. With wet teacloths wrapped round their faces the two Gardaí again began to force their way upstairs through the inferno in a crawling position. The sound of a man's voice reached them and but when at last they got to the door of the flat it was jammed. Garda Ainsworth lay on his back on the landing and kicked at the lower half of the door until it gave way. Nobody emerged, so McConologue and Ainsworth were forced to crawl into the room and search through the smoke until they came upon the trapped terror-stricken man crouched in a corner. The nearest exit was a window below which was a shed, and the two Gardaí managed to get the man through it and onto the shed roof. Ambulance staff then took over and treated the man for shock and smoke inhalation.

On 6 July 2000 Justice Minister John O'Donoghue presented Sergeant McConologue with his Scott Bronze Medal during a ceremony at the Garda College, Templemore. Garda Ainsworth received his Scott Bronze Medal while serving with the United Nations. Both officers are still serving.[210]

Jeremiah McCabe, Detective Garda 15860G
Benjamin O'Sullivan, Detective Garda 15636A

Born in Ballylongford, County Kerry, on 22 November 1943, Jerry McCabe had been a tradesman before joining the Garda Síochána on 9 September 1964. Ben O'Sullivan, born at Mourneabbey, Mallow, County Cork, on 7 April 1944, had worked in farming before joining the Guards on 6 May 1964.

Detective O'Sullivan was driving and Detective McCabe acting as observer on the morning of 7 June 1996 as they escorted the post office van on its cash delivery at Adare, County Limerick. Both officers had an Uzi submachine gun as well as their sidearms. Just before 7 a.m. the truck stopped at Adare Post Office and the two Gardaí pulled up a few feet behind. As the truck driver prepared to unload the mail a jeep crashed at full speed into the rear of the detectives' unmarked car, breaking Detective O'Sullivan's arm and jamming him against the steering wheel. Simultaneously a silver Mitsubishi car came alongside and crashed into both vehicles. Five armed masked men jumped out and raked the policemen's car with high-velocity weapons, killing Detective McCabe and severely wounding Detective O'Sullivan. Both officers were trapped in the car and had no opportunity to defend themselves. The killers then decamped in the Mitsubishi in the direction of Rathkeale.

Detective Jerry McCabe was posthumously awarded the Scott Gold Medal. His family attended the presentation ceremony at the Garda College, Templemore, on 6 July 2000 to receive the medal on his behalf. Also present to receive his second Scott Gold Medal (see pp 164–5 above for the earlier incident) from Justice Minister John O'Donoghue was Detective Garda Ben O'Sullivan, whose recovery from his injuries had been slow and painful. Detective O'Sullivan continued on in service until his retirement on 6 February 2001 after a career of 36 years and 277 days.[211]

Andrew J. Callanan, Garda Sergeant 22477D
Born in Tipperary on 8 January 1963, Andy Callanan joined the Garda Síochána on 13 April 1982.

Soon after 4 a.m. on the morning of 21 July 1999 Sergeant Callanan was putting his paperwork in order at Dublin's Tallaght Station before going off shift. A colleague, Garda John Malone, got up to investigate a noise coming from the public area. He was met by the extraordinary sight of a man carrying a sword, Japanese flares and a damaged plastic petrol can. The man lifted the can onto the desk where it immediately began to leak fumes and petrol, and told the astonished Guard that he must evacuate the building. As Malone ran back to the inner office to raise the alarm the man lit the two flares. Sergeant Callanan, who had grabbed a fire extinguisher, rushed into the reception area in time to see the man ignite the leaking petrol. Callanan began spraying him with the fire extinguisher when the petrol in the can exploded setting the entire public area ablaze, including Callanan himself. A Guard who had been standing in the doorway between the inner and outer offices was blown the length of the building. Garda Malone, who tried to get to the Sergeant, was driven back by the searing heat which had built up within seconds in the relatively confined area. By the time his colleagues reached him Andy Callanan was dead.

Sergeant Callanan was posthumously awarded the Scott Gold Medal at a presentation ceremony in Templemore on 6 July 2000, attended by members of his family who accepted the medal on his behalf from Justice Minister John O'Donoghue.[212]

Thomas Lehane, Garda 26011H
Patrick F. O'Hara, Garda 23686A
Thomas Lehane was born in New Jersey, USA, on 24 February 1971, and had been a trainee manager before attesting for the Gardaí on 7 February 1994. Patrick O'Hara, a Dubliner born on 16 January 1961, joined the Gardaí on 21 September 1983.

On 23 November 1998 Gardaí Lehane and O'Hara were on mobile patrol when they came upon a robbery-in-progress at a building society in Malahide, County Dublin. Confronted by the Guards one of the two raiders pushed a shotgun against Garda O'Hara's chest before driving off in a powerful car. With O'Hara at the wheel the two officers pursued the getaway vehicle, keeping it in sight until the robbers eventually lost control and crashed. The chase continued on foot with occasional pauses as the armed raider periodically turned and menaced the two Gardaí with the gun. Before long O'Hara and Lehane overtook the culprits and disarmed them. The gun was found to be loaded.

Gardaí Lehane and O'Hara received their Scott Silver Medals from Justice Minister John O'Donoghue at the Garda College, Templemore, on 6 July 2000. Patrick O'Hara left the force on medical grounds in November 2001. Garda Lehane is still serving.[213]

Laurence Bergin, Garda 22816H
Born in Cashel, County Tipperary, on 30 December 1962, Laurence Bergin had been a clerk before deciding on a career in the Garda Síochána on 21 July 1982.

Early on the morning of St Patrick's Day 1999 Garda Bergin was on mobile patrol in Clonmel with Garda Elaine Corkery when they were alerted that a woman had fallen into the River Suir at Old Bridge. On-lookers at the scene told them that the woman had been swept under the bridge. Using his torch to guide him through the darkness, Garda Bergin lowered himself into the icy waters. After a moment he glimpsed the woman's head as it broke the surface some twenty feet from him. He shouted to her and she began to swim towards the sound of his voice. But when she had covered half the distance she was again caught by the current and swept back downriver. Garda Bergin renewed his search and eventually caught sight of her hand moving some distance from him. Pausing only to invest in the precaution of a rope around his waist he swam determinedly until he reached the woman. She was barely conscious by the time he lifted her onto his shoulder. He swam against the powerful current until he gained the river bank. After hospital treatment the woman recovered fully from her experience.

On 6 July 2000 Garda Laurence Bergin received his Scott Bronze Medal from Justice Minister John O'Donoghue at the Garda College, Templemore. He is still serving.[214]

Padraic Powell, Garda 26623L

A Dubliner born on 12 November 1972, Padraic Powell had worked as a storeman before becoming a member of the Garda Síochána on 2 April 1997.

On 18 May 1998 Garda Powell was on mobile patrol with Garda James Keogh on Dublin's Ballyfermot Road when word reached them of a house on fire at Drumfinn Road. A daunting sight met them at the scene, the house almost invisible through a pall of thick smoke and the front sitting room burning fiercely. At an upstairs window a terrified woman was trying desperately to escape. Other Gardaí from nearby stations were arriving also. With the help of a neighbour's ladder the woman was rescued from the upper floor. Neighbours also thought it possible that children might still be trapped inside. Garda Powell forced the front door and ran through the smoke and flames to a back bedroom where two children aged 12 and 14 lay senseless. Hearing his shouts for help other Gardaí rushed in and the children were carried to safety. The woman and the children all made a full recovery.

Garda Padraic Powell received his Scott Bronze Medal from Justice Minister John O'Donoghue at Templemore on 6 July 2000. He is still serving the community.[215]

Aiden McGuinness, Garda Sergeant 21042M
John Dollard, Garda 25420G

Aiden McGuinness was born at Ballyshannon, County Donegal, in 1955 and had been a lifeguard before joining the Gardaí on 11 January 1978. John Dollard, a Dubliner born on 26 July 1969, had been a student until he joined the force on 19 November 1992.

Sergeant McGuinness was on patrol with Garda John Dollard in Dublin's Amiens Street on the morning of 30 May 1996. As they passed by a newsagents on the busy city centre thoroughfare their attention was attracted by the apparent absence of any staff in the shop, even though it was clearly open for business. As the two Guards entered the shop to investigate they were suddenly confronted by two raiders who stepped from the shadows brandishing a handgun and a screwdriver. McGuinness and Dollard, themselves unarmed, instantly tacked the robbers, grappling with them until they were overpowered, disarmed and taken into custody.

Sergeant McGuinness and Garda Dollard were presented with their Scott Bronze Medals by Justice Minister John O'Donoghue at a ceremony in Templemore on 6 July 2000. Both officers are still serving.[216]

Dominick Reilly, Detective Garda 17918C
Brendan O'Donovan, Detective Garda 22800A
Dominick Reilly from Belmullet, County Mayo, born on 29 November 1950, had been a labourer before attesting for the Garda Síochána on 16 June 1971. Brendan O'Donovan, born in Limerick City on 17 May 1962, had worked as a post office clerk until he joined the force in 1982.

The two detectives were on mobile patrol in the Castletroy area of Limerick on the evening of 18 September 1999. As they passed a supermarket on the Dublin Road they noticed two young men on a motorcycle who were, to say the least, behaving suspiciously. One of them was carrying a double-barrel shotgun and, as the officers watched, he got off the bike and went into the shop. Reilly and O'Donovan rushed after him and entered the shop in time to see him threatening the staff. As they came in the officers identified themselves as armed Gardaí and ordered the robber to lie on the floor. The youth turned and pointed his weapon straight at the detectives. O'Donovan fired a shot in his direction and in fright the youth dropped the gun; he was then arrested.

Detective Gardaí Reilly and O'Donovan were presented with their Scott Bronze Medals at Templemore on 1 October 2001 by Justice Minister John O'Donoghue. Both officers are still serving.[217]

John Mulligan, Detective Inspector 17472F
John Gantly, Detective Inspector 21982G
Fearghal Pattwell, Detective Garda 24765M
John Mulligan from Dunfanaghy, County Donegal, was born on 6 August 1950 and had been a clerk until deciding on a career in the Guards on 25 June 1969. Born on 17 July 1960 at Bray, County Wicklow, John Gantly had been a student before he joined the force on 14 May 1980. Fearghal Pattwell was

born at Blackrock, Cork, on 28 November 1969, and had also been a student until joining the Garda Síochána on 1 June 1990.

These three detectives were members of a party of Gardaí who went to a flat at Dublin's New Brunswick Street on the morning of 15 January 1998 to execute a search warrant. They identified themselves as armed Gardaí but, as there was no response from inside the flat, the party forced an entry to a narrow hallway. While Detective Mulligan kept an eye on the doorway Detectives Gantly and Pattwell approached a door just ahead of them. Both officers were then fired on through the door from inside the room, pellets from a sawn-off shotgun peppering Pattwell's arm and shoulder and Gantly's face. Detective Mulligan rushed into the hallway and dragged the badly injured Pattwell to safety. Detective Gantly, notwithstanding his facial injuries, proceeded into the room followed by other Guards and arrested seven criminals. Two loaded firearms and seven knives were recovered in the raid.

All three detectives received their Scott Bronze Medals from Justice Minister John O'Donoghue at Templemore on 18 October 2001. They are still serving: John Mulligan was promoted Superintendent in 2002, John Gantley became an Inspector in 1998 and a Superintendent in 2007, and Fearghal Pattwell a Sergeant in 1999.[218]

Gerard McGrath, Garda 23327G

Born in Dublin on 6 September 1962, Gerard McGrath had been a clerical assistant before joining the Gardaí on 26 January 1983.

He was off duty on the afternoon of 8 November 1997 and at the shopping centre in Dublin's Castleknock district when he spotted two youths in a car outside a chemist shop both of whose faces were swathed in scarves. As he watched they ran from the car into the shop. He followed them inside, identified himself as a Garda and ordered them to lie on the floor. One of the raiders swung at McGrath with a syringe but missed. The two then beat a retreat to their waiting car followed by McGrath. They managed to lock the door before he reached them but McGrath smashed his way through the driver-side window. He tried to pull the driver out but the youth suddenly pushed open the door and ran, knocking the Guard momentarily off balance. Recovering quickly McGrath caught up with the raider and knocked him off his feet. Help was summoned and both raiders were taken into custody.

On 18 October 2001 Justice Minister John O'Donoghue presented Garda McGrath with his Scott Bronze Medal. He had been promoted Sergeant in 1998. Today he still serves the community.[219]

James Joseph Hennessy, Garda 23753A

Seamus (Shay) Hennessy, born in Waterford City on 19 December 1963, had worked as an architectural technician before attesting for the Garda Síochána on 5 October 1983.

On the morning of 5 June 1998 word reached Garda Hennessy that a woman had plunged into the River Lee at Pope's Quay, Cork. He ran to the scene there he saw a man throw a lifebuoy towards a woman in the water. The woman vanished from sight and Garda Hennessy jumped in. As he swam towards her she re-surfaced, but the current was very strong. He caught her before she could again disappear or be swept downstream and swam with her to the bank. But as they neared the bank the woman began to resist him. Garda Hennessy held on determinedly until she was safely landed. After hospital treatment the woman fully recovered but remained ungrateful to Garda Hennessy who had risked his own life to save her.

His bravery was recognized, however, at Templemore on 18 October 2001 when Justice Minister John O'Donoghue presented him with his Scott Bronze Medal. He continues to serve the community.[220]

Patrick Melody, Garda 26692B

Born in Ennis, County Clare, on 16 March 1971, Patrick Melody had worked as an aircraft technician before joining the Gardaí in 1996.

Garda Melody was on motorcycle patrol in Dublin's Inchicore district in the early hours of 17 July 2001. At Emmet Road a man who had just entered his house and closed the door behind him was suddenly hit in the neck and back by pellets from a sawn-off shotgun blasted through the door by a man standing outside. Garda Melody heard the shots and arrived at the scene in time to see the masked assailant, shotgun in hand, running towards a waiting car. The gunman pointed the weapon directly at him forcing Melody to take evasive action. The gunman dived into the car and sped off towards Inchicore. Garda Melody, who was unarmed, took off after the car which was travelling at a high speed, keeping it in sight while he relayed its location to Command and Control. Before very long Gardaí brought the car to a halt and arrested the gunman and an accomplice. The shotgun was also recovered.

At a ceremony in Templemore on 21 November 2002 Justice Minister Michael McDowell presented Garda Patrick Melody with his Scott Silver Medal. He is still serving.[221]

Michael Fitzgerald, Detective Garda Sergeant 21839A
Michael Fitzgerald, born in 1959 in Ennis, County Clare, had been a plumber until he joined the Guards on 31 December 1978.

Detective Sergeant Fitzgerald was a customer in a shop at a service station on Dublin's Ballyboden Road on the morning of 13 January 2001 when a man approached the counter assistant with a handgun and demanded money. The detective struck the gunman a blow over the hand and seized hold of him. The would-be robber struggled very violently and a shot was fired from his gun. Sergeant Fitzgerald's wrist was lacerated and the gunman managed to tear himself out of the officer's grasp and escape. He was, however, eventually identified and apprehended.

Detective Sergeant Michael Fitzgerald received his Scott Bronze Medal from Justice Minister Michael McDowell at Templemore on 21 November 2002. He is still serving the community.[222]

Ciaron Barry, Garda 26632K
Born at Enniskerry, County Wicklow, on 27 March 1972, Ciaron Barry was a draughtsman before joining the Gardaí in 1996.

Garda Barry was on beat duty at Dublin's Temple Bar area on the night of 6 January 2001 when a message reached him that a man had jumped into the River Liffey near O'Connell Bridge. When he arrived at the bridge a few minutes later other Gardaí and firemen were trying to locate the man. Eventually he was spotted floating downriver. A lifebuoy was thrown to him but the strong current was dragging him under the surface and he could not reach it. Garda Barry ran down the quays and, without even pausing to remove his clothing, scrambled down a ladder set into the quay wall and jumped into the river. He managed to grab hold of the man and swam back to the quay wall with him, clutching the ladder as he waited for help to arrive. The man later made a full recovery.

Garda Barry was presented with his Scott Bronze Medal by Justice Minister Michael McDowell at the Garda College, Templemore, on 21 November 2002. He still serves the community today.[223]

James J. Nolan, Garda Sergeant 24660C
Thomas Murphy, Detective Garda 21733F
James Nolan, born in Burren, County Clare, on 13 February 1964, had worked as a labourer until joining the Gardaí on 10 December 1986. Thomas Murphy was born in Limerick in 1960 and had been a sales assistant before he joined the force on 3 October 1979.

The two colleagues were on mobile patrol in Limerick's Henry Street area on the night of 25 January 2000 when they were alerted to a robbery at a nearby shop. They arrived in time to surprise the raider as he emerged, shotgun in hand, from a restaurant opposite the shop. He took to his heels, pursued by Nolan and Murphy. Detective Murphy drew his handgun and identified himself and Nolan as Gardaí. The man, however, kept running. As the officers narrowed the distance between them and their quarry, the robber at intervals turned and pulled the trigger but the shotgun repeatedly failed to fire. Eventually he discarded it over a nearby wall, upon which the two Gardaí pounced on him and took him into custody.

Detective Sergeant James Nolan (who had already received a Scott Bronze Medal in 1997 – see pp 177–8 above) and Garda Thomas Murphy received their Scott Bronze Medals from Justice Minister Michael McDowell at a ceremony in Templemore on 21 November 2002. Both officers are still serving.[224]

Colm Finnerty, Probationer Garda 29529K

Born at Carrick-on-Shannon on 3 April 1979, Colm Finnerty had worked as a machine operator before attesting for the force on 19 June 2003.

Probationer Garda Finnerty was on mobile patrol in Dublin on 7 December 2002 when he received a message that a man had plunged into the River Liffey at Sean Heuston Bridge. When he reached the bridge he saw that there were in fact two men in the water and that a strong current was on the point of carrying them away. Finnerty jumped into the freezing water and swam towards them. They had sunk below the surface but he dived down, grabbed the men who were locked together in a tight embrace, and dragged them to the surface. He separated them with difficulty only to have one of the panic-stricken men seize him round the waist and drag him under again. Eventually Finnerty managed to get both men over to the ladder set into the quay wall. He now discovered that a third man, intent on helping him, had jumped in and was himself in difficulties. Finnerty swam towards the man who was being swept away, caught him and dragged him back to the quay wall. All three men made a full recovery.

At the Garda College, Templemore, where Colm Finnerty was yet to have his own passing-out parade, Justice Minister Michael McDowell presented him with his Scott Gold Medal on 23 October 2003.[225]

Raymond Costello, Garda 26579K

Raymond Costello, born in Cork City on 21 November 1972, had been a sales assistant before joining the Gardaí on 5 December 1996.

Garda Costello was on mobile patrol in Dublin's Drumcondra district on the night of 28 January 2001 when he noticed fire brigade and ambulance personnel attending an incident at Binns Bridge. On inquiring he was told that a short time earlier a man had jumped into the canal. The man had taken hold of a ladder which was lowered to him by firemen but he had then let go of it and had drifted into the middle of the canal; he was now at the point of drowning. As the man sank beneath the surface Garda Costello, with a rope tied around his body, entered the water (which was at least a dozen feet in depth). Three times Garda Costello dived underneath the muddy frozen water until he finally found the man and pulled him back to the ladder. He then transferred the rope from his body to that of the rescued man allowing the firemen to haul him up onto the bank. Sadly the man did not recover.

On 23 October 2003 Garda Raymond Costello received his Scott Silver Medal from Justice Minister Michael McDowell. He is still serving the community.[226]

Kieran McNamara, Detective Garda 19562F

A native of Newmarket-on-Fergus, Kieran McNamara was born on 31 July 1952 and had worked as a factory operative before joining the force on 3 April 1974.

Detective McNamara was on foot patrol in Loughrea, County Galway, on 1 March 2002, when he was directed to investigate the apparently suspicious behaviour of a man outside a building society premises on Main Street. He went into the offices and paused to speak to a customer who was on his way out. As he did so two masked men armed with a knife and a hammer ran past him. McNamara ran after the man with the knife and tackled him. After a violent struggle he disarmed the man and placed him under arrest. The other would-be raider fled to a parked car where a third man drove them both from the scene. The two were later apprehended.

At a ceremony in Templemore on 23 October 2003 Detective Garda Kieran McNamara received his Scott Bronze Medal from Justice Minister Michael McDowell. He still serves the community today.[227]

Gerard Collins, Garda 25545K
Darran Kirwan, Garda 26343E

Born in Thurles on 12 May 1972, Gerard Collins had been a student before becoming a Garda on 9 June 1993. Darren Kirwan, from Longwood, County Meath, was born on 17 September 1971 and had been an engineering draughtsman before joining the force on 28 March 1996.

The two colleagues were on mobile patrol in Dundalk, County Louth, in the early hours of 15 January 2002 when a report was relayed to them that a man was sitting on the Castletown Bridge and threatening to throw himself in the river. When they arrived at the bridge they saw the man sitting as described, facing the river with his feet dangling over the side. Seeing the two Guards coming towards him he warned them to stay back and threatened that he would jump there and then. In fact a moment or two later the man did jump without warning into the freezing waters. Collins and Kirwan saw that the current was dragging the man into the central channel and that within minutes he would be swept into Dundalk Bay. They both jumped in and swam towards the spot where they last caught sight of him. When they reached him he was near to drowning and the two Guards had the greatest difficulty in keeping hold of him as they battled against the freezing temperature and the strong current. At last they succeeded in bringing him to the safety of the river bank.

Garda Collins was presented with his Scott Bronze Medal by Justice Minister Michael McDowell on 23 October 2003 at Templemore. Garda Kirwan, also awarded the Scott Bronze Medal, unfortunately was unable to attend the ceremony. Both have since been promoted Sergeant and are still serving.[228]

REFERENCES

1 *Guth an Gharda*, 21 August 1924, 10–14. *Irish Times*, 19 August 1924.

2 *Garda Review*, January 1926, 91–2.

3 *Garda Review*, August 1926, 625–6.

4 Ibid., 626.

5 Ibid., 626.

6 *Garda Review*, August 1927, 911–12.

7 Ibid., 912–13.

8 Ibid.

9 *Garda Review*, May 1928, 580–3; *Garda Review*, August 1928, 860–70. Paddy Hanly, 'The sea did not have them', *Iris an Gharda*, April 1959, 393–5.

10 *Garda Review*, August 1928, 868–70.

11 Ibid., 870.

12 *Garda Review*, September 1929, 1038–9. *Garda Review*, January 1932, 141–2.

13 *Garda Review*, September 1929, 1038. *Garda Review*, January 1932, 143.

14 *Garda Review*, September 1929, 1038.

15 *Garda Review*, July 1930, 756–7. *Garda Review*, January 1932, 143.

16 *Garda Review*, January 1932, 143.

17 Ibid.

18 Ibid. See also the brief entry on Joseph Kelly in *Iris an Gharda*, February 1959, 239, by Paddy Hanley.

19 *Garda Review*, June 1933, 773–4.

20 Ibid., 775, 777.

21 Ibid., 777.

22 *Garda Review*, September 1933, 1096–7; 1102–5. Paddy Hanly, 'Supt. Fennelly's daring deed', *Iris an Gharda*, May 1959, 475–7.

23 *Garda Review*, September 1933, 1105–6; 1096–7.

24 Ibid., 1106; 1096–7.

25 Ibid., 1106–7; 1096–7.

26 *Garda Review*, August 1934, 1019–21. Paddy Hanly, 'Sergeant Wynne's gallant deed', *Iris an Gharda*, June 1959, 561–3.

27 *Garda Review*, August 1934, 1023–4.

28 Ibid., 1021–3.

29 *Garda Review (Supplement)*, September 1935, 1190–1.

30 Ibid., 1191–2.

31 *Garda Review*, December 1937, 79–81. Paddy Hanly, 'Midnight drama in Stephen's Green', *Iris an Gharda*, July 1959, 641–3.

32 *Garda Review*, December 1937, 81.

33 Ibid., 81–3.

34 Ibid., 83.

35 Ibid., 83–5.

36 Ibid., 85.

37 *Garda Review*, January 1940, 222–3.

38 Ibid., January 1940, 223.

39 Ibid., 223–4.

40 Ibid., 224.

41 *Garda Review*, November 1941, 1088–9. NAI, D/J 4/438, part 1, M.J. Kinnane, Commissioner, to J. Berry, Justice, 7 December 1941 (with enclosure).

42 Ibid., 1089–91.

43 Ibid., 1091; also NAI, D/J 4/438, part 1, Kinnane to Berry, 7 December 1941.

44 *Garda Review*, December 1942, 44–6. NAI, D/J 4/438, part 1, T.J. McCarthy, Commissioner's Office, to J.J. McCarthy, Private Sec., Minister for Justice, 29 November 1942 (with enclosure).

45 Ibid., 46–7; also NAI, D/J 4/438, part 1, McCarthy to McCarthy, 29 November 1942.

46 *Garda Review*, December 1944, 75, 77. Paddy Hanly, 'The story of the Scott Medal winners 1943', *Iris an Gharda*, August 1959, 713, 715.

47 *Garda Review*, July 1948, 604–7. Paddy Hanly, 'The heroes of '47', *Iris an Gharda*, March 1959, 13–15.

48 *Iris an Gharda*, May 1960, 449, 451. NAI, D/J 4/438, part 2, Sgt. J. Ryan, Garda Station, Bandon, to Superintendent, Bandon, 9 May 1959; C.P. Donovan, Superintendent, Bandon, to Chief Superintendent, Bandon, 13 May 1959; D. Costigan, Commissioner, to Secretary, Justice, 15 October 1959.

49 Ibid., pp 449, 451, 453. NAI, DJ 4/438, part 2, P. Gerin, Superintendent, Dublin Metropolitan Division, 'C' District, to Deputy Commissioner, Dublin Castle, 22 May 1959.

50 *Iris an Gharda*, June 1961, 567, 569. NAI, D/J 4/438, part 2, D. Costigan, Commissioner, to Oscar Traynor, Minister for Justice, 7 April 1961.

51 Ibid., 567.

52 *Iris an Gharda*, June 1962, 537. NAI, D/J 4/438, part 2, ('Awards … to …').

53 Ibid., 539. NAI, D/J 4/438, part 2 ('Award … to Garda John O'Connor').

54 Ibid., 539. NAI, D/J 4/438, part 2 ('Award … to Garda Jeremiah Connolly').

55 *Iris an Gharda*, May 1963, 415. NAI, D/J 4/438, part 2, Sgt. M. Gleeson, Garda Station, Goresbridge, Kilkenny District, to Superintendent, Kilkenny, 18 June 1962; W.J. McConville, Chief Superintendent, Louth/Meath Division, to Commissioner, 8 January 1963; D. Costigan, Commissioner, to Charles J. Haughey, Minister for Justice, 23 February 1963.

56 Ibid., 417. NAI, D/J 4/438, part 2 ('Award … to Garda Aidan Murray').

57 *Iris an Gharda*, November 1965, 621.

58 Ibid.

59 Ibid., 619.

60 *Iris an Gharda*, November 1966, 753, 755.

61 Ibid., 757.

62 Ibid., 755.

63 *Iris an Gharda*, July 1967, 409–10.

64 Ibid., 411, 413.

65 NAI, D/J 2005/147/157 ('Award of Scott Silver Medal to Sergeant Martin K. Walsh').

66 *Iris an Gharda*, October 1970, 7. NAI, D/J 2005/147/258 ('Award of Scott Silver Medal to Garda Philip Brady').

67 NAI, D/J 2005/147/158 ('Award of Scott Medals (Silver) to Gardai James Callaghan, 11011, and Mark Fitzgerald').

68 Ibid., ('Award of Scott Medal (Bronze) to Garda Michael B. McGann').

69 Liz Walsh, *The final beat: Gardaí killed in the line of duty* (Dublin, 2001), 3–7.

70 NAI, D/J 2005/147/158 ('Award of Scott Medals (Gold) for bravery to (1) Sergeant James B. Griffin, 15118, Union Quay Station, Cork, and (2) Garda John F. Murray, 15608, Bridewell Station, Cork').

71 *Garda Review*, December 1973, 6. NAI, D/J 2005/147/158 (copy of citation).

72 Ibid., 6. NAI, D/J 2005/147/158 (copy of citation).

73 *Garda Review*, December 1973, 4. NAI, D/J 2005/147/158 (copy of citation).

74 *Garda Review*, December 1973, 5. NAI, D/J 2005/147/158 (copy of citation).

75 *Garda Review*, December 1973, 5. NAI, D/J 2005/147/158 (copy of citation).

76 *Garda Review*, October 1974, 27. Garda Archives (hereinafter GA), copy of citation.

77 *Garda Review*, October 1974, 27. GA, copy of citation.

78 *Garda Review*, November 1975, 17. NAI, D/J 2005/147/159, E.P. Garvey, Commissioner, to A. Ward, Department of Justice, 24 September 1975, enclosing draft full citation in respect of English, McGowan and Madigan).

79 *Garda Review*, November 1975, 18. NAI, D/J 2005/147/159. E.P. Garvey, Commissioner, to A. Ward,

Department of Justice, 24 September
1975, enclosing Appendix 'A' to
timetable of awards ceremony for 2
October 1975.

80 *Garda Review*, November 1975, 16.
NAI, D/J 2005/147/159. E.P. Garvey,
Commissioner, to A. Ward,
Department of Justice, 24 September
1975, enclosing Appendix 'A' to
timetable of awards ceremony for 2
October 1975.

81 *Garda Review*, November 1975, 18.
NAI, D/J 2005/147/159. E.P. Garvey,
Commissioner, to A. Ward,
Department of Justice, 24 September
1975, enclosing draft full citation in
respect of Kane, Counihan and
Mitchell.

82 *Garda Review*, November 1975, 17.
NAI, D/J 2005/147/159. E.P. Garvey,
Commissioner, to A. Ward,
Department of Justice, 24 September
1975, enclosing Appendix 'A' to
timetable of awards ceremony for 2
October 1975.

83 *Garda Review*, November 1975, 17–18.
NAI, D/J 2005/147/159. E.P. Garvey,
Commissioner, to A. Ward,
Department of Justice, 24 September
1975, enclosing draft full citation in
respect of Duffin, Heneghan and
O'Loughlin.

84 *Garda Review*, November 1975, 16.
NAI, D/J 2005/147/159. E.P. Garvey,
Commissioner, to A. Ward,
Department of Justice, 24 September
1975, enclosing draft full citation in
respect of Garda Moroney.

85 *Garda Review*, November 1975, 16–17.
NAI, D/J 2005/147/159, E.P. Garvey,
Commissioner, to A. Ward,
Department of Justice, 24 September
1975, enclosing draft full citation in
respect of Garda Cosgrove.

86 *Garda Review*, August 1976, 3. NAI,
D/J 2005/147/159, E.P. Garvey,

Commissioner, to A. Ward,
Department of Justice, 6 July 1976,
enclosing Appendix 'A' to timetable of
the awards ceremony for 16 July 1976.

87 *Garda Review*, August 1976, p 3. NAI,
D/J 2005/147/159. E.P. Garvey,
Commissioner, to A. Ward,
Department of Justice, 6 July 1976,
enclosing Appendix 'A' to timetable of
the awards ceremony for 16 July 1976.

88 *Garda Review*, August 1976, 3. NAI,
D/J 2005/147/159. E.P. Garvey,
Commissioner, to A. Ward,
Department of Justice, 6 July 1976,
enclosing Appendix 'A' to timetable of
the awards ceremony for 16 July 1976.

89 Liz Walsh, *The final beat*, 39–59.

90 *Garda Review*, December 1977, 15.
NAI, D/J 2005/147/160. E.P. Garvey,
Commissioner, to A. Ward,
Department of Justice, 11 November
1977, enclosing draft full citation in
respect of Sergeant Callanan.

91 *Garda Review*, December 1977, 15.
NAI, D/J 2005/147/160. E.P. Garvey,
Commissioner, to A. Ward,
Department of Justice, 11 November
1977, enclosing draft full citation in
respect of Sergeant Sexton.

92 *Garda Review*, December 1977, 15.
NAI, D/J 2005/147/160. E.P. Garvey,
Commissioner, to A. Ward,
Department of Justice, 11 November
1977, enclosing draft full citation in
respect of Sergeant Neill.

93 *Garda Review*, December 1977, 15.
NAI, D/J 2005/147/160. E.P. Garvey,
Commissioner, to A. Ward,
Department of Justice, 11 November
1977, enclosing draft full citation in
respect of Detective Daly.

94 *Garda Review*, December 1977, 14–15.
NAI, D/J 2005/147/160. E.P. Garvey,
Commissioner, to A. Ward,
Department of Justice, 11 November
1977, enclosing Appendix 'A' to

timetable of the awards ceremony for 24 November 1977.

95 *Garda Review*, April 1998, 7, 9. GA, copy of full citation dated 12 November 2007. Personal communication, Mr Anders to the author, 4 May 2007, enclosing copy of earlier citation dated 10 November 1999.

96 GA, official account of incident.

97 GA, personal account by Mr Grier, 22 March 2007.

98 GA, copy of full citation, 8 November 1978.

99 GA, draft full citation, 8 November 1978.

100 GA, copy of full citation, 8 November 1978.

101 GA, copy of full citation, 8 November 1978.

102 GA, copy of full citation, 28 May 1979.

103 GA, draft full citation, 28 May 1979.

104 Personal communication to the author from Mr McCarthy, 1 May 2007. GA, official recommendation for Scott Medal, John A. Carey, D/Super-intendent, Union Quay, Cork, to Chief Superintendent, Cork ER, 6 May 1979. *Cork Examiner*, 23 February, 4, 5, 25 April 1979. *Irish Times*, 4 June 1980.

105 GA, draft full citation, 29 May 1980.

106 Personal communication, Detective Superintendent Lynch to the author, 30 August 2007.

107 GA, draft full citation, 29 May 1980.

108 *Garda Review*, September 1982, 17.

109 *Garda Review*, September 1981, 15. GA, personal statement by Sergeant Stokes, 16 October 2007.

110 GA, copies of statements of evidence to the Special Criminal Court by Sergeant Prenty and Garda Duffy at the trials of Leonard McAteer and James Tracey.

111 GA, official report on the murders of Detective Garda Morley and Garda Byrne on 7 July 1980. Liz Walsh, *The final beat*, 76–90.

112 GA, official report on the murder of Detective Garda Quaid and the attempted murder of Detective Garda Lyttleton on 13 October 1980. Liz Walsh, *The final beat*, 91–102.

113 GA, official report on the attempted murder of Detective Gardaí Daly and Curran on 30 December 1980. Paul William, *Crime Lords* (2nd edition, Dublin, 2004), 271–4.

114 GA, personal statement by Detective Sergeant Doyle, 4 April 2007.

115 *Garda Review*, September 1982, 16–17.

116 GA, personal statement by Garda Costello, 28 August 2007.

117 GA, draft full citation, 4 June 1981.

118 *New Ross Standard*, 18 April 1980.

119 GA, copy full citation, 4 June 1981.

120 *Garda Review*, June 1984, 4.

121 *Garda Review*, November 1983, 12. GA, official recommendation for Scott Medal.

122 GA, copy full citation, 15 October 1985. See also the feature article in the *Garda Review* for November 1985, and the account in Sean Flynn and Padraig Yeates, *Smack: the criminal drugs racket in Ireland* (Dublin [c.1985]), 98–105.

123 *Garda Review*, September 1982, 16.

124 *Garda Review*, November 1983, 13. GA, official recommendation for Scott Medal.

125 *Garda Review*, September 1982, 15–16.

126 *Garda Review*, November 1983, 12. Liz Walsh, *The final beat*, 103–16. GA, official recommendation for Scott Medal.

127 *Garda Review*, November 1983, 13. GA, official recommendation for Scott Medal.

128 *Garda Review*, June 1984, 4.

129 *Garda Review*, November 1983, 12–13. GA, official recommendation for Scott Medal.

130 *Garda Review*, June 1984, 4–5. GA, copy full citation (undated).

131 *Garda Review*, July/August 1985, 5. GA, copy full citation (undated).

132 *Garda Review*, July/August 1985, 5. GA, official account of incident of 15 November 1983.

133 *Garda Review*, July/August 1985, 5. GA, official account of incident of 24 June 1983.

134 *Garda Review*, July/August 1985, 4–5; also the feature article in *Garda Review*, November 1985. GA, copy full citation (undated).

135 *Garda Review*, July/August 1985, 5. GA, statements of evidence by Sergeant Mullarkey and Garda Scanlon, by Dr. P.F. Magill of Mullingar General Hospital, and evidence of identification of culprits by Sergeant Mullarkey [all 1984].

136 *Garda Review*, December 1986, 9. GA, official report of aggravated burglary at the Royal Oak on 20 June 1985, signed by Sergeant Gerard Creagh, Bridewell, Dublin.

137 *Garda Review*, January 1987, 8–9. Liz Walsh, *The final beat*, 177–90.

138 GA, official report on the 'Murder of Detective Garda Frank Hand, CDU, and armed robbery at Drumcree Post Office, Co. Meath, on 10 August 1984'. Liz Walsh, *The final beat*, 156–76.

139 *Garda Review*, January 1987, 11, 13.

140 *Garda Review*, January 1987, 11.

141 *Garda Review*, January 1987, 9,

142 *Garda Review*, January 1987, 14. GA, official recommendation for Scott Medal (dated 22 January 1986); also, official account of the incident (undated).

143 *Garda Review*, January 1987, 14.

144 GA, Crime File 6952; also memorandum by Sergeant Walter O'Connell, 1992, regarding the petition for release by Christopher Griffin. Superintendent M.J. Francis, Store Street Station, Dublin, to Chief Super-intendent, D[ublin] M[etropolitan] A[area], 23 February 1987, supple-mentary to his official Scott Medal recommendation of 13 January 1987 in respect of Detective Garda Dolan.

145 *Garda Review*, December 1988, 20.

146 *Garda Review*, December 1988, 22.

147 *Garda Review*, December 1988, 21.

148 GA, draft full citation (undated).

149 *Garda Review*, December 1988, 20.

150 *Garda Review*, December 1988, 20.

151 *Garda Review*, December 1988, 21.

152 *Garda Review*, December 1988, 22.

153 *Garda Review*, December 1988, 22.

154 *Garda Review*, December 1988, 21.

155 *Garda Review*, December 1989, 19. GA, 'Statement of Garda Martin Caine, 21206G, Ronanstown Garda Station, made to Sergeant Gerard P. O'Carroll and Garda John Doyle at St. James Hospital on Sunday the 7th December, 1986'.

156 *Garda Review*, December 1989, 18.

157 *Garda Review*, December 1989, 17–18.

158 GA, official recommendation for Scott Medal, signed by Detective Inspector J. Canning, 19 February 1989.

159 GA, official account by Superintendent C.P. McCarthy, Killaloe, County Clare, of the 'Armed raid on sub-post office at Caher, Co. Clare on Friday the 6th May, 1988, and subsequent shoot-out with Gardai at Feakle, Co. Clare', addressed to Martin G. Linnane, State Solicitor, Ennis, County Clare and dated 30 August 1988. Also, official statements regarding the incident made to Superintendent McCarthy on 21 May 1988 by Gardai Condren and Kelly.

160 GA, official recommendation for Scott Medal, signed by Superintendent PMA Sheil (undated).

161 *Garda Review*, December 1989, 21.

162 *Garda Review*, December 1989, 21.

163 *Garda Review*, December 1989, 19.

164 *Garda Review*, December 1989, 19.

165 *Garda Review*, December 1990, 8.

166 GA, 'Statement of evidence of Garda Gerry O'Grady, 21747F, of Cabra Station' (undated but clearly c1988).

167 GA, personal statement by Sergeant Donnelly, 11 December 2007.

168 GA, official report of 'Attempted robbery at Allied Irish Bank, Ranelagh, on 8th January 1990'.

169 *Garda News*, December 1991/January 1992, 11–12.

170 GA, official report of 'Armed robbery at JR Byrne & Sons Ltd, Robinhood Industrial Estate, Dublin 12, at 12,30pm on 28th April, 1990'.

171 *Garda News*, December 1991/January 1992, 11.

172 *Garda News*, April 1993, 37.

173 *Garda News*, April 1993, 37.

174 *Garda News*, April 1993, 41.

175 *Garda News*, April 1993, 39.

176 GA, official report of 'Arrest of man in possession of loaded .22 Stephens rifle between 1am and 2am on 16th November, 1990'.

177 *Garda News*, April 1993, 41.

178 *Garda News*, April 1993, 40–1.

179 *Evening Press* and *Irish Press*, 13 December 1991; *Leitrim Guardian*, 27 March 1993.

180 GA, official report 'RE: Exceptional courage by a Garda in discharge of his duties – Garda John O'Neill, 24328M, Tallaght Station', from the Chief Superintendent's Office, Crumlin, Dublin 12, dated 14 May 1993.

181 *Garda News*, April 1994, 40.

182 GA, official report, 'Arrest of two criminals, one armed, following an armed robbery at Dorset Street Post Office, on 23rd November, 1990'.

183 *Garda News*, April 1994, 40.

184 *Garda News*, April 1994, 41.

185 *Garda Review*, June/July 1995, 12.

186 *Garda Review*, June/July 1995, 12–13.

187 *Garda Review*, June/July 1995, 15.

188 *Garda Review*, June/July 1995, 14.

189 *Garda Review*, June/July 1995, 13.

190 *Irish Independent*, 7 July 1993. GA, official recommendation for Scott Medal (copy unsigned and undated).

191 GA, official 'Statement of Declan Sheeran of Ballyfermot Garda Station, Dublin 10, taken on 1 August 1993 by Patrick Flynn, D[etective] Garda, Ballyfermot'.

192 *Garda Review*, March 1996, 14–15.

193 *Garda Review*, March 1996, 16.

194 *Garda Review*, March 1996, 16.

195 *Garda Review*, March 1996, 16.

196 *Garda Review*, March 1996, 16.

197 *Garda Review*, March 1996, 15.

198 *Garda Review*, March 1996, 15.

199 Personal communication, Superintendent Ward to the author, 15 May 2007.

200 *Garda Review*, May 1997, 57, 59.

201 *Garda Review*, May 1997, 59.

202 *Garda Review*, May 1997, 59.

203 *Garda News*, August 1998, 7, 9.

204 *Garda News*, August 1998, 7.

205 *Garda News*, August 1998, 9.

206 *Garda Review*, August 1998, 9; *Garda News*, August 1998, 13.

207 *Garda Review*, August 1998, 8; *Garda News*, August 1998, 11.

208 *Garda Review*, August 1998, 8.

209 *Garda News*, August 1998, 11.

210 *Garda Review*, August 2000, 33; *Garda News*, July 2000, 7.

211 *Garda News*, July 2000, 5–6. Liz Walsh, *The final beat*, 191–224.

212 *Garda News*, July 2000, 5–6. Liz Walsh, *The final beat*, 225–33.

213 GA, personal statement by Garda Lehane, 28 June 2007.

214 *Garda News*, July 2000, 9.

215 *Garda News*, July 2000, 9.

216 *Garda News*, July 2000, 7.

217 GA, copy full citation, 26 September 2001.

218 *Garda Review*, December 2001, 65. GA, copy full citation, 26 September 2001.

219 GA, copy full citation, 26 September 2001.

220 *Garda Review*, December 2001, 65. GA, copy full citation, 29 June 2000.

221 *Garda Review*, December 2002/January 2003, 46; *Irish Independent*, 23 November 2002.

222 *Garda Review*, December 2002/January 2003, 47; *Irish Independent*, 23 November 2002.

223 *Garda Review*, December 2002/January 2003, 47; *Irish Independent*, 23 November 2002.

224 *Garda Review*, December 2002/January 2003, 46–7; *Irish Independent*, 23 November 2002.

225 *Garda Review*, Yearbook 2003, 24–5.

226 *Garda Review*, Yearbook 2003, 25.

227 *Garda Review*, Yearbook 2003, 25.

228 *Garda Review*, Yearbook 2003, 27.

INDEX